Gorbachev and His Generals

Gorbachev and His Generals

The Reform of Soviet Military Doctrine

EDITED BY

**William C. Green and
Theodore Karasik**

Westview Press
BOULDER, SAN FRANCISCO, & OXFORD

This Westview softcover edition is printed on acid-free paper and bound in library-quality, coated covers that carry the highest rating of the National Association of State Textbook Administrators, in consultation with the Association of American Publishers and the Book Manufacturers' Institute.

Published in 1990 in the United States of America by Westview Press, Inc., 5500 Central Avenue, Boulder, Colorado 80301, and in the United Kingdom by Westview Press, Inc., 36 Lonsdale Road, Summertown, Oxford OX2 7EW

Library of Congress Cataloging-in-Publication Data
Gorbachev and his generals : the reform of Soviet military doctrine /
edited by William C. Green and Theodore Karasik.
    p.   cm.
  ISBN 0-8133-7898-2
  1. Soviet Union—Military policy. 2. Gorbachev, Mikhail
Sergeevich, 1931–   . 3. Civil-military relations—Soviet Union.
I. Green, William C., 1941–   . II. Karasik, Theodore William.
UA770.G665   1989
322′.5′0947—dc20   89-29113

Printed and bound in the United States of America

The paper used in this publication meets the requirements
of the American National Standard for Permanence of Paper
for Printed Library Materials Z39.48-1984.

10   9   8   7   6   5   4   3   2   1

Contents

Preface

This collection of works is built around a common theme: how the reforms and political currents sweeping through Soviet society relate to the many indications of change in Soviet military doctrine. At first glance, the relationship is clear: the Soviet military is undergoing changes similar in nature to those in the rest of the Soviet political and social structure. But as the chapters in this book make clear, there is a far more subtle dynamic taking place that bears heavy implications for the future of U.S.-Soviet relations. As a result, this book is intended for a much larger circle of readers than specialists in Soviet political-military relations. Ideally, it should be of value to all readers interested in long-term Soviet approaches to strategic issues.

In his five years as General Secretary of the Communist Party of the Soviet Union, Mikhail Gorbachev has launched initiatives that are leading to major changes in Soviet government, economy, and society. These changes have already begun to touch the military, and it is possible that the next decade could see the Soviet Armed Forces dramatically transformed. One factor that could accelerate, delay, or derail this process of changes is Soviet military doctrine.

"Doctrine" is a term that requires explanation, since it is used differently by the Soviet and American Armed Forces. In the Soviet sense it indicates the formal Party-military consensus over the external threats facing the Soviet Union, the approaches by which they are countered, and the resources and organization needed by the Armed Forces to react to them. The Party apparently adopted the use of doctrine in this sense, as a "contract" with the military, in the late 1950s.

For the next twenty years, Soviet military doctrine apparently remained relatively stable. The strategic and technological environment underwent considerable changes in this period. But the Soviet military responded with gradual and piecemeal modifications to military doctrine rather than major revision. By the early 1980s, many American analysts were detecting signs of dissatisfaction with existing doctrine in Soviet military writings. They felt that at the point of Gorbachev's accession to power Soviet military doctrine was at last being subjected to major revision.

Gorbachev's personal and far-reaching approach to reform raises many questions in regard to his relations with the Soviet military. Some of the most important include issues such as whether military doctrine is guiding Soviet military reform or simply catching up with it, how the Soviet military intends to match its diminishing share of resources to its increasing need for high technology, and how the ideological strictures that have confined the Soviet military can be maintained under conditions of glasnost. The most significant, of course, are the issues of how closely the Soviet military supports Gorbachev's policies of reforms, what degree of control Gorbachev maintains over the Soviet military, and whether the military leadership could lend their support to Gorbachev's opponents.

The editors decided to produce this book after long discussions at two conferences, the October 1988 Air Force Intelligence Agency Conference on Soviet Affairs in Washington, D.C., and the November 1988 conference of the American Association for the Advancement of Slavic Studies in Honolulu, Hawaii. We felt that a current work needed to be assembled that would address the foregoing questions, and we developed an outline that in our opinion connected most of the issues associated with Gorbachev's reforms and Soviet military doctrine.

We would like to thank our colleagues who participated in the debates surrounding the issues found within this book, for as the reader will discover, the views presented here are diverse. However, it is important to point out that the opinions expressed in this book are those of the authors and do not represent the views of their employers or sponsors; they accept full responsibility for the content. Finally, we want to thank our wives, Ann Green and Eve Karasik, for their support and understanding.

William C. Green
Boston, Massachusetts

Theodore Karasik
Los Angeles, California

1

Soviet Military Doctrine: Continuity and Change?

William F. Scott

Is Soviet military doctrine now of "a purely defensive character?" Are Soviet forces maintained only at a level of "reasonable sufficiency?" Kremlin leaders make major efforts to convince the outside world that fundamental changes are occurring in Soviet military policies. They are heralded as part of General Secretary Mikhail Gorbachev's "new thinking."

But there is nothing new in these expressions. Gorbachev's predecessors implemented these slogans to change Western perceptions of Soviet military power. What is new is the skill of the public relations campaign to sell Gorbachev as the driving force behind glasnost and perestroika. To confuse the situation further, many words have different meanings in the Soviet Union than in the West. Military doctrine is a case in point.

In the United States military doctrine simply is a set of principles for the use of forces in combat. We have a "Navy doctrine," "tactical doctrine," "Air Force doctrine," and so on.

In contrast, in the Soviet Union military doctrine is the military policy of the Communist Party of the Soviet Union (CPSU). Its edicts have the force of law. As stated by Marshal of the Soviet Union Nikolai Ogarkov, military doctrine is to answer the following five questions:

1. What is the degree of probability of future war, and with what enemy will one have to deal?

2. What character might the war take that the country and its Armed Forces might have to wage?

3. What goals and missions might be assigned to the Armed Forces in anticipation of such a war, and what Armed Forces is it necessary to have in order to fulfill the assigned goals?

4. In what way, proceeding from this, should military structuring be accomplished, and in what way should the army and the country be prepared for war?

5. By what methods should the war be conducted, if it breaks out?[1]

If one studies Marshal Vasilii Sokolovski's *Military Strategy*, written in the 1960s, it will be found that all of these five questions were discussed in this work, although not specifically identified. It was not until 1974 that they first were spelled out by Marshal Andrei Grechko, then the Soviet Minister of Defense.[2] In 1982 Marshal Ogarkov made slight changes to Grechko's wording, but the essence of the five questions remained the same. The 1986 *Military Encyclopedic Dictionary* defines military doctrine as the military policy of the CPSU, and it "is concerned with the essence, aims, and character of a possible future war, the preparation of the country and its armed forces for it, and the methods by which it will be fought."[3] This basically covers the points made both by Grechko and Ogarkov.

In theory, Soviet military doctrine is formulated by the Central Committee. In actual fact, policy guidelines for doctrine probably come from the shadowy Defense Council. This body, headed by the Party's General Secretary, is concerned with the preparation of the entire nation for the possibility of future war, to include its industry, population, and armed forces.[4] Soviet theorists stress a two-sided military doctrine, the political and military-technical. The political side dominates. New technology, leading to new weapons, forces change in the military-technical side.

The Defensive Nature of Soviet Military Doctrine

Soviet spokesmen seek to convince the West that their military doctrine consists of a "purely defensive character," even claiming that this always was the case. They do not now admit that throughout most of the 1970s Soviet military textbooks specified that their military doctrine was "offensive." For example, the 1971 *Officer's Handbook* stated that "Soviet military character has an offensive character" (*Sovetskaia voennaia doktrina nosit nastupatel' ni kharakter*).[5] This changed, however, not because of any policy set by Gorbachev but as a result of policies during Brezhnev's tenure as General Secretary.

For example, in May 1980, the Political Consultative Committee (PCC) of Warsaw Treaty Organization (WTO) General Secretaries issued a declaration that they "have not, have never had and will not have any other strategic doctrine other than a defensive one."[6] In Soviet terminology "strategic doctrine" is not the same as "military doctrine," although the distinction is not altogether clear. Marshal Ogarkov, both in 1981 and 1982, following the 26th Party Congress stressed the Soviet Union's "defensive military doctrine."

Continued assertions in the 1980's about military doctrine being "defensive," in contrast to material written earlier, probably confused Soviet officers. To clarify this, a 1987 military textbook, *The Military-Theoretical Heritage of V.I. Lenin and Problems of Contemporary War*, explained that the offensive remains the primary method of waging war.[7] However, in its political aspect, war will be waged only for defensive purposes. Since the political side of doctrine dominates, the change in wording from "offensive" to "defensive" posed no problem.

The Concept of Reasonable Sufficiency

Many in the West hope that current statements by Soviet leaders about their forces being maintained at a level of "reasonable sufficiency" mean a change in Soviet thinking. This concept, however, was expressed long before Gorbachev became the Party's General Secretary. At the 1980 meeting of the WTO PCC, the final declaration stated that the member nations "invariably advocate safeguarding the military balance *at ever lower levels*, for reduction and elimination of the military confrontation in Europe."[8] Elsewhere the declaration called for "renunciation of the use of force or threat of force, limitation of forces and arms of each state or group of states *solely to suit defense needs* [emphasis added], and mutual renunciation of attempts at gaining military supremacy." Essentially, this is what is said today.

Kommunist Voorushennykh Sil, the official journal of the Main Political Administration (MPA) of the Soviet Armed Forces, often indicates the ideological line that the Party directs the Armed Forces to follow. Since mid-1987 this journal has published a continuous series of articles discussing the concept of reasonable sufficiency. All the authors make clear that Soviet nuclear forces must be able to deliver a retaliatory strike on an opponent, regardless of the possible scenario under which an opponent's first strike is made.

This Soviet emphasis on "reasonable sufficiency," made at a time when there are hopes in the West for a meaningful arms control agreement with Moscow, is carefully studied by NATO defense specialists as well as by the Chinese. Soviet spokesmen now press the matter of "reasonable sufficiency" in television programs and radio broadcasts. NATO political leaders and scholars trek to Moscow to hear more about this new Soviet view on the required level of military forces.

Soviet spokesmen are very vague on the meaning of "reasonable sufficiency." Colonel (ret.) Lev Semeiko, formerly on the faculty of the Frunze Military Academy and currently a member of Dr. Georgi Arbatov's Institute of the USA and Canada, made one of the more coherent explanations. In Semeiko's view, the concept of reasonable sufficiency is not for the present, rather it "is oriented to the future and carries a charge of ideas for long-term action." However, it will not become a reality until "nuclear weapons and other types of mass destruction weapons" are eliminated. He went on to say that:

> Sufficiency does not preclude but, on the contrary, presupposes the presence of strategic parity; that decisive factor in preventing war. It is necessary to have within the framework of parity a reasonably sufficient military potential capable of reliably ensuring the security of the USSR and its allies. This means that under contemporary conditions we are obliged to have a guaranteed potential for nuclear retaliation designed to prevent an unpunished nuclear attack under any, even under the most unfavorable, nuclear attack scenarios. In any situation, an answering strike must unacceptably damage the aggressor.[9]

Using Semeiko's words, one might state that "sufficiency" is all the NATO nations ever wished to achieve; a sufficient military potential capable of reliably ensuring the security of NATO, to include a guaranteed potential for nuclear retaliation!

Even Gorbachev's "new thinking" is a takeoff from what was written before his designation as General Secretary. A 1984 book by Anatolii Gromyko, *Novoe Myshlenie v Iadernyi Vek*,[10] provided many of the concepts expounded today. Some Soviet theorists now state that the "new thinking," which generally is attributed to Gorbachev, actually began in 1956, when Khrushchev announced that war between communism and capitalism was no longer inevitable.[11] This condition, Khrushchev added, was due to the powerful new weapons possessed by the Soviet Union. As Soviet military power grew, later writers stated that the Soviet Union would "force" peaceful coexistence on the "imperialists." "Reasonable sufficiency" must maintain this capability.

While many in the United States take seriously the Soviet use of "sufficiency" when applied to military forces, Soviet writers were more critical when the expression appeared in a text delivered by former United States President Richard Nixon. In a 1971 article, for example, Colonel V.V. Larionov, then of the Institute of the USA and Canada, chided Nixon's use of sufficiency in his 1970 foreign policy message. The "sufficiency" concept as a basis for building up the armed forces, Larionov explained "is variable and dependent on subjective appraisals."[12] But at the same time it is a very useful expression, which can "satisfy the hawks and placate the doves simultaneously." If only United States analysts would be so critical of the current Soviet usage of the term!

Even though there is no clear evidence of a new Soviet military doctrine, there are attempts by Kremlin leaders to make certain changes in the economic structure of their nation and to convince the West that a new era is beginning in international affairs. It is most difficult to determine what is actually taking place. Disinformation remains a trademark of Soviet actions.

Debates and Disinformation

Since the mid-1950's the idea of internal Soviet military "doctrinal" debates dominated United States' perceptions of Soviet military writings. Generally, the debates are perceived as between Soviet "hawks" and "doves," or the bad guys and the good. In the 1960s the debates were thought to be between the "modernists" who favored emphasis on nuclear weapons and "traditionalists" who stressed conventional forces. In the 1960s, as today, anyone who could produce evidence, real or imaginary, of the Kremlin leadership moving away from reliance on nuclear weapons found a ready hearing. The following item published in the *Washington Post* in 1967 is illustrative:

> London: An article by Soviet Marshal Ivan Yakubovski, new commander of the Warsaw Pact forces, declaring that soldiers and conventional weapons remain East Europe's primary defense, was seen yesterday as marking the end of former Soviet Premier Khrushchev's "massive retaliation" policy. Analyzing Yakubovski's remarks, which appeared in the Soviet newspaper *Red Star*, Victor Zorza of the *Manchester Guardian* said the statement represents the first official Soviet admission that Khrushchev's concept of relying on nuclear arms had been abandoned. It had been in decline since Khrushchev's ouster in 1964.[13]

The 1967 *Washington Post* article represented a completely misleading but popular view at that time. Yakubovski, as CINC (commander in chief) of the WTO forces, could scarcely be expected to write that the Armed Forces of Eastern European satellites, armed with non-nuclear weapons, had no role. At the same time he made it clear that nuclear weapons would be decisive in the event of a future war.[14] This article was timed to coincide with the beginning of WTO summer field exercises. Yakubovski repeated the standard expression, found in major articles of that period: "Units and subunits must be prepared to fight with or without the use of the nuclear weapon." But the idea of internal Soviet doctrinal debates then was in vogue and the "traditional" Soviet leaders had to be shown as winning. In actual fact, during this period the Soviet Union built up its nuclear forces with unprecedented speed.

Another popular view in the United States is that debates take place between senior Soviet military and Party leaders; the military wants more weapons, the Party wants resources to improve the economy. Too often it is forgotten that senior military officers also are senior Party members. Where only one in ten of the adult population belongs to the CPSU, nine out of every ten military officers are card-carrying Party members. The military is an instrument of the Party, which in turn depends on the military for its survival.

The Soviet Union is a military superpower, nothing more. Soviet military doctrine is established by the Party, not by the military. The Soviet minister of defense and the commander of the Moscow Air Defense District were fired by the Party leadership in 1987 after a German teenager landed a light aircraft on Red Square. While some military leaders may disagree with established policies, they do not do so without having the backing of a segment of the Party leadership. A Soviet party-military debate is about as likely as the chairman of the United States Joint Chiefs of Staff disagreeing in public with the President of the United States.

Perceptions of Soviet internal military debates tend to make the Soviet leadership, both military and Party, "seem like us." Soviet authorities, probably the KGB, may help to foster this illusion. For example, Moscow now issues an *APN Military Bulletin*, conveniently printed in English for those who do not read Russian. The May 1977 issue carried an article entitled "Debate on Warsaw Pact and Military Doctrine in the USSR and Socialist Pluralism."[15] This particular article is an excellent example of Soviet disinformation.

The article argues that a major internal doctrinal debate is now in progress. While the new Soviet doctrine is defensive, there are different views. "Civilian analysts," such as Andrei Kokoshin and Vitalii Zhurkin, are portrayed as more moderate than the military officers. For example, Kokoshin, a corresponding member of the Soviet Academy of Sciences, "believes that the reduction in the size of troops and armaments is not enough." Neither Kokoshin nor Zhurkin were identified as being members of the Institute of the USA and Canada, a leading Soviet center of information and disinformation. Both Kokoshin and Zhurkin speak excellent English, they host foreigners in Moscow, and they frequently travel abroad. The purpose of the *APN Military Bulletin* probably is to convince its foreign readers of "socialist pluralism" and of the sincerity of Gorbachev's "new thinking."

Now, as in the past, Kremlin leaders seek to mold foreign opinion in their favor. For this, many Soviet books and journals are published in foreign languages. Some, like *Socialism: Theory and Practice*, are to advise the Party faithful abroad of current Politburo policies. A journal such as *Soviet Military Review*, published in English, Spanish, and other languages, is both to inform and disinform. One reading this journal would likely have a very benign view of the Soviet Armed Forces. Many of the most sensational articles about changes in the Soviet Union, and criticisms of the existing order, appear in the English-language edition of *Moscow News*.[16] Russian-language editions of this newspaper are virtually impossible to obtain in the Soviet Union. But the English-language edition is freely available, both in Moscow and in Washington, D.C., where it can be purchased at some newsstands.

Those in the West who try to follow current Soviet writings on defense issues should first research the origins and purposes of the Institute of the USA and Canada, as well as similar bodies such as the Institute of World Economy and International Relations (IMEMO) and the new Institute of Western Europe. The stated purpose of these institutes is "to determine the most effective ways and means to ensure the victory of socialism over capitalism."[17] Each institute publishes its own journal, with the table of contents published in English. Like the Soviet *APN Military Bulletin* and *Moscow News*, these journals also both inform and disinform. They frequently carry articles on Soviet military doctrine, carefully crafted to create the impression desired by the leadership.

At present, as at times in the past, the Soviet leadership is in turmoil. Soviet secrecy and disinformation are such that we have little real knowledge of what is actually happening, glasnost notwithstanding. We can only guess at who supports whom and the strength of the opposition.

But in Soviet military affairs, we find that certain basics appear to remain, regardless of the power struggle at the top. Soviet concern with the "correlation of forces in the world arena" or, in military terms, the laws of war may be the primary focus of Kremlin actions.

The Laws of War

The training of the Soviet leadership, whether they be industrial managers, Party *apparatchiki*, or military officers, is political and conceptual. All will have studied Marxism-Leninism. Whether or not they personally believe these teachings is one thing; their actions must conform to them. The relationship between political, economic, scientific, moral, and military factors is constantly stressed. This provides a conceptual basis for actions, whether they are political or military.

In particular, Soviet officers are required to study Marxist-Leninist philosophy throughout their careers. Their military doctrine, strategy, force development, organization, and combat roles are explained in Marxist-Leninist terms. Soviet law requires the establishment of a department of scientific communism, headed by a general or an admiral, in each military academy.

One reason for the ideological indoctrination to which the Soviet "nomenklatura" are subjected since earliest childhood is to give them a common world outlook (*mirovozrenie*). As a result of this indoctrination, it is not surprising that Soviet theoreticians formulate the "laws" of war.

These laws, which have a major impact upon military doctrine, are not about "rules of engagement" or the treatment of prisoners of war. Rather, they are laws that, according to Marxist-Leninist teachings, determine which side will win and which side will be defeated. Soviet officers are told that "the known laws of war are taken into account by the military policy of the Party, they are expressed in the military doctrine of a socialist state, serve as the basis of military science and lie at the base of the principles of waging war."[18]

Laws of war are "objective" and therefore apply equally to both warring sides. Soviet theorists assert that, although the laws exist, not all are discovered or correctly interpreted. They claim that the scientific methodology made possible by Marxist-Leninist teaching permits them to identify and to apply these laws in a manner impossible for military leaders in capitalist nations.

There is no set number of laws, nor agreement on how they are stated. A number of current Soviet writings explaining the laws of war state that the course and outcome of war are dependent upon the economic, scientific-technical, moral-political, and military potentials of the warring states.[19]

The necessity for "perestroika" (restructuring) of the Soviet economy stems from Soviet concern that the "correlation of forces" or, in military terms, the "laws of war," may be moving against them. Since the beginning of the Soviet state, Soviet military textbooks have sought to show the superiority of the Soviet system's economy, science and technology, moral-political behavior, and military power. These are the four areas with which the laws of war are primarily concerned.[20] Gorbachev now admits that something is wrong. To put things right there must be a restructuring of the entire Soviet society, from industry to the Armed Forces. An examination of these laws helps to explain Gorbachev's priorities.

First, the economic potential of the Soviet Union is of major concern. Speeches by Soviet leaders and articles in the daily press admit that the economy is in serious trouble. Visitors to the Soviet Union, even in this period of glasnost, are still confined to a limited number of cities which offer special facilities for foreign tourists and official guests. Even these selected areas show a depressed economy. Availability of food is no better than it was in 1962.[21] Promises of adequate housing never materialized.

If domestic shortages are not enough, the foreign economic scene is equally troubling to the Kremlin rulers. While the Soviet Union has stagnated, nations such as Japan and South Korea have become major industrial powers. And now China in only the last decade has made remarkable industrial progress. The Kremlin might notice that over 30,000 Chinese students are now studying in the United States alone. More and more, in comparison with its potential opponents, the Soviet Union is appearing as an under-developed nation. If its leaders believe that the economic potentials of warring states are the first law of war, priority must be given to improving the economy.

Second, the scientific-technical potential in the Soviet Union shows little progress. There was a time in the early 1950s and 1960s when Soviet successes in ballistic missiles and space exploration convinced the Soviet people and the world of their scientific-technical superiority. The Soviet leadership now faces reality. Shortcomings in science and technology are admitted in the Soviet press. For example, in a *Pravda* article, the President of the USSR's Academy of Sciences, Gurii Marchuk, made a startling admission. He stated that "our real potential for fundamental research is approximately five times lower than America's." He went on to say that "although the overall number of scientific workers in both countries [the Soviet Union and the United States] is approximately the same, the capital-labor ratio of U.S. scientific workers in the United States is...at least three times higher."[22] Marchuk even admitted that "the fall in our proportional contribution in world science cannot fail to be alarming." This loss in scientific-technical potential represents another law of war working against the Soviet Union.

Third, the moral-political potential of Soviet society is in question. A number of Soviet writers and senior military officers decry the growing pacifism among the youth. Corruption is rampant and is admitted to a startling degree. In general, the population is indifferent to the pleas of the leadership. Young people, in particular those in the large cities where foreigners are permitted to visit, are cynical. By the early-1980s drunkenness reached new levels, resulting in severe restrictions being placed on the sale of alcohol. Past Soviet writings asserted that their system, based on Marxism-Leninism, assured moral-political superiority over the "imperialists." Such writings are more circumspect today.

The fourth law of war, the military potential, is the only area in which the Soviets are successful. But the cost is great, consuming approximately 20 percent of the Soviet gross national product. For the present, the Soviet Armed Forces are equal to, and in some areas superior to, those of any potential opponent. But looking down the road to the year 2000 and beyond, the Kremlin leadership may be alarmed. Follow-on weaponry will be dependent upon a modernized economy, a revitalized science and technology, and a more capable work force. Senior Soviet officers appear to be aware of the importance of perestroika to their military forces. This has been explained in the Soviet press as, for example, in the following article which appeared in *Krasnaia Zvezda*, the official newspaper of the Soviet Ministry of Defense:

> The backbone, the load-bearing wall of our country's defense capability, is the Soviet economy....The programs drawn up under the Party's leadership for the radical modernization of the national economy and the resolute acceleration of scientific and technical programs have their defense aspects. The priority development of machine building, electronics, the nuclear industry, laser technology, information science and other sectors

2

Assessing Soviet Military Literature: Attempts to Broker the Western Debate

William C. Green

This chapter is a review of some attempts by U.S. strategic writers to find a methodological solution to a problem that polarized analysis on an important strategic issue. Until the rise of Mikhail Gorbachev thoroughly shook up Western evaluations of Soviet strategic intentions, U.S. analysts of the Soviet military were locked in a sterile debate over whether the Soviet Union had realistic plans for nuclear combat. Evaluating this debate and several methodological works that attempted to resolve it gives valuable insights into the limits of Western Sovietology. These insights will be of great use, regardless of whether Gorbachev succeeds in his program of reform or the Soviet Union is sieged by reactionary backlash or a confused political situation emerges where no consistent policy line governs Soviet behavior. American strategic thinkers have for many years been strongly divided in their assessment of the fundamental nature of Soviet nuclear weapons policy. One side holds that the Soviet view of nuclear weapons is essentially the same as that held by the United States: that nuclear weapons use is far too destructive and uncontrollable to figure in actual military planning. Hence, the Soviet Union values nuclear weapons primarily for their deterrent value. The other side holds that some or most Soviet authorities find the potential for tactical or strategic advantage in the actual use of nuclear weapons. In this view, then, the Soviet Union has a nuclear war-fighting or war-winning strategy. Not surprisingly, there are extremes to both of these positions.

Some advocates of the "deterrence" school, for example, hold that Soviet nuclear weapons policy is governed by the theory of "mutual deterrence," essentially the policy referred to as Mutual Assured Destruction (MAD) in the American context. Some advocates of the "war-fighting" school hold that there is a Soviet politico-military consensus over the employment of nuclear weapons in combat and that Soviet arms control and strategic policy rests upon expanding the conditions in which advantageous nuclear weapons use might occur.

This Western debate is all the sharper because of the ambiguity of Soviet statements and actions concerning its nuclear weapons policy. Twenty years ago, when the serious study of Soviet nuclear intentions began, both Soviet declaratory and operational policy supported the views of the nuclear war-fighting school much more clearly than they do currently.[1] Nevertheless, advocates of the deterrence school found little trouble in identifying Soviet statements and deployment patterns to support their position. Today, although we have seen two decades of arms control negotiations and heard numerous statements by Soviet political and military leaders as to the defensive nature of Soviet military doctrine, advocates of the war-fighting position are able to point to evidence that enables them to dismiss indications to the contrary as disinformation.

It is important to recognize that all U.S. assessments of Soviet nuclear weapons policy rest on evaluating the relative authoritativeness of conflicting evidence. As Eric Beukel noted several years ago, they are *interpretations*:

> It is important to make clear that the dispute [over deterrence or warfighting] which dominates much American debate on strategic weapons policy *vis-a-vis* the Soviet Union concerns a *Western interpretation* of Soviet statements and weapons deployments.[2] (Emphasis in the original.)

Many U.S. strategic analysts not directly involved in this debate are disturbed that both sides rest their arguments on the same evidence; many partisans of one interpretation or the other are angered and frustrated that their opponents are taking good sources and twisting their significance. As early as 1978 Fritz Ermarth stated:

> Things have progressed beyond the point where it is useful to have the three familiar schools of thought on Soviet military thought arguing past each other: one saying "Whatever they say, they think as we do;" the second insisting, "Whatever they say, it does not matter;" and the third contending, "They think what they say, and are therefore out for superiority over us."[3]

Given this background, it is not surprising that a number of attempts to broker the Western debate over Soviet nuclear weapons policy have been published. In reviewing these sources, it is important to pass over works written by partisans of one interpretation for the purpose of validating their own view or debunking the other. It is also important to avoid those that attempt to resolve the U.S. debate by offering, without regard to the claims of one interpretation or the other, a "correct" way to formulate judgments on Soviet beliefs.

Instead, this chapter offers an examination of the relatively small number of works that evaluate both major U.S. interpretations with at least a show of impartiality. These works are methodological in nature; that is, they attempt to resolve the debate by pointing to problems in analytical technique that would either discredit one side or demonstrate that the question of the nature of Soviet nuclear weapons policy itself had no validity.

An exhaustive search of the literature revealed five such evaluative works. All were produced within a three-year period; that is, between 1982 and 1984. Their appearance at this time is understandable, for the preceding decade had seen the question of Soviet nuclear weapons policy injected into the internal American political process in connection with some highly contentious issues. It reflected on such matters as detente; the SALT II Treaty; the vulnerability of U.S. ballistic missile forces, especially the MX missile basing problem; and the nuclear "freeze" campaign. Furthermore, there is some evidence that the four successive works were produced directly in response to the first.

Reviewing these evaluative works yields a number of interesting results, indicating, above all, whether a methodological solution to this problem is possible, short of an even more dramatic change in Soviet politics than those we are seeing today or whether these two interpretations of Soviet nuclear weapons policy are rooted in the political viewpoints of their advocates and hence must remain locked in sterile debate. In conducting this review, one set of sources was deliberately omitted. This source is an evaluative work by the current author, which was built upon prior research involving detailed examination of Western views of Soviet nuclear weapons policy.[4] Its major conclusion was that the debate was political rather than methodological in nature and rested upon preconceptions on the part of the analysts in regard to the likelihood and relative destructiveness of nuclear war and/or their views on the nature of the Soviet political system.

The Garthoff-Pipes Debate

In 1978, Raymond Garthoff, then U.S. Ambassador to Bulgaria, published an article in the journal *International Security*, in which he described his views on fundamental Soviet attitudes toward strategic deterrence, nuclear warfighting, and arms control.[5] In 1982, Richard Pipes, then a member of the National Security Council Staff, submitted a critique of this article to the journal *Strategic Review*. Although four years had passed, the journal's editors thought the issue still timely enough to stage a debate between these two analysts.[6] Accordingly, they reprinted Garthoff's original article, along with Pipes' critique and a rebuttal by Garthoff.[7] Subsequently, the journal published reactions from two other scholars, Albert Weeks and Gerhard Wettig.[8] This "Garthoff-Pipes Debate" marks the first attempt in which the debate dividing the U.S. strategic community over the character of Soviet nuclear weapons policy was submitted to public scrutiny *as a debate*.

Garthoff's original article began by noting that the basis for possible strategic arms limitation has been questioned on the grounds that the Soviet Union does not accept the concept of mutual deterrence. Garthoff reviewed Soviet statements and actions that he saw as bearing on the subject and concluded that since the late 1960s, when SALT was launched, the Soviet political and military leadership has recognized that the strategic balance provides mutual deterrence; that the strategic balance is basically stable but requires continuing military efforts to assure its continuation; and that strategic arms limitations can make a significant contribution to reducing otherwise necessary military efforts. More broadly, Garthoff saw the Soviet leaders as believing that peaceful coexistence is the preferable alternative to an unrestrained arms race and to recurring high-risk political and military confrontation.

Pipe's critique began with the statement that three separate types of evidence had to be drawn upon in order to adduce Soviet strategic doctrine and intentions: authoritative material on the overall political and military objectives of the Soviet government, the literature on its strategic doctrine, and data on actual Soviet strategic programs and deployments. Pipes not only found Garthoff's essay flawed in its evaluation of these three types of sources, but he specifically accused Garthoff of selective use of sources and out-of-context quotations. Pipes concluded that Garthoff was searching so strongly for evidence to support his thesis that he interpreted any evidence that the Soviet Union acknowledged the unavoidability of retaliation to mean that it subscribed to the doctrine of mutual deterrence.

Garthoff's strongly worded rebuttal began with the contention that there was no contradiction between Soviet recognition of the catastrophic consequences of nuclear war and the Clausewitzian/Leninist contention that war is a political phenomenon. He agreed that discussion of military programs was necessary in analyzing Soviet strategic thinking and asserted that it would not have changed his conclusions. Garthoff accused Pipes himself of superficial understanding of fundamental Marxist-Leninist sources on war. He concluded with a point by point discussion of each of the quotes Pipes accused him of taking out of context, reaffirming in each case that the statement in question confirmed Soviet commitment to mutual deterrence. In sum, he dismissed Pipe's critique as "acid, darkly suggestive, but irrelevant" and as "Pipes-dreams."[9]

The two follow-on articles picked up on points their authors felt should have been covered by the participants in the debate, although Garthoff came in for considerably more criticism than Pipes. Albert Weeks saw the Garthoff-Pipes debate as illuminating major premises in the controversy over Soviet strategic doctrine and intention but attacked both authors for falling short of covering all the issues. He felt that they failed to address squarely a number of persistent themes in Soviet military writings, including the insistence on superiority in all military sectors, the primacy of the political and military offensive, and an undertone that rang disturbingly of preemptive war, even though it did not necessarily reflect a ready strategy-in-place for such a conflict. He felt that these themes seemed to drown out any adduced symptoms of Soviet interest in the concepts of mutual deterrence and U.S.-Soviet strategic parity. If such symptoms did exist, he felt, they probably reflected the Soviet "peace" offensive rather than any change in military thought. He felt that definitive assessment of the ultimate Soviet strategic intentions was impossible but that the available evidence as well as prudence should incline analysis in the direction of worst case assumptions.

Wettig's response was similar. After noting that the Garthoff-Pipes debate demonstrated how differing interpretations could be drawn from the same Soviet sources, he went on to observe how this illuminated the dangers of reading into Soviet statements the same motives and concepts that shape Western strategic views and hopes. He believed that for reasons of both ideology and historical experience, the Soviet Union could not accept any notion of shared security with its opponents, be it "mutual deterrence" or Mutual Assured Destruction. Nor, he felt, could it accept a theory of armed force that once invoked would be directed at anything short of victory. He qualified these observations by stating that at the level of the strategic nuclear relationship with the United States, the Soviet leaders recognized the massive dangers standing in the way of translating these concepts into achievable reality.

In the end, the Garthoff-Pipes debate was not a truly evaluative work as this study is defining the term since there was not (and could not be, given the format) an effort made to systematize the results along methodological lines. Nevertheless, it made glaringly obvious a major contention within the strategic community over Soviet strategic intentions. The need for some form of resolution was strongly spelled out.

Walt

Perhaps the first of the true evaluative works appears in a 1983 research memorandum produced by Stephen M. Walt entitled *Interpreting Soviet Military Statements: A Methodological Analysis* from the Center for Naval Analyses. The central premise of this paper is that one of the main reasons for the failure of efforts to resolve such differences is the lack of an explicit set of procedures to use in making inferences about Soviet beliefs from the statements available in the Soviet press. In short, Walt contends, the debate over Soviet military doctrine remains confused and dysfunctional, and scholars do not even agree on *why* they disagree. To develop a methodological consensus, he believes that a model of the inferential process must be developed that is sufficiently general and comprehensive to permit the various assumptions, pieces of evidence, guesses, and conclusions made by different analysts to be exposed and compared.

Walt characterizes his paper as a first step towards developing such a model and stresses that he intended it "to begin a dialogue within the analytical community." Revealing the sources of disagreement among a number of prominent interpretations of published Soviet statements, he believes, will indicate what additional types of evidence might be used to resolve interpretative disputes.

This study begins with a lengthy discussion of content analysis drawn heavily from the work of Ole Holsti and other political scientists specializing in this subject.[10] On the basis of this abstract analysis, Walt constructs a Model of Soviet Communications. The purpose of this model is to contrast the picture of Soviet military doctrine constructed by various analysts with the way the inferential process should proceed.

Walt demonstrates the usefulness of the model for distinguishing between various Western interpretations of Soviet military by examining two specific topics: the Soviet view of nuclear deterrence and Soviet doctrine regarding limited nuclear war. His stated purpose is not to determine who is right and who is wrong but to discriminate between the arguments, indicating points of disagreement and noting gaps in the evidence.

He initially selected the works of Raymond Garthoff, Stanley Sienkiewicz, Fritz Ermarth, Richard Pipes, Leon Goure, Richard Soll, John Erickson, and James McConnell for assessment. Walt sees Pipes, Erickson, Goure, and Soll as maintaining that the Soviet Union rejects the concept of mutual deterrence and that the Soviet Union believes nuclear war would be unlimited in character. The other analysts are seen by Walt as taking opposing points of view. For a variety of reasons, he excludes Pipes, Erickson, Ermarth, and Sienkiewicz from his analysis.

In contrasting the views of the remaining analysts in a one-on-one, round-robin fashion, Walt is able to find many points in which they disagreed or had gaps.

On the basis of these comparisons, Walt concludes that the general lack of agreement within the field of Soviet military analysis could be narrowed. He feels that the sources of disagreement are frequently identifiable, as are particular types of evidence that could be used to resolve the disputes. Walt feels that even his primitive model is a help and that other scholars could help to refine it.

Hart

Douglas Hart, in the spring 1984 issue of *Washington Quarterly*, published "The Hermeneutics of Soviet Military Doctrine." Hermeneuts were members of the early Church who interpreted the worship service for congregations that did not understand Latin or Greek and are an apt symbol for analysts of Soviet military doctrine since "discussions of Soviet doctrine in the Western analytical community have come to resemble arguments over scriptural interpretations."[11] Hart sets himself to examine the impact of "hermeneutics" for interpretation of Soviet military doctrine upon the formulation of U.S. defense and arms control policy. Policy makers require, in Hart's view, the services of hermeneuts for interpretation of Soviet military doctrine because the typical decision maker does not understand Russian, has no time to read the fraction of material that gets translated, and lacks the expertise to discern trends and watersheds in the stylized, ideology-laden literature of Soviet military theory.

To determine the impact of the hermeneutics of Soviet military doctrine, Hart examines what he sees as the different interpretations. He finds six, which he terms Primitivism, Convergence, Neoclausewitzianism, Talmudism, Imperialism, and Eclecticism. Hart sees a major problem with the manner in which these different interpretations affected U.S. policy. As long as decision makers face an artificial choice posed by analysts who adhere to unilateral interpretations of Soviet military thought, policy makers have no reason to consider arguments other than whether or not an interpretation supports a pre-established policy goal.

Hart's depiction of six schools of interpretation, rather than the two assumed for this study, presents no major problems of incompatibility. He sees the study of Soviet doctrine as polarized between the Primitivist and Convergence interpretations, on the one hand, and the Neoclausewitzian, on the other.[12] The remaining three interpretations, by contrast, he sees as helpful ways out of this quagmire, even though they do not have large followings, because they create the possibility of side-stepping debate on a contentious but sterile issue.

Hart identifies the Primitivism school as a holdover from the period when the United States felt smugly superior about its strategic forces and concepts. The essence of primitivism is a conviction that Soviet strategic thought is backward and hence unimportant; as Soviet strategists become better acquainted with nuclear realities, their thinking will converge with that of the United States. In the Primitivist view, arms control is important as a means of educating the Soviet Union in superior concepts of strategy. Hart has chosen Paul Warnke, Roman Kolkowicz, and Donald Hanson as representatives of this interpretation.[13]

Hart sees his Convergence interpretation as an offshoot of Primitivism, differing from it only in its assumption that the confluence of U.S. and Soviet strategic thought has already occurred. Hart characterizes Convergence as viewing "Soviet military doctrine as caught up in the dialectical tension created by the horrors of nuclear war and exigencies of Marxist-Leninist ideology."[14] For several essentially ideological reasons, adherents of the Convergence interpretation assert, the Soviet Union cannot make its support of mutual deterrence as clear as it might otherwise. Hart portrays Convergence theorists as seeing the chief utility of arms control in promoting understanding of the difficult situation the Soviet Union is in, owing to its inability to express its views clearly. In the short run, however, there should be no impediment to significant agreements on offensive strategic weapons since each nation maintains forces in excess of what it requires for mutual deterrence. He lists Raymond Garthoff as representative of the Convergence interpretation.

Neoclausewitzian is Hart's term for the warfighting interpretation, which he defines as the assertion that Soviet military doctrine endorses the political utility of nuclear war. His assessment is that Neoclausewitzians find Soviet military thought both radically different from and clearly superior to the U.S. strategy of mutual deterrence. They rely heavily on Soviet military writings, which they take as an accurate reflection of Soviet nuclear weapons policy. However, they are quick to draw an unclear distinction between doctrine, which should be interpreted literally, and propaganda, which they dismiss. For Neoclausewitzians arms control, Hart concludes, is a means for degrading an opponent's advantages. Hart cites Richard Pipes as representative of the Neoclausewitzian interpretation; he employs heavy sarcasm in discussing this view.

Hart's Talmudic, Imperial, and Eclectic interpretations are havens for those who attempt to sidestep the deterrence/warfighting debate. Advocates of the Talmudic view hold that Soviet doctrine is an elite communication devise designed to exclude the general population from strategic discourse. By the employment of semiotic tools, chiefly "semantic variation," "surrogate discussion," and "ideological strictures," the knowing analyst can tap into flexible and ongoing Soviet strategic planning. This is tied closely to the cycle of five-year plans. Adequate mastery of these techniques, contend the Talmudists, would give the United States the ability to predict developments in Soviet weapons programs and, if necessary, interfere with them. James McConnell, of the Center for Naval Analyses, is identified by Hart as the chief advocate of the Talmudic approach.[15]

The Imperial interpretation, in Hart's schemata, asserts that Soviet military doctrine is an instrument for controlling satellite nations. Soviet doctrine, with its emphasis on preparing the armed forces for war and the mechanics of modern, including nuclear, conflict, is designed to reinforce the cohesion of the Warsaw Pact. Christopher Jones is the exponent of this view selected for examination by Hart.[16] The Eclectics hold that Soviet military doctrine is not monolithic; that it reflects evolving and sometimes conflicting views on modern war. David Holloway is selected by Hart as a representative member of this group.[17] Unlike the Imperial school, the Eclectics refuse to recognize any underlying theme for Soviet military thought. Instead, they "claim that the Soviet political and military leadership have hedged their bets concerning the utility of nuclear war in an age of parity."[18]

Hart indicates that he finds the last of these interpretations the most convincing and the most helpful for U.S. policy makers, although he sees no reason why the last three cannot work in conjunction. He sees them as free of the sweeping characterizations of the entire discipline of Soviet military thought that in his view mar the other three interpretations.

Hart sums up the problem this way: If analysis of Soviet military doctrine is to become a useful tool for policy making, all-inclusive, single-factor, interpretive models must be eschewed in favor of less ambitious mechanisms that focus on specific aspects of Soviet military thought.

Herspring

Dale Herspring attempts to clarify the issue by contrasting three different analysts' views on several questions encompassed by the debate.[19] Herspring defines the Western debate over Soviet strategic policy as an argument between two groups of Western analysts. On one side are those who assert:

> that the USSR seeks primarily to defend its own security and sees its strategic weapons largely as a deterrent. Others take a more skeptical view. They contend that the USSR wishes to gain strategic superiority and plans to use its strategic weapons as an instrument for actively advancing Soviet policy.[20]

Herspring sees the debate as encompassing four areas of key importance. These include: 1) Soviet views toward mutual deterrence; 2) Soviet attitudes toward winning a nuclear war; 3) Soviet perceptions of strategic parity; and 4) the role of arms control in Soviet strategic policy. On each of these points he examines the writings of three prominent analysts of Soviet strategic policy, Raymond Garthoff, Richard Pipes, and John Erickson.[21] Although Herspring does not say so, it is clear that he sees their views as representative of three clear tendencies in the field as a whole. By contrasting their views on these issues, Herspring attempts to lay out their differences in a systematic fashion. He cautions that he is not attempting to resolve the debate. But it is clear from many of his comments that he regards the very process of setting their views on display as demonstrating the relative validity of one as opposed to the others.

Garthoff, according to Herspring, holds that mutual deterrence is the basis of Soviet strategic policy. He sees Soviet efforts in the strategic area primarily as aimed at maintaining a mutual deterrent capability, not at gaining strategic superiority, and he maintains the Soviet leadership recognizes that the strategic balance is unlikely to change significantly.[22] Herspring feels that Garthoff tends to pass over the question of Soviet war fighting or war winning capability by vaguely attributing any such capability as might exist to augmenting the credibility of deterrence and giving Moscow a contingent resort should deterrence fail.[23]

Garthoff believes that the Soviet leaders have accepted the existence of strategic parity since the early 1970s and that it is the basis for their acceptance of mutual deterrence. However, the Soviet Union is suspicious and concerned over American intentions and growing capabilities.[24] Herspring quotes Garthoff as viewing strategic arms control as tied closely to the Soviets desire to maintain overall strategic parity. He cites the Anti-Ballistic Missile (SALT I) Treaty as an example where the Soviet Union sought to prevent the United States from regaining "a position of superiority that could imperil the still unstable state of mutual assured destruction and mutual deterrence."[25]

Herspring finds Pipes completely opposed to Garthoff on almost every issue. Pipes asserts that the Soviet Union rejects the very basis upon which the Western concept of mutual deterrence rests.[26] The Soviet Union does not believe that the costs of a nuclear war necessarily outweigh the gains and totally rejects the concept of mutual vulnerability. While Pipes holds that the Soviet Union would prefer to avoid a nuclear war if at all possible, its outcome would not be suicide. Herspring notes that Pipes does not directly address the question of whether the Soviet Union believes it could employ the threat of nuclear weapons use for political purposes but suggests that his categorization of Soviet policy as Clausewitzian implies that he feels this is so. Herspring also notes that Pipes claims that Soviet policy is counterforce oriented and implicitly criticizes him in stating that the "only purpose Pipes attributes to such a doctrine is fighting and winning a nuclear war."[27]

Pipes, in Herspring's view, holds that the Soviet Union does not accept parity as a mutually desirable condition. "They do not want to give the US the capability of deterring them, and to judge from the heavy military input into their strategic policy, they feel that the only viable option is military superiority."[28] As a result, the strategic balance is by definition unstable. On this basis, Pipes questions the value of strategic arms control. "While Pipes does not say so explicitly, his argument suggests that, for Moscow, arms control negotiations are primarily aimed at enhancing Soviet strategic capabilities and, if possible, helping the Kremlin achieve strategic superiority."[29] On the other hand, Pipes does leave open the possibility that arms control might be in the US interest, provided that a more realistic view was taken of Soviet nuclear weapons policy.

John Erickson plays a significant role in Herspring's analysis. He states that Erickson's views "come out somewhere between Garthoff and Pipes."[30] Yet Herspring's descriptions of Erickson's views show them to generally fall closer to Garthoff than to Pipes. While Erickson agrees with Pipes that the Soviet Union is unwilling to trust its security to another country, he does not see this as meaning that the Soviet Union rejects mutual deterrence. Indeed, he sees deterrence as a key or even central component of Soviet strategic policy. But unlike the American concept of deterrence, which is to prevent war by threat of retaliation, the Soviet concept, according to Erickson, is to minimize the incentives for attacking the USSR.[31]

Erickson agrees with Garthoff in holding that any nuclear war-fighting capability the Soviet Union may possess is fully compatible with a deterrence strategy. Soviet statements that it would survive and prevail in a nuclear war are, in Erickson's view, ideologically motivated. He believes that Soviet military writings demonstrate full recognition of the tremendous destruction the Soviet Union would suffer in a nuclear exchange.[32]

Herspring notes that Erickson does not directly address the question of parity. But Erickson holds, with Garthoff, that the Soviet Union is deeply suspicious of U.S. efforts to upset the strategic balance. "While Erickson would agree with Pipes that the nuclear balance is inherently unstable, he would assign primary responsibility to the US, not Moscow."[33] On this basis, while admitting that Erickson does not directly discuss the role of arms control in Soviet policy, Herspring concludes that he would say that the Soviet Union would take a skeptical view of it, while nevertheless pushing ahead on its research and development programs to avoid falling behind the United States.[34]

Herspring apparently holds that Garthoff and Pipes are articulate spokesmen for two opposing views that each have strengths and weaknesses. By introducing Erickson as a third, "moderate" view, Herspring is able to lay out the areas in which he feels the extremes lack plausibility. On the whole, it would appear that Herspring feels that Garthoff's views are more valid than Pipes, if a bit too optimist. At no point in his essay does he imply criticism of Erickson's views.

Lambeth

Benjamin S. Lambeth lays out what he terms a "preliminary stocktaking of Western research on Soviet strategic policy" in a 1984 note entitled *The State of Western Research on Soviet Military Strategy and Policy*. His work begins with a brief survey of Western research on the subject since the early 1950s, then turns to an examination of the key issues in contention in the Western debate. Lambeth dismisses the "Garthoff-Pipes Debate" over Soviet strategic policy as essentially concerning different dimensions of Soviet military thought, Garthoff being preoccupied with the political component of Soviet military doctrine and Pipes with the military-technical side, concerning what to do if deterrence fails. "As the following discussion will point out, there is no necessary contradiction between stress on deterrence by the Soviet political leadership and dominance of concern over offensive war waging in the Soviet military literature."[35]

Instead, Lambeth feels that it is the core nature of the Soviet Union, including military strength, external motivations, and the "threat" implications for the West, rather than Soviet doctrine in isolation that lies behind the U.S. debate. One side he terms simply "conservatives," accusing them of having a narrow fixation on doctrine without regard to content and indulging in "uncritical quote-mongering."[36] The other he refers to more vaguely as those who take a "prismatic approach that posits a "natural" divergence between Party and military views concerning the Soviet security dilemma."[37]

Lambeth identifies a number of major points of contention between these opposing schools. These include the question of war as a continuation of politics, the offensive orientation of Soviet military doctrine, strategic superiority as a Soviet force posture goal, and the argument over deterrence vs. warfighting. He discusses these questions with little direct reference to the actual analysts who hold to one side or the other on each of these points of contention. In concluding this phase of his study, he notes that more and better work is being done in studying the Soviet military than ever before. Yet he laments the fact that this research is so unconnected and contends that real understanding is not possible until the analytic community forges a consensus on these issues or is able to get beyond them.

In the final portion of his study, Lambeth attempts to lay down a basis for future debate by dealing with some problems of interpretation and some important rules of evidence; in short, a methodological framework. These include the trouble with translations, which he sees not only as leaving the analyst at the mercy of the translator, but also as abdicating control over one's data base. He holds that context is critical since the institutional and political origins of a particular Soviet spokesman, as well as the current nature of each source and its pertinency to the subject at hand, can affect the authoritativeness of any Soviet statement. He asserts that staffers of Soviet civilian research institutes who "specialize" in foreign and international security affairs are of marginal relevance. Lambeth reminds his readers that Soviet statements have to be judged by Soviet ability or willingness to carry them out. Set against this, he adds, is force posture as a mirror to Soviet intent; that is, Soviet ability to use forces in ways not clearly spelled out in their military writings. Lambeth contends that there is too great a willingness on the part of Western commentators to assume a Soviet policy "debate" is occurring because they have found two conflicting statements on the same issue and that evidence for debate takes much more sophisticated analysis. Finally, he takes up the case of the "Tula Line," the issue of whether a shift in high-level Soviet policy rhetoric from the late 1970s represents a real change in Soviet thinking or is merely a propaganda campaign.

Lambeth concludes his study with the thought that there is no more evidence to be gained from Soviet political-military literature on large questions bearing on the Western strategic debate. He advocates a shift in analytical attention to the norms, practices, and processes that constitute actual Soviet military behavior. He describes several areas in which he would like to see such research take place. In sum, he calls for moving beyond "quotational exegesis toward increasingly integrated looks into the Soviet armed forces as they actually are."[38]

Conclusions

These studies share a number of common features. The authors are badly split on the most important issue: how can methodological reform improve analysis. The editors of *Strategic Review* and Herspring leave their readers to draw their own conclusions after laying out the positions of the opposing sides. Walt is optimistic that methodological reform alone can mend the split. Both Hart and Lambeth seem to feel that the issue of the fundamental character of Soviet nuclear weapons policy is both too superficial and too deeply divisive for easy resolution. Instead, they recommend evading this central issue, focusing instead upon specific questions of military or strategic analysis.

Can this safely be done? Currently analysts of Soviet strategic affairs seem to be taking the Lambeth/Hart prescription seriously for few works on the central issue have appeared in the last few years. Much of this is due, no doubt, to the numerous initiatives in the strategic area launched by Gorbachev. Yet the issues of concern seem, ultimately, too fundamental to be sidestepped. Sooner or later, probably in renewed debate over U.S. strategic arms control or force structure, this issue is likely to be revived. No amount of methodological reform can prevent this for the issue is of basic premises about the Soviet Union, not analytical technique. And regardless of the success of Gorbachev's policies, few U.S. analysts are likely to change the premises of their beliefs on Soviet behavior, so long as the global strategic environment is dominated by two nuclear superpowers.

Notes

[1]I mark this study as beginning with the publication of William R. Kintner and Harriet Fast Scott's *The Nuclear Revolution in Soviet Military Affairs*, (Norman, OK: University of Oklahoma Press, 1968).

[2]Eric Beukel, "Analyzing the Views of Soviet Leaders on Nuclear Weapons," *Cooperation and Conflict*, Vol. 15, June 1980, p. 74.

[3]Fritz W. Ermarth, "Contrasts in American and Soviet Strategic Thought," *International Security*, Fall 1978, p. 140.

[4]See, for example, William C. Green, *Soviet Nuclear Weapons Policy: A Research and Bibliographic Guide*, (Boulder, CO: Westview Press, 1987).

[5]Raymond L. Garthoff, "Mutual Deterrence and Strategic Arms Limitation in Soviet Policy," *International Security*, Summer 1978, pp. 112-147.

[6]Garthoff, prior to joining the Foreign Service, conducted ground breaking research on Soviet military doctrine in the 1950s. He appears to have coined the term "mutual deterrence" to disassociate his understanding of Soviet views from the controversy surrounding the term "Mutual Assured Destruction." Pipes, an eminent historian of

revolutionary Russia at Harvard University, chaired the controversial "B Team," a panel of outside experts that in 1976-77 reviewed CIA sources used to prepare the National Intelligence Estimate on Soviet strategic forces. Shortly afterwards he published an article with the provocative title "Why the Soviet Union Thinks It Can Fight and Win a Nuclear War," *Commentary*, July 1977, pp. 21-34. The editors of *Strategic Review* correctly concluded that it was a matter of extreme concern that two such highly credentialed authorities on Soviet strategic policy should disagree on such a fundamental issue.

[7]"A Garthoff-Pipes Debate on Soviet Strategic Doctrine," *Strategic Review*, Fall 1982, pp. 36-63.

[8]Albert L. Weeks, "The Garthoff-Pipes Debate on Soviet Doctrine: Another Perspective," *Strategic Review*, Winter 1983, pp. 57-64; Gerhard Wettig, "The Garthoff-Pipes Debate on Soviet Strategic Doctrine: A European Perspective," *Strategic Review*, Spring 1983, pp. 68-78.

[9]"Garthoff-Pipes Debate...," p. 60.

[10]Ole Holsti, *Content Analysis for the Social Sciences and Humanities*, (Reading, MA: Addison-Wesley, 1969).

[11]Douglas Hart, "The Hermeneutics of Soviet Military Doctrine," *Washington Quarterly*, Spring 1984, p. 77.

[12]*Ibid.*, p. 86.

[13]Paul Warnke, "Testimony before the U.S. Congress, Senate Committee on Banking, Housing, and Urban Affairs," *Civil Defense*, January 8, 1987, (Washington, D.C.: Government Printing Office, 1979); "The Real Paul Warnke," *The New Republic*, March 26, 1977; Roman Kolkowicz, "Soviet-American Strategic Relations: Implications for Arms Control," in Kolkowicz, et al., *The Soviet Union and Arms Control: A Superpower Dilemma*, (Baltimore, MD: Johns Hopkins University Press, 1970); Donald Hanson, "Is Soviet Strategic Doctrine Superior?" *International Security*, Winter 1982/1983.

[14]Hart, *op. cit.*, p. 78.

[15]James B. McConnell, *The Interacting Evolution of Soviet and American Military Doctrines*, (Alexandria, VA: Center for Naval Analyses, M-80.1313.00, September 17, 1980).

[16]Christopher Jones, "Soviet Military Doctrine and Warsaw Pact Exercises," in Derek Leebaert (ed.), *Soviet Military Thinking*, (London: George Allen and Unwin, 1981); Jones, "Soviet Military Doctrine: The Policy Dimension," in William Kincade and Jeffrey Poor (eds.), *Negotiating Security*, (Washington, D.C.: The Carnegie Endowment for International Peace).

[17]Dale Herspring, "Soviet Strategic Policy: Some Western Views," *Naval Intelligence Quarterly*, March 1984, pp. 17-24.

[18]Hart, *op. cit.*, p. 85.

[19]Dale R. Herspring, "Soviet Strategic Policy: Some Western Views," *Naval Intelligence Quarterly*, March 1984, pp. 17-24.

[20]*Ibid.*, p. 17.

[21]Herspring takes Erickson's views from "The Soviet View of Deterrence: A General Survey," *Survival*, November-December 1982, pp. 242-251. The other works by Garthoff and Pipes are adopted from works previously mentioned in this chapter.

[22]Herspring, *op. cit.*, p. 18.

[23]*Ibid.*, p. 19.

[24]*Ibid.*, p. 21.

[25]*Ibid.*, p. 22.

[26]*Ibid.*, p. 18.

[27]*Ibid.*, p. 20.

[28]*Ibid.*, p. 21.

[29]*Ibid.*, p. 23.

[30]*Ibid.*, p. 18.

[31]*Ibid.*

[32]*Ibid.*

[33]*Ibid.*, p. 22.

[34]*Ibid.*, p. 23.

[35]Benjamin S. Lambeth, *The State of Western Research on Soviet Military Strategy and Policy*, (Santa Monica, CA: The RAND Corporation, N-2230-AF, October 1984), p. 15.

[36]*Ibid.*, p. 16.

[37]*Ibid.*, p. 16.

[38]*Ibid.*

3

Civil-Military Relations Under Gorbachev: The Struggle over National Security

Thomas Nichols and Theodore Karasik

The chapters in this volume describe the turbulent changes occurring in various areas of Soviet defense policy.[1] From the military uses of space to the length of a draftee's service, the Soviet defense establishment is undergoing scrutiny, and, thanks to glasnost (openness), it is alive with debate and disagreement. Underlying these many disagreements, however, is a chronic and more fundamental problem, one that strikes at the very nature of the Party's authority in military affairs.

This conflict is not over policy; Soviet civilian and military leaders confer and cooperate on a host of prosaic issues. But the resolution of these lesser questions does not carry implications for power and authority in the Soviet system raised by the struggle over military doctrine and national security policy itself. Thus the issue is not policy; it is power.

The struggle over control of Soviet national security policy is not new; since the Russian revolution tension between the leadership and the military dominated civil-military relations. Although Iosif Stalin managed to circumvent these tensions (through the most efficient means possible, i.e. murder), every Soviet leader since has faced the dilemma created by a lack of authority over military issues. Nikita Khrushchev's failure to dominate the military in the 1960s and Leonid Brezhnev's unwillingness to oppose military priorities in the 1970s heightened the anxiety over control of the military. Soviet President Mikhail Gorbachev and his followers, like Khrushchev, chose to confront this chronic source of conflict, and the present period may be the final stage in the evolution of the Soviet civil-military relationship: either the civilians will fail and the defense agenda will be dominated by the military, or they will succeed and the Soviet military will be relegated, like its Western counterparts, to provide options and advice but not participate directly in politics.

The debate is marked by three phases: the introduction of the *novoe myshlenie,* or new thinking, in 1986; the creation of a new military doctrine in 1987; and the current disagreements over the concept of reasonable sufficiency. These are considered chronologically, as each phase provides context for the next.

Origins of the New Thinking

Gorbachev's plans for domestic economic and political reforms, unveiled almost immediately upon his appointment as general secretary of the Communist Party of the Soviet Union, necessitated either unwilling subordination or political acquiescence on the part of the military. Perhaps seeking to avoid Khrushchev's reputation for thoughtless blundering, Gorbachev tried to make his reform of defense policy intelligible to both Soviet military elites and the West with a set of concepts that are known as new thinking. The new thinking, which made its appearance in the wake of the April 1985 Plenum, served two purposes: first, it signaled Gorbachev's desire (and provided him a rationalization) for better relations and improved arms control with the West, and second, it served as the philosophical groundwork for a civilian offensive aimed at wresting control of the security agenda from the military.

Early Aspects of the New Thinking

Neither Gorbachev himself nor his spokesmen ever sought to delineate exactly what is comprised in the new thinking. The contours and implications of the new thinking, however, are easily deduced, as was no doubt intended by its author. Throughout 1985 and 1986, Gorbachev revealed the foundations of this idea through comprehensive statements.

An important and fundamental aspect is how Gorbachev redefines Soviet security needs. In his estimation, the desirability of detente and the inherent reasonableness of the West are first and foremost. In his first day in power, Gorbachev told the Central Committee:

> We will firmly follow the Leninist course of peace and peaceful coexistence. The Soviet Union will always answer good will with good will, trust with trust. But all should know that we will never forego the interests of our *Rodina* and her allies. We value the successes of the detente in international tensions achieved in the 1970s, and are ready to participate in the continuation of the process of starting the peaceful, mutually beneficial cooperation between states on the bases of equal rights, mutual respect and non-interference in internal affairs.[2]

Gorbachev officially initiated his reform program at the April 1985 Plenum of the Central Committee, one of the key political events of this decade. He also expanded on his foreign policy concepts. Despite the efforts of "certain circles in Washington," Gorbachev told the members of the Central Committee:

Our readiness to improve relations with the United States of America is well-known....There isn't some sort of fatal unavoidability of confrontation of the two nations. If the positive as well as negative experiences of the accumulated history of Soviet-American relations, recent as well as distant history, are interpreted, then it follows that the most reasonable path is to find the way leading to the smoothing of relations, and to build bridges of cooperation, but to build them from both sides.[3]

Here, Gorbachev went beyond denying the inevitability of war by rejecting the inevitability of confrontation.[4] At both the Plenum and afterwards, Gorbachev stated that he was aware of the West's recalcitrance but held out the hope that the American position could be corrected.[5] Indeed, Gorbachev's speeches throughout 1985 contain, side by side, excoriations of American stubbornness and hopes of American reasonability.

Eight months later, some of the implications of this new view were explained. "The USSR and the US," Gorbachev said,

will have to reach a common understanding of what level of weapons on each side could be considered relatively sufficient....We are convinced that this level of sufficiency is much lower than that which the USSR and the United States in fact possess at the moment.[6]

Thus, Gorbachev began a program to revitalize international security. However, the details of Gorbachev's thinking emerged in greater clarity at the 27th Party Congress in February 1986.

The 27th Party Congress

A new Soviet leader's first Party congress is always his opportunity to place his stamp on foreign and domestic policy; for Gorbachev it was no different. The first foreign policy theme taken up by Gorbachev at the 27th Congress was his own interpretation of the problems of international security:

The character of present weapons does not leave a single state with the hope of defending itself only by military-technical means, in other words, through the creation of new weapons, even the most powerful. The guaranteeing of security ever more appears as a political problem, and it can be resolved only by political means. Above all, the will is needed to embark on the path of disarmament.[7]

The key aspects of this passage are that it undercuts longstanding military arguments about the dangerous and radical impact of new weaponry and, perhaps most important, it explicitly establishes the problem of security as within the exclusive purview of politicians ("security is ever more a political problem") rather than soldiers. Gorbachev reinforced this point by arguing that new weapons systems shorten the time to make "*political* decisions on the questions of war and peace" during a crisis. (Emphasis added)[8]

In a return to language similar to that of the days of the Soviet reliance on collective security in the 1930's, Gorbachev emphasized that security must be mutual in the case of Soviet-American relations and general in the case of international relations at large. He then moved on to admit the dangerous aggressiveness of the United States military-industrial complex but countered by noting that "the interests and goals of the military-industrial complex are not entirely one and the same with the interests and goals of the American people, nor with the underlying national interests of that great nation."[9]

Finally, Gorbachev sought to move the debate on security away from strictly military considerations. In the tradition of Western socialists and social-democrats, Gorbachev embraced a functionalist definition of security that argued for striking at the causes of conflict rather than on armaments to defend against conflicts. In essence, he argued that the cause of peace cannot be furthered without "a thoroughgoing system of international economic security," a phrase that also appeared, predictably enough, in Gorbachev's welcoming remarks before his 1985 meeting with former West German Chancellor Willy Brandt.[10]

These themes were quickly taken up by Gorbachev's supporters and allies, particularly among what are now known as the "*institutchiki*," the small, fledgling group of civilian defense analysts who work at various Soviet think tanks such as the Institute of USA/Canada or IMEMO, the Institute of International Economy and International Relations. Senior figures such as former United States ambassador and now foreign policy advisor Anatolii Dobrynin, Politburo Member and Foreign Minister Eduard Shevardnadze, Politburo Member Aleksandr Yakovlev, and others lead these *institutchiki* through the defense policy debate.

The new line taken by Gorbachev in 1985 and 1986 contained two basic implications, one foreign and one domestic: reduced military expenditures and acceptance of asymmetrical arms agreements. The domestic aspect also saw an increase on the attacks on the military in society and on virtually all military privileges, including the draft. While this was coupled with a general desire for greater flexibility in arms control, the Gorbachev group apparently had little idea how their proposed changes would materialize in actual practice.

The Early Military Reaction

If Gorbachev hoped that his statements at the 27th Party Congress would serve to head off some of the emerging military opposition to his pronouncements, he clearly misjudged how the military might react. Indeed, the lack of clarity in the Gorbachev program did not prevent an attack from the military regarding this new policy orientation. (In Eastern Europe as well there were indications of opposition to the new line.)[11] Several Soviet senior officers voiced doubts in the wake of the Congress in early 1986, and criticism grew in intensity into the summer. Former Ground Forces CINC (Commander in Chief) Evgenni Ivanovskii, for example, argued that the West could not live peaceably with the USSR:

> Now when the imperialist states spurn the peace-loving, clear and honorable proposals of the Soviet government, strengthen military preparations, and seek to carry the arms race into space, it is especially necessary that our tireless struggle for peace be organically combined with the readiness to rebuff any aggressor.[12]

Colonel General V.S. Nechaev of the MPA (Main Political Administration) also agreed. "The ruling circles of the United States," he wrote in the spring of 1986, "have not rejected the course of stirring up war hysteria."[13] Likewise, Nechaev referred to the failure of arms initiatives and the dangerous attitude it reveals: "The Soviet Union, of course, cannot fail to take into account the militaristic actions of the United States."[14] Ironically, both Ivanovskii's and Nechaev's comments appeared in a series of pamphlets whose ostensible purpose was to explain and support the work of the Congress.

Deputy Minister of Defense for Armaments, Army General Vitalii Shabanov, also put it bluntly that summer:

> Through the fault of imperialistic circles in the USA the international situation remains complicated. The aggressiveness of imperialism not only is not decreasing, but on the contrary, it is getting greater.[15]

Later in the year, Shabanov returned to the theme of expenditures; he pointed out that the expense involved in the production of the first Soviet ICBMs was great but that Western aggressiveness left the Soviets no choice. At the same time, he admitted point blank that the Soviets, like the Americans, planned for a first strike, but again, as a matter of necessity.[16]

Through the spring and summer of 1986, military alarmism continued unabated. Military authors wanted their audience to remember not only the dangers of conventional conflict but also the possibility of all-out nuclear war. One author, Colonel V.A. Zubkov, added a nuclear twist to a growing number of military warnings about surprise attack. Zubkov wrote in March 1986 that the West planned the nuclear destruction of both military and civilian targets, and he used this threat to argue for greater militarization of the economy:

> The possibility of the surprise unleashing of war by the imperialist states demands the supporting of high mobilizational readiness not only of the armed forces, but also of the nation's economy. The necessity of high readiness of the domestic economy is defined by the fact that in a future war the conditions of economic mobilization and work of the rear is significantly more complex. The militarist circles of the USA and NATO are planning on the massive use of rocket-nuclear weapons not only against groupings of forces and military objectives, but also against the rear and throughout the entire depth with the goal of the destruction or the essential undermining of military-economic potential, disruption of the system of economic communications and control, and the demoralization of the population.[17]

Zubkov hinted that the only barrier to this mobilizational requirement was political will, not Soviet capabilities. "A level of development of science and technology has been achieved in our country," he wrote near his conclusion, "that allows the successful solving of the most complex technical problems and the creation in a short period of any kind of weapon on which the aggressors are counting."[18]

Throughout the summer of 1986, other officers joined in with presentations that integrated the threats of nuclear attack and general conventional war into even more nightmarish scenarios.[19] One officer even raised the formerly off-limits topic of nuclear victory. At an October 1986 conference on the role of social scientists in relation to the 27th Party Congress, then MPA Colonel General Dmitrii Volkogonov took the offensive against what he apparently saw as serious dangers of moral relativism and irresoluteness. He first warned that the imperialists are in a position to launch a war they cannot win, and he then moved to a more serious problem. Volkogonov noted that "in the Party program, a clear-cut problem was formulated" and put before the Armed Forces. How, he asked, can the Armed Forces be tasked to "smash any aggressor," while "at the same time, it is asserted in one of our journals that the wisdom of Soviet military doctrine lies in the fact that the word "victory" has disappeared there. I think," he added, "that we cannot agree with this interpretation."[20]

Thus, the Soviets entered 1987 in disarray. The new thinking failed to permeate the ranks of the Soviet military because no clear agenda for security policy took hold. Even the meetings between Gorbachev and former United States President Ronald Reagan failed to generate results that Gorbachev could then present as evidence of the correctness of his approach. By 1987, the Soviet defense establishment became a doctrinal mess. The leadership failed in two major efforts. The first was an attempt at an overall civilian redefinition of the security environment. The second, related goal was to reestablish the Party leadership, and Gorbachev personally, as the unambiguous source of military doctrine. The military's acceptance of Gorbachev's philosophy was ritualistic at best and accompanied by clear signs of doubt and dissent.

By 1987, glasnost added an edge to the attacks on Gorbachev's policies as military critics became more and more direct. Former WTO (Warsaw Treaty Organization) CINC Marshal Viktor Kulikov expressed his frustration at Gorbachev's nonconfrontational policy. Interviewed in the newspaper *Trud*, Kulikov warned that "today, Europe is the most explosively dangerous place on Earth." The choice of alternatives, for him, is no choice at all:

> Regrettably, the voice of reason does not reach everyone. We propose peace to them, they propose war to us. Therefore, it has been necessary for us to buttress the possibilities of our diplomacy with the possibilities of our Armed Forces. Their high combat might is a factor of huge significance. They restrain the imperialists from the wish to set us up in a test of forces.[21]

Little wonder that these comments (made in observance of Army-Navy Day) were relegated to *Trud* rather than *Pravda*.

Army General Valentin Varennikov, a longtime deputy chief of the General Staff, prepared an even more dedicated attack on the new thinking even as Kulikov was giving his interview. Varennikov's views had a new importance because of his promotion to CINC of the Ground Forces on February 22, 1989. (This post, according to some in Moscow, was gained through "old-boy" political connections in the Central Committee.) Varennikov's article contained the classic style of official Soviet dissent: criticism cloaked behind an initial outburst of obsequious approbation. Among other things, Varennikov began by referring to the Armed Forces as "equipped with everything necessary," as well as to the new thinking, "at whose foundation lies the Leninist principle of peaceful coexistence of states with different social structures, and a concrete accounting of the realities of the nuclear-space age."[22] Varennikov soon dispensed with ritual, however, and turned sharply critical. He repeated the Congress formulation on the primacy of politics and then followed it directly by warning:

> But the Soviet Union cannot fail to take into account that in practice imperialism still leans on military aspects, on the arms race. The USA and the other NATO countries are not heading for agreement. To the contrary, they are striving in every way possible to break out into the lead in the military-technical aspect.[23]

Varennikov also revealed a very different view of the United States than that shown by the General Secretary. While Gorbachev was disappointed with the Reykjavik summit and the Administration's actions, his evaluation of it was generally cool-headed and showed a certain amount of awareness of the relationship between Reagan's behavior and American domestic politics.[24] However, Varennikov's explanation attempted to define American behavior at Reykjavik: "reactionary forces are forming the policy of the USA."

Two concrete political signs appeared in early 1987 that trouble existed between the leadership and the military. The first was Gorbachev's surprising public confirmation of himself as head of the Defense Council:

> The Soviet leadership and the country's Defense Council, which I am instructed to head, constantly keep the problems of the security of the country, of that of our allies, and of universal security, at the center of attention.[25]

This direct claim is unusual for a Soviet leader, and Gorbachev probably felt it necessary in order to shore up his authority.

This event coincided with an apparent bow to political sensitivities by then Deputy Minister of Defense and Chief of the General Staff Marshal Sergei Akhromeev on the front page of *Sovetskaia Rossiia*. Akhromeev noted that the Plenum, Gorbachev's February 16 peace conference speech, and Gorbachev's recent foreign policy initiatives all pointed up the realities upon which the new thinking is based:

> (I)n the modern nuclear-space age, the guaranteeing of security appears ever more to be a political problem. It can never be guaranteed through military-technical means, even through the creation of the most powerful offensive or defensive forces, including a "space shield."[26]

In other words, one year later to the month, Akhromeev endorsed, word for word, Gorbachev's statements from the 27th Party Congress, dampening the more dire predictions made about SDI and rebalancing the definition of military doctrine in favor of the social-political rather than the military-technical side. Moreover, Akhromeev explicitly bowed to civilian supremacy. Resolution of these pressing security problems, he said, "can and should" be done through political means.

In retrospect, it is evident that a major purpose of Akhromeev's *Sovetskaia Rossiia* piece served as a preview of the new military doctrine that would be unveiled in May 1987. "Soviet military doctrine," he wrote, "is created and developed in accordance with the policy of the CPSU, and the principles of the new political thinking. Thus, the 27th Party Congress confirmed the defensive trend of Soviet military doctrine," in particular by approving a policy of no first use of nuclear weapons.

Two other noteworthy attempts to neutralize criticism occurred early in 1987. One was the direct intervention of the MPA Chief, Army General Aleksei Lizichev, himself. Lizichev was tasked with what can only be considered as a rearguard defense of the new thinking in the pages of *Kommunist*.[27] The opposition to the new thinking in defense circles is revealed indirectly by Lizichev's defensive response:

> To any sensible person it is clear that peace-loving initiatives, coming from a powerful state, are not evidence of weakness but rather are a manifestation of the necessity in the modern era for new political thinking.[28]

Lizichev was aware of the conservative argument and anticipated it by admitting to recent American recalcitrance; he even drew a parallel between the modern era and those dangerous days after the Russian Revolution and went so far as to call the world situation "explosively dangerous." (For him, however, all of this made obedience to the Party's demands on the military even more paramount.)[29]

Lizichev also confronted the problem of alarmism directly. Military expenditures are always dictated by defense needs, he said, and he followed this point with a discussion of the Soviet demobilizations after the Civil War and World War II:

> And today expenditures on defense, the number of personnel in the Army and Navy, the quantity and quality of weapons and military equipment are defined exclusively by the demands of the Fatherland and the collective defense of the gains of socialism. In our country, nothing more is being done than is necessary.[30]

Lizichev was not speaking in the abstract; there were those who obviously disagreed with what is "necessary." Lizichev admitted that there is danger in carelessness, complacency, and "naive pacifism" but warned that there is similar danger in overestimating the "potentialities" of imperialism's aggressive circles.[31]

This was not the first time one of the more recently appointed officers attempted to label the new thinking as a threat to Soviet foreign policy. SRF (Strategic Rocket Forces) CINC General Yuri Maksimov, marking Rocket Forces/Artillery Day on Soviet television in November 1986, foreshadowed Lizichev's rhetoric:

> Our peace-loving course is dictated not by weakness, but by our consciousness of a high responsibility for the fate of mankind, and rests on taking full account of the realities of the contemporary state of affairs in the international arena.[32]

Although Maksimov also referred to the "threat of war which now exists," it is evident that the new thinking created much more controversy in the military than was revealed in the press, glasnost notwithstanding.

A New Military Doctrine

On May 28-29, 1987, the Political Consultative Committee (PCC) of the Warsaw Treaty Organization (WTO) met in Berlin to discuss military doctrine.[33] The meeting produced a document, simply titled "On Military Doctrine" in the Soviet press. The document was not revolutionary in any detailed way since it outlined the "new" WTO doctrine only in broad strokes.

Of course, Gorbachev led the Soviet delegation. Other participants listed as official members of the Soviet mission included then President and Politburo Member Andrei Gromyko, Prime Minister and Politburo Member Nikolai Ryzhkov, Eduard Shevardnadze, then Minister of Defense and Candidate Politburo Member Sergei Sokolov, and Central Committee Secretary Vadim Medvedev (then a Gorbachev appointee in charge of Soviet-East bloc party relations, promoted directly to full Politburo member in September 1988). Of these, only Gromyko and Sokolov could be thought of as possible opponents of the new doctrine, and their positions, weakened since 1985, guaranteed that they could not significantly harden the final document. Ryzhkov, only the month before, supported the new thinking explicitly (and with none of the more conservative pro-defense attitudes exhibited at times by conservative Egor Ligachev).[34]

The Berlin Declaration appeared in the Soviet press on May 31, 1987, and contained six major proposals:

1. A moratorium on nuclear testing (a sore point with the Soviet military), as the first step to later moratoria on development and production and finally to liquidation of all nuclear weapons and consequently to a halt to SDI.

2. Liquidation of all chemical weapons "and other types of weapons of mass annihilation." (Ostensibly, this could be taken to mean conventional as well as nuclear systems.)

3. Reduction of forces in Europe to levels at which neither side can successfully execute a surprise attack "or begin offensive operations in general."

4. Creation of a workable arms control regime, including verification both through national technical means as well as on-site inspection by international bodies (and not, it should be noted, by American or Soviet teams).

5.   Creation of nuclear and chemical-free trust building zones on land and at sea, disbanding of bases on foreign soil, withdrawal of troops to national borders, and the mutual renunciation of force as an instrument.

6.   Eventual liquidation of the WTO and NATO, as an extension of the view that the "continuing division of Europe into opposing military blocs is abnormal," and supplanting them with an "all-embracing system of international security."[35]

It is not difficult to find Gorbachev's fingerprints all over the Berlin Declaration, whatever the official press may say about "consultation." (This does not mean, however, that the Eastern Europeans granted unanimous accord to the new thinking but only that the Soviets, and in this case the General Secretary, dominate the PCC on key questions.)[36]

Reactions to the Berlin Declaration

The Berlin Declaration on doctrine was accepted widely in the military press, but questions similar to those posed by Kulikov in March 1987 reappeared nonetheless.[37] One military observer asked in July 1987 why the West did not respond to the new doctrine. His answer, like Kulikov's, asserted that the West is simply unprepared for a defense-dominant world. Answering his own question, the writer claimed that the West realizes what would result from a comparison of doctrines: "the military doctrine of the NATO nations has a far from defensive character; its key element, flexible response, pursues offensive, aggressive goals."[38] Another sign of problems was the fact that it took the military press almost four months to publish even a short article on educating the troops about the new doctrine; usually, such study notes appear within days of official announcements, and the article carried neither a signature nor identification as an MPA piece.[39]

Actually, taken in the context of military rhetoric in 1986 and 1987, the Berlin Declaration in retrospect seems more a defensive maneuver by Gorbachev rather than a bold new stroke. The idea of the "defensive" character of Soviet military doctrine was, after all, emphasized at the 27th Party Congress, and the opposition to it on the part of the military is clear right up to the May 1987 meeting itself. Indeed, looking back, it is a fair question to ask why Gorbachev waited until late May to hold the PCC meeting; it gave the military group repeated chances to make their case in the press on Soviet V-E Day (May 9).

Marshal Kulikov realized this, for he seized the opportunity to argue themes that were very much out of step with the Berlin Declaration (assuming he knew of its existence). No doubt he did; he even pointed out that the United States did not give "a constructive answer" to the last PCC overture, approved at a 1986 meeting in Budapest.[40] In Kulikov's view, this was hardly the time to try and reason with the West:

The problem of saving ourselves, of saving our future, now stands before mankind in its full magnitude. Never before has the situation been so close to that dangerous borderline, across which is the destruction of everything alive, as today. And blame for this totally and fully rests with imperialism. Its policy is the policy of the most reactionary, militaristic, aggressive forces of modern times.[41]

Kulikov's interview ran in *Izvestiia* on Victory Day, but he used the opportunity to reemphasize the dangers of being duped by arms control rhetoric. He praised Soviet arms initiatives, as usual, and then added:

Regrettably, while admitting in words the inadmissability of nuclear war, the ruling circles of the United States and the imperialist states continue their material preparation for it. Dreams of world hegemony hypnotize the leading figures of the USA.[42]

Virtually nothing had changed since Kulikov's March interview in *Trud*; if he knew of the impending PCC meeting, he either criticized it or attempted to derail it. While Gorbachev pushed defensiveness, Kulikov countered that only the ability and willingness to use force had restrained United States "reactionaries" so far.[43]

Once the Berlin declaration appeared, Kulikov used it as well to return to this point, this time in the Bulgarian military press. "NATO's threat to the socialist countries is completely real," he said, citing President Reagan's June 1987 West Berlin speech as proof. Then:

I shall stress that this [speech by Reagan] was explicitly said after the allied socialist countries declared at the Berlin meeting of the Political Consultative Committee that they will never and under no circumstances begin military actions against any state or alliance first, providing that they are not themselves the target of an armed attack.[44]

While Kulikov painted this not so subtle portrait of the General Secretary as militarily naive, even Marshal Akhromeev began expressing reservations. Akhromeev's Victory Day declaration was far more supportive of Gorbachev, and Akhromeev's style is more nuanced and his outlook is more progressive than Kulikov's. However, this more polished style did not conceal his fears:

Reactionary forces in the USA and some of its allies are trying not to curb the arms race. [They are] perfecting...nuclear weapons. [This] is absurd and criminal....and [they] are trying to attain world supremacy.[45]

The obvious difference between Kulikov and Akhromeev is that the former Chief of the General Staff realized the potential for negotiation with the reasonable elements in the West, and that made a major difference in his view of Gorbachev's policies. Kulikov, by contrast, argued explicitly that in the West, the "inmates are now running the asylum" and hopes for dialogue are based more on wishes than reality.

After the Berlin Declaration, the leadership recognized the absence of significant gains in reform of Soviet military doctrine. Apparently sensitive to a possible image problem, an anonymous Soviet analyst made some rather bold statements while on a visit to Western Europe. The anonymous "high-ranking Soviet" indicated that all was not going smoothly back in Moscow. "We are no longer talking about winning the war...but about how to prevent it, to which end a doctrine of "sufficiency" was being developed." Not that it has been easy to do:

> (I)n all areas, the Soviet Union is currently involved in a thoroughgoing reevaluation of its military posture. That does not sit well with a good many people. But the leadership's necessary political decision will be implemented.[46]

The message to the West was clear: change is underway, despite the signs of struggle.

The Debate Over Reasonable Sufficiency

Since 1987, the Soviet civil-military defense debate fractured into a number of distinct arguments, but the most important concerns the size and direction of the Soviet armed forces into the next century. This is the debate over the right to define "reasonable sufficiency."

Reasonable sufficiency lies within the framework of the new thinking. In essence, proponents of reasonable sufficiency take the new thinking argument into the practical realm, arguing that Soviet security can be maintained at a lower level of armaments and that strictly symmetrical, tit-for-tat responses to Western arms programs are not necessary. The Soviet formulation maintains that the Soviet Union will not seek a greater level of security than other nations but at the same time cannot accept military inferiority; however, there is still some confusion over what constitutes "inferiority" and specifically over whether it should be interpreted in a strictly numerical sense. This kind of imprecise language means that the definition of reasonable sufficiency remains flexible and thus continues to elicit substantial debate within the Soviet military.

Soviet military leaders view Gorbachev's definition of reasonable sufficiency in several forms. A pro-Gorbachev group (small though it is) articulates a version of reasonable sufficiency somewhat similar to that advocated by Gorbachev himself. Unlike Gorbachev, however, this group sees in reasonable sufficiency a rejection of unilateral or asymmetrical initiatives in arms control, while agreeing that strategic parity may not be required either. These leaders still see the West as a threat to Soviet interests but also see political methods as the primary means of achieving security. They also consider a reduction in defense spending to be necessary in order to create a healthy Soviet economy.

A more undecided group of military leaders promotes a variant of the concept by referring to "sufficient defense" (*dostatochnaia oborona*) rather than reasonable sufficiency. Here it is acknowledged that the military needs to reform in the abstract, but this is coupled with stiff opposition to the dramatic reductions in defense spending as advocated by Gorbachev. This group likewise rejects unilateral and asymmetrical responses in arms control but also supports strategic parity.

Oppositionist military leaders resort to a standard phrase, "reliable defense" (*nadezhnaia oborona*), in Soviet military literature in their rejection of the Gorbachev program. Reliable defense describes traditional Soviet thinking on security issues. This position rejects Gorbachev's intention to alter Soviet military doctrine and advocates that defense expenditures should be maintained or even grow. Its advocates argue that Soviet forces must prevent large-scale destruction of the homeland during wartime and be able to defeat and destroy Western aggression on Western soil. These Soviet military leaders argue for reforms in the military that serve to strengthen discipline and improve weaponry and equipment.

The genesis of reasonable sufficiency, like that of the new thinking, is rooted in a decision by the political leadership to achieve foreign and domestic reforms. Besides its rhetorical value, the civilians no doubt saw one other strength in the concept: After Gorbachev and his supporters introduced the term "reasonable sufficiency," the military seemed unable to coordinate its responses.

Gorbachev spoke about reasonable sufficiency on several occasions. At first, Gorbachev's comments appeared to lack specific content. For example, at a meeting of the Supreme Soviet in 1985, just eight months after assuming the post of General Secretary, Gorbachev mentioned reasonable sufficiency in vague terms:

> The USSR and the US will have to reach a common understanding of what level of weapons on each side could be considered relatively sufficient....We are convinced that the level of this sufficiency is much lower than that which the USSR and the United States in fact possess at the moment. This means that weighty practical steps for the limitation and reduction of weapons are perfectly possible, measures that not

only will not lessen, but will strengthen security both for the USSR and the US, and the entire strategic stability of the world.[47]

In a report to the 27th Party Congress, Gorbachev gave the first detailed explanation of reasonable sufficiency. In this explanation, Gorbachev broke away from the concept of strategic parity and argued for reducing nuclear arsenals and also suggested the need for a reduction in defense spending:

Our country stands for...restricting military potentials within the bounds of reasonable sufficiency. Security...can only be mutual, and if one considers international relations as a whole, it can only be universal.[48]

In addition, Gorbachev's emerging ideas on reasonable sufficiency appeared in the 27th Party Congress program. The program emphasized in very strong terms that the party had a dominant role in military affairs and also indicated a lower priority for defense needs for the first time:

The basic foundation of the strengthening of the defense of the socialist homeland is the Communist Party's guidance of military construction and the Armed Forces. Policy in the field of defense, and the country's security policy, and Soviet military doctrine, which is purely defensive in nature, are worked out and implemented with the party playing the guiding role.[49]

A year after the 27th Party Congress, Gorbachev continued to advance the concept of reasonable sufficiency. In a speech to the Trade Union Congress in February 1987, Gorbachev stated:

Now when the opponent's gamble on our backwardness has taken a serious shaking, imperialism is switching the emphasis on to something else: preventing the implementation of our plans for transformation, hindering them, slowing them down, and foiling them by the arms race....But we will not take a single step over and above the demands and requirements of reasonable, sufficient defense.[50]

However, Gorbachev's speech to the United Nations on December 7, 1988 focused on the unilateral withdrawal of equipment and troops from the Soviet periphery in conjunction with achieving reasonable sufficiency:

The reductions will be made on a unilateral basis....By agreement with our allies in the WTO, we have made the decision to withdraw six tank divisions from the GDR, Czechoslovakia, and Hungary, and to disband them by 1991....

The Soviet forces in those countries will be cut by 50,000 persons, and their arms by 5,000 tanks. In addition, in the European part of our country and on the territory of our European allies, the Soviet Armed Forces will be reduced by 10,000 tanks, 8500 artillery systems, and 800 combat aircraft.[51]

Three aspects of this compressed overview of Gorbachev's position on reasonable sufficiency are particularly noteworthy. First, it indicates Gorbachev's willingness to intervene in military affairs, even to the point of Khrushchev-like efforts at massive reductions. Second, it also shows that Gorbachev is powerful enough, or at least feels he is powerful enough, to implement his ideas. Finally, it reveals definite differences with the military concept of "sufficiency"; in particular, no mention is made of the need for the concept to be based on reciprocal measures in the West, something which the military insists upon from the start.

Dobrynin, Yakovlev, and the Civilians

Both Anatolii Dobrynin and Aleksandr Yakovlev are active participants in the drive to enshrine the idea of reasonable sufficiency in Soviet security policy.[52] Although they rarely refer to reasonable sufficiency, their actions suggest that they play an important role in defining the defense agenda.

Dobrynin became the first leader to propose an enhanced civilian role in the Soviet national security debate. In an article in *Kommunist*, Dobrynin stated that "immediate scientific analysis to [determine] the questions of what is the reasonable sufficiency in lowering the level of military potentials [is needed]."[53] Although civilians did not immediately respond at that time, some did participate in the creation of civilian think tanks designed to address the issues raised by reasonable sufficiency. For example, under Dobrynin's direction, the International Department created a special section dealing with arms control. Headed by Lieutenant General Viktor Sharodubov, who took part in the Soviet delegation to the SALT talks on INF, and staffed by civilian specialists, this body strengthens arms control expertise in the International Department and ensures that several points of view are incorporated into the policy process. This should eventually provide Gorbachev with a source of information on defense security issues.[54]

The early military reaction to reasonable sufficiency was predictably negative; more alarming, however, was the fact that civilian analysts were probably incapable of rebutting military arguments with any intellectual authority. Major General Yuri Lebedev, chief of the Treaty and Legal Directorate of the General Staff, and his coauthor, A. Podberezkin, admitted as much when they noted that the experiences of recent years indicated that Soviet political analysts still are not competent to discuss military doctrinal matters.[55] This poor preparation, perhaps coupled with a continued lack of support for reasonable sufficiency even by some civilians as well as the ongoing complaints from supporters of the military, was probably a catalyst behind Yakovlev's earlier challenge to Soviet civilian foreign policy specialists to undertake analyses of military doctrine. This appeal seemed to be stronger than the one articulated by Dobrynin:

> The concept of sufficiency of military potentials, including under the conditions of a complete elimination of nuclear weapons, a concept which was advanced by the 27th CPSU Congress, needs to be revealed and filled with substance. Of no less importance is the task of analyzing, in conjunction with the military specialists, our military doctrine, the strategic essence of which is based on the policy of averting nuclear war.[56]

The civilian policy establishment answered Yakovlev's call with several articles on everything from strategic stability to the appropriate role of the armed forces, but the civilian analysts will nonetheless enter the 1990s at something of an intellectual disadvantage vis-a-vis their military colleagues.

Before Gorbachev's rise to power, Soviet civilian analysts did not comment on Soviet military affairs. Thus, both Dobrynin's and Yakovlev's "invitations" provided civilians with sanctions to participate. The causal relationship here is important to understand. At this point, it does not appear that Gorbachev acted on ideas generated by the civilian analysts; rather, it seems that the civilians perceived "more freedom" to conduct certain areas of analysis in the wake of Gorbachev's statements and proposals.

Several civilians, who represent prestigious Moscow-based institutes with close ties to Gorbachev and Yakovlev, entered the debate espousing broad points of view. First, the former director of the Institute of World Economics and International Relations and current Chairman of the Supreme Soviet's Council of the Union, Evgenni Primakov, a close associate of both Gorbachev and Yakovlev, argued that the USSR requires only a qualitative parity, which he defined in the McNamaresque language of finite deterrence as the ability to inflict "unacceptable damage" on an aggressor in response to a nuclear first strike.[57] In addition, Primakov also argued that military strength between the superpowers should be reduced to levels acceptable to both sides.[58] Second, three members of the Institute of the USA and Canada (IUSAC), Deputy Directory Vitalii Zhurkin (now director of the new Institute of Western Europe), section head Sergei Karaganov (now deputy director of the Institute of Western Europe), and senior researcher Andrei Kortunov (head of the international security department at the IUSAC), argued for reasonable sufficiency in Soviet military doctrine. The authors also noted that a reduction in military spending would release economic resources for Gorbachev's reform program ("The need to shift to sufficiency is also the result of economic factors"). Furthermore, they advocated unilateral cuts in Soviet forces and criticized the current policy of maintaining armed forces capable of countering all potential enemies.[59]

Other prominent Soviet commentators sought to redefine the nature of the Western threat. For example, *Izvestiia* political commentator Aleksandr Bovin suggested in a November 1987 article that the traditional Soviet assessment of the West's intentions to wage war to eliminate socialism might be incorrect. He argued that in the nuclear age there exists a desire for self-preservation, even in Washington. In addition, Chief of the Central Committee International Department Valentin Falin noted the political ramifications of implementing reasonable sufficiency.[60] He stated that the problem of security had became mostly political, and military solutions are impossible to achieve. Falin also articulated his views on the Soviet television program "Studio Nine" on October 9, 1988; in a roundtable discussion on reasonable sufficiency, which also included then First Deputy Chief of the General Staff Vladimir Lobov, Falin defined reasonable sufficiency according to the definitions stated by Gorbachev. However, Lobov (who replaced Anatolii Gribkov as WTO chief of staff on February 25, 1989) countered by advocating sufficient defense. Thus, Soviet television has also become the latest forum for defining Soviet security issues and promotes discussion of these issues by millions of television viewers.[61]

A Divided Ministry of Defense

The Soviet leadership's drive towards reasonable sufficiency and reform created a division of opinion in the Soviet military.[62] For his part, Akhromeev adhered closely to Gorbachev's intended use of reasonable sufficiency, with the notable exception of his insistence that the concept must be influenced by Western actions; a corollary Gorbachev seems to have accepted at least rhetorically. Akhromeev, of course, played a key role in arms control negotiations including those leading to the successful conclusion of the INF treaty. In a May 9, 1987 article in *Krasnaia Zvezda* Akhromeev joined the civilians by arguing for political means to prevent war and seemed to suggest that an additional military buildup would be unnecessary. He also attacked his fellow officers for not participating in the new thinking.

Even Akhromeev possessed few choices, however, and he reached those limits on December 7, 1988 when he retired.[63] There is plenty of evidence to support the belief that Akhromeev opposed unilateral cuts for some time. The day before his resignation, he wrote in the Bulgarian press:

> Errors in evaluating the likely nature of aggression and in forecasting the possible results of such an aggression are always dangerous and, especially given the defensive nature of our strategy, may entail serious consequences.

Even worse, in his view:

Certain influential circles in the West are now more realistic in evaluating the situation in the Soviet Union and within its Armed Forces, as well as the disastrous consequences which the arms race may produce for world peace. Other, no less influential circles, however, are relying, as in the past, on the "position of strength" as regards the Soviet Union, *and are trying to frighten our country and to extort one-sided actions from us.* (emphasis added)[64]

This was not new from Akhromeev: it was basically what he told the Party *aktiv* meeting at the General Staff in August 1988.[65] He made this statement even earlier, in January:

In conditions of the constant military threat being created by the active military preparations of imperialism, defense sufficiency cannot be interpreted one-sidedly, without regard to the developing correlation of forces. It would be even more of a mistake to understand it as unilateral disarmament, a unilateral lessening of our defense.[66]

Furthermore:

The limits of defense sufficiency are not set by us, but by the practical actions of the United States and the NATO bloc and their attempts to have a military capability that would ensure military superiority over us.[67]

In March 1988 Akhromeev delivered a stinging attack on NATO policies and argued that "in reality [i.e., despite NATO claims], there is an approximate parity [*paritet*] between the WTO and NATO in the area of armed forces and conventional weapons." Note that he did not use the usual word, *ravnovesie* (equilibrium), choosing instead the cognate for parity, with its more strictly numerical connotations.[68] This did not bode well for a General Secretary who wanted to move security issues away from strict bean-counts.

Divisions in the General Staff were no less raucous or confusing. Lobov, as seen above, argued for sufficient defense, stating that sufficient defense is necessary in "maintaining, training, and using armed forces" while pursuing arms control agreements.[69] He also took a more conciliatory line, however, on the subject of asymmetries, a key barrier to many officers' acceptance of reasonable sufficiency. Unlike others (including such notables as CINC of the Soviet Navy Admiral Vladimir Chernavin), Lobov accepted the idea that there are legitimate asymmetries that might concern NATO strategists.[70] Another Deputy Chief of the General Staff, Colonel General Makmut Gareev, advocated reliable defense.[71] He cited a growing threat from imperialism and the need to preserve parity with NATO and the United States.[72] Gareev, like his co-religionist Colonel General Volkogonov, also attacked those who believe in the conceptual underpinnings of the putative Western threat. For example, Gareev sounded off during an interview with *Argumenty i Fakty*:

> In all branches of activity of the Armed Forces many new and complex questions arise. A fundamental question (is) about the reality of the military threat to us from the imperialist states. Certain press organs have begun to cast doubt on the presence of such a threat, and consequently, on the necessity of defense measures, of the defense of the Fatherland....Positive international changes...(must also be considered along with) military preparations of the imperialist states.[73]

Furthermore, Gareev stated that a real military threat continues to exist. He admitted that Soviet doctrine is indeed defensive but apparently only during the initial repulsion of aggression. Finally, Gareev asserted that NATO simply isn't ready to deal with the USSR in good faith.[74] (This latter point, echoed by a *Krasnaia Zvezda* reviewer in September 1988, said that "realistic tendencies" in NATO military policy are not yet dominant.)[75]

Other signs of trouble existed within the General Staff. Akhromeev's then senior deputy, Varennikov, in the 1987 piece cited earlier, identified reasonable sufficiency as "a reliable defense and the strengthening of parity between the USSR and the United States."[76] Major General V.A. Kuklev, apparently yet another new arrival to the General Staff, also exhibited some ambiguity about the Gorbachev program.[77] His responses during an interview about the Moscow summit were entirely uncontroversial, approving of the business of the summit while chiding then President Reagan for lecturing the USSR about human rights.[78] Recently, however, Kuklev challenged Western estimates of the European balance. Moreover, Kuklev made an observation on the meaning of unilateralism (and by extension, on reasonable sufficiency) that may catch on among the military: He stressed that the Soviet action is unilateral but added that "we have the right to expect an adequately significant answer from the other side."[79] Major General Lebedev voiced his ire over Western reaction to Gorbachev's cuts, saying that unilateral reductions were not a propaganda move, nor did they injure Soviet security interests. He felt they were deeply significant, and he was upset at the implication that they were not: "However, judging from some statements in the West, their scale and depth are not yet acknowledged by everyone."[80]

Akhromeev's replacement, Chief of the General Staff General Mikhail Moiseev, not only failed to impose some unity on the situation, but also actively joined the ranks of the skeptics.[81] Moiseev echoed Gareev word-for-word recently:

Thus, the presence of a military threat on the side of imperialism is a fundamental question. And from this, whatever the social opinion around it will be, the success of much depends on the realization of the party directives on defense. Meanwhile, some authors in our publications try to cast doubt on the reality of the military threat and on the rectitude of defense measures that have been adopted.[82]

And:

Precipitousness in any matter is dangerous. And this is all the more so when we are talking about the preservation of peace and the defense of the nation. Here it is especially important, as they say, "not to lose touch with the earth." Their reality is that the USA, for example, has not given up, and is not thinking of giving up, even one of its military-technical programs. Moreover, they are talking about equipping their armed forces with the kind of weapons systems for which the search for counter measures will demand many times more time and resources from the Soviet Union. Thus the matter here is not that some sort of "imaginary military threat" to our country was invented, as some think, by military men, but in the urgent necessity of a search for new ways to guarantee the reliable defense of the peaceful labor of the Soviet people.[83]

Moiseev attempted to support two essentially conflicting arguments: one that accepts limits on military growth, the other that warns of a harsh "reality" in which the West will quickly outpace the USSR in the race for military-technical superiority. Meanwhile, Gorbachev's statements repeatedly downplayed the dominance of technology in military affairs; either Moiseev disagreed or was unaware of the implications of his statement.

Meanwhile, other senior officers were either at odds with the military opposition or chose to restrain themselves. Yazov's successor at the Soviet Ministry of Defense cadres desk, General Dmitrii Sukhorukov, is somewhat evasive in this exchange when asked if Gorbachev's reductions would hurt the nation's defense capability: "With regard to reductions in the Armed Forces, the chief problem in cadre policy in the army and navy will be to ensure their full combat readiness on the basis of our defensive doctrine. Basic efforts will be directed toward instilling in officers a high feeling of responsibility."[84] In other words, perhaps: My job is cadres, and I'm not going to answer the question. It is important to remember that when Lebedev answered the same questions, he responded with a flat denial, unlike Sukhorukov.

Another indication of some sort of problem within the General Staff is noted in Kulikov's speech at the General Staff party conference:

In his speech, MSU V. Kulikov...stressed that...the plans for combat preparedness in a series of military districts do not correspond with the abilities of the troops. In new conditions a new mechanism of discharge of duties is needed at all levels. New. Something that allows the attainment of qualitative parameters to be guaranteed. There is no alternative.

Kulikov continued:

A subject of special concern in the current period was the work of the General Staff and all of its *podrazdelenii* and party organizations on the elimination of shortcomings noted by the Central Committee of the party in June 1987. And in the report as well as in the speeches it was noted that the work conducted has been great. But this is only a part of the matter. Approaches have changed principally not only in the organization of duty [i.e. *boegodezhurstva*] and service in the troops, including the solving of extraordinary problems in peacetime, but also in the theoretical bases of a whole series of standing conceptions. In consideration of the defensive military doctrine, plans are being reworked, and documents and regulations are being defined more precisely and perfected; other work is being carried on as well.[85]

Kulikov, unfortunately, did not elaborate on the Central Committee's criticisms, but it seemed that directorates charged with military science (Gareev again) were slow to react to new changes: Remember, June 1987 is also the same month the WTO announced the new doctrine in Berlin.

Moiseev partly confirmed this possibility:

One of the most complex problems of military science is the prevention of war. Such a task was never before put before our Armed Forces. It requires deep scientific research and working out of concrete recommendations to the organs of direction, to the troops and the naval forces. It has been put before us to generalize experience and realize in practice the tenets of a defensive military doctrine, and to work out unified views and prevention of aggression. Together with this, *it must be noted that military-scientific organizations called upon to provide preliminary deep working through of these questions often lag behind.* In part, one of the questions that has been insufficiently worked through is connected with the organization and conduct of combat actions of a defensive character.(emphasis added)[86]

This "lag" may be behind Marshal Kulikov's cryptic statement about remedying "shortcomings" in General Staff work. Apparently, the General

Staff planners decided to oppose reform by refusing or neglecting the work necessary to support reform. This naturally casts doubt on the claims of Akhromeev and others who assured the public that the ramifications of the new doctrine had been worked out long in advance of the 1987 PCC meeting in Berlin.

Yazov is a more confusing case, in that he seemed to endorse both the concepts of sufficient defense and reliable defense. He defined sufficient defense as the minimum necessary and the highest quality of armed forces and armaments capable of ensuring the country's defenses.[87] However, Yazov does not endorse asymmetrical and unilateral arms control initiatives. Instead, he defended parity as the decisive factor in preventing war and advocated that Soviet forces cannot remain static. In addition, Yazov asserted that "(the Soviet Union is) not the one who sets the limits of sufficiency, it is the actions of the United States and NATO which support a symmetrical response."[88] Moreover, in his 1987 book, *Na strazhe sotsializma i mira*, he stated that "the reliable defense of the Soviet people relies on the success of all tasks given to the army and the navy based on Soviet military doctrine."[89] This is most likely an expression of the tension between Yazov's loyalties to the leadership and his instincts as a career field commander.

Kulikov's replacement as WTO CINC, General Petr Lushev, argued that parity is necessary and stated that any army must "train to use all the weapons, all the means and methods of warfare that the enemy possesses or may possess."[90] By contrast, of course, Lushev's support of reliable defense is tepid compared with the vitriol of his predecessor.[91] A more extreme example is Soviet PVO (Air Defense Forces) CINC General Ivan Tretiak, who does not support Gorbachev's reasonable sufficiency or, indeed, any form of sufficiency. He expressed publicly his disregard for defense cutbacks and charged that unilateral defense cuts should never be implemented and that the USSR should not be lured into arms control agreements.[92] Tretiak, according to analysts in Moscow, is currently engaged in a specific debate on reasonable sufficiency with USA/Canada academic Lev Semeiko. Semeiko recently returned fire on this issue in the pages of *Kommunist*, and his exposition of reasonable sufficiency is probably the most authoritative look at the problem yet from a civilian analyst.

A New Battle: Semeiko and the Military

Semeiko admits from the outset that "reasonable sufficiency" contains no meaning yet.[93] This naturally should raise yet more doubts about the military claim that Soviet forces are already being restructured along these lines.

Semeiko's central concern appears to be the relationship between parity and stability. He attacks the definition of "nuclear parity" given in the *Military Encyclopedic Dictionary* (edited by Akhromeev in 1986) as too imprecise: "But just what kind of equality [*ravenstvo*] are we talking about, and according to which indicators of military potential?"[94] Needless to say, Semeiko is setting up the argument that the military, i.e., strictly quantitative, view of stability and parity is insufficient. Not that the qualitative aspect, he says, is unimportant, but it shouldn't be the dominant factor.

Semeiko moves on to discuss actual limits on strategic weapons. Even if forces could be reduced to 6000 warheads, he argues that this is still "a gigantic number." Instead, he points out that:

> Soviet and American scholars and experts, independently of each other, have [defined as a better reduction] approximately 500-600 single warheads, mobile, and therefore less vulnerable, ICBMs. In the specialists' opinions, such a nuclear potential [without SLBMs or heavy bombers] is fully sufficient, remaining at the utmost minimum, to guarantee a [second-strike capability]; that is, to fulfill the functions of military-political deterrence [*sderzhivaniia*] and to ensure the stability of the situation.[95]

In what seems to be an answer to some of Gorbachev's critics, Semeiko argues that an innovative idea like reasonable sufficiency requires an "untraditional...asymmetrical...flexible" policy. Any other path allows the West to dictate the path and direction of the arms race.[96] He then moves on to conventional weapons. They are no less important than nuclear weapons; after all, "nuclear weapons, with their gigantic power, cannot occupy territory." One puzzling comment here, given Semeiko's position as cheerleader for the new thinking: "It is the conventional troops themselves that are capable of using the results of the use of nuclear arms in the course of their own subsequent combat actions. Nonnuclear war can escalate into a nuclear war."[97] This betrays some pre-new thinking strategy on Semeiko's part, in that he seems to accept a rational combat role for some nuclear weapons.

In a surprising moment of direct criticism, Semeiko attacks Minister of Defense Yazov's formulation of conventional sufficiency. Yazov defines sufficiency in conventional arms as "the quantity and quality of armed forces capable of reliably guaranteeing the collective defense of the socialist commonwealth." Semeiko's retort:

> As we can see, this arrangement is sufficiently flexible and so does not fix any kind of concrete level of strength of conventional forces. This, strictly speaking, cannot be allowed, for such a definition will always depend upon the character of the military confrontation.[98]

In other words, the military is only using the terminology of reasonable sufficiency to serve its own ends.

At one point Semeiko dives into the terminological quandary surrounding the sufficiency debate. "Is there," he asks, "a difference between the general concepts of "reasonable" and "defensive" sufficiency?" Semeiko admits that there are differing opinions on this, but his own inclination is to regard them as forces sufficient for defense at the lowest (and therefore most rational) level.[99]

A recent military counterattack at the problem appeared at the same time in *Vestnik PVO*, the journal of the Air Defense Forces.[100] The differences between Semeiko's views and those of Colonel Skorodenko are striking. Skorodenko (who is also a professor of history) wrote prominently on this subject before; he is no friend of the new thinking or the new doctrine, as this article confirms.

Skorodenko begins with the standard genuflection toward the constructive and defensive character of socialist military doctrine, citing recent Soviet arms proposals as examples, including the cuts announced by Gorbachev at the UN in December 1988. But, "We note that in response the USA has not abandoned even one of its own military programs."[101] Chief of the General Staff Moiseev made the same complaint in February 1989.[102]

Thus,

an important part of the military doctrine of the WTO is the dialectical mutual link between its peace loving policy and its readiness and decisiveness to jointly defend its own revolutionary gains against the encroachments of imperialism.[103]

This forces the WTO, "in conditions where effective international political mechanisms" of war prevention have not been created, to rely on their own "defensive potential." Furthermore:

[The WTO members] consider the currently existing military-strategic parity to be the decisive factor in the prevention of war. The allied states support their armed forces at such a level and in such a composition that would allow them to repel any attack from without. These measures are of a necessitated character; they are necessary so that the sense of self-preservation will overcome a potential aggressor with the intention of unleashing nuclear war against us.

The meaning for reasonable sufficiency should also be clear from this: "It is fully evident that the limits of reasonable sufficiency of the military potential of the USSR and the WTO depend upon the position and the actions of the USA and of NATO as a whole."[104]

A New Development: The Committee for Defense and Security

One innovation in the battle over national security in the Soviet Union designed to increase civilian control is the creation of a state committee to control defense matters. Under the Supreme Soviet, the Committee for Defense and State Security was formed on June 10, 1989. The chairman of the commission, Vladimir Lapygin (a leading figure in the Soviet military-industrial complex and one of the designers of the Buran Space Shuttle), supports reform of the Soviet military. In an interview with *Izvestiia* on June 26, 1989, Lapygin argued that the Soviet armed forces can become a professional (i.e., volunteer) army and that such an army would be much better than the present one because "recent conscripts are unable to cope with increasingly sophisticated military technology." However, Lapygin warned that creating a professional army must be studied closely.[105]

Lapygin also supports the transition of the Soviet army from an offensive to defensive organization. His committee must control and oversee the entire military apparatus and its defense decision making processes:

> The committee will examine very important programs for the development of the Army and Navy and the branches and categories of troops with due regard for our military doctrine and their reasonable and reliable sufficiency to ensure strategic stability....We will analyze how the demands connected with enhancing quality parameters in military building are being realized. To this end we will listen to the defense minister, other ministers working for defense, and top military leaders. If necessary, we will go out to the troops."[106]

Lapygin also comments on a few areas previously considered taboo. First, he supports glasnost in Soviet military affairs and agrees with his interlocutor that there are "too many unjustified secrets and secrecy."[107] Second, he bluntly makes the case for breaking down institutional barriers to control. The military will fall under the Committee's jurisdiction in that it "will consider the budget and maintenance problems" within the army, and, as chairman, he feels that he has "the right to invite any head of a ministry or industry" for discussions.[108] Finally, Lapygin takes a slap at Yazov's lack of authority on the cutting of 175,000 former students of higher education. He states that Yazov "did not demonstrate the appropriate flexibility" needed to achieve such a cut.[109]

The Supreme Soviet approved the composition of the Committee for Defense and State Security on June 16, 1989; it consists of several military personnel. The most famous, Marshal Akhromeev, reported to the Committee upon his return to Moscow from the United States; other military personnel belonging to the committee include a model Afghan veteran, Colonel Ruslan Aushev, Deputy Minister of Defense Vitalii Shabanov, a former Deputy

Minister of Radio Industry, and regimental commander V.N. Ochinov, who was elected deputy chairman of the Committee.[110] Although the Committee for Defense and State Security should become one of the most powerful bodies within the revamped Supreme Soviet, it is off to a rocky start. For example, there is no meeting room for the Committee for its first session; it possesses no staff and does not know how to organize one; and it does not know how or where to store classified military and intelligence information. In addition, even if they wanted to recommend changes in the Soviet military budget, very few members know what a military budget looks like and probably would not know where to make cuts. The Committee bears watching, however; even the Soviet public seems to believe that it will accrue the powers promised when created.[111]

Conclusions

The making of Soviet national security policy is currently being transformed from an ossified, mechanistically ideological process into a civil-military free-for-all not seen since the early 1960s. The creation of the new thinking, the promulgation of a "new" military doctrine, and the debate over reasonable sufficiency all reflect a struggle between two groups with fundamentally clashing world views for the right to define the strategic course of the USSR into the next century.

Gorbachev's early attempts at creating the appropriate philosophical atmosphere for the reform of national security policy failed. Instead, since 1987, the leadership has relied on two more reliable methods of wresting control of the military agenda: they have publicly committed the Soviet Union to arms initiatives that achieve domestic as well as foreign goals and they have finally decided to remove many senior military officers from their posts. In the last year, a huge turnover occurred in almost every major defense post in the USSR. However, the level of tension between the Gorbachev leadership and the military is so significant that even personnel turnover is emerging as a mixed blessing. The officers taking over senior positions are no more or less flexible than their predecessors (with the exception, of course, of Kulikov's replacement), and this may be an indication that Gorbachev is swiftly running out of military allies.

Gorbachev's trump card, of course, is the diffusion of power he is seeking to create by enlarging the circle of defense policymaking. In the past few years, the Soviet defense community grew to accommodate some outside opinions, and now there is even a structure in place for parliamentary control. If Gorbachev remains in power, it is likely that the military monopoly on defense will be broken for the foreseeable future. However, until that monopoly is overcome, the military possesses means and the will to subvert crucial aspects of military reform, and it frequently shows an inclination to do so, even in direct contravention of the Party line. The debate is not over, nor will it be until the senior Soviet military leaders either voluntarily or forcibly accept a role as executors of policy rather than participants in policymaking.

Notes

[1]The opinions expressed in this chapter are those of the authors and do not reflect the views of the RAND Corporation or its sponsors.

[2]Mikhail Gorbachev, *Izbranne rechi i stat' i*, (Moscow: Politizdat, 1987), Vol. 2, p. 131.

[3]*Ibid.*, p. 171.

[4]Gorbachev avoided this formulation a month later when he told a group of World War II veterans that, despite the efforts of "some influential forces" in the West pressing for military superiority, "we do not consider war as fatally inevitable." *Ibid.*, p. 183.

[5]*Ibid.*, p. 171. See also Gorbachev's remarks in Warsaw, April 26, 1985, pp. 176-179.

[6]*Pravda*, November 28, 1985, p. 1.

[7]Gorbachev, *op. cit.*, Vol. 3, p. 245.

[8]*Ibid.*

[9]*Ibid.*

[10]*Ibid.* For the Brandt speech, see Vol. 2, p. 238.

[11]East German Minister of Defense Heinz Kessler made reference in the Soviet press to NATO preparations for a surprise attack throughout the depth of the WTO and the necessity for a near-combat footing even as the 27th Party Congress took place. See *Krasnaia Zvezda*, February 26, 1987, p. 11. Kessler did not attend the Congress; he made his remarks in an article on the 30th anniversary of the GDR National People's Army.

[12]Evgenni Ivanovskii, *Na strazhe rodiny*, (series: Resheniia XXVII S"ezda KPSS— v Zhizn') (Moscow: Izdatel'stvo DOSAAF, 1986), p. 88. Conversations with Soviet civilian analysts during a seminar in the USSR in May 1989 confirmed the general direction of the views of Ivanovskii and others.

[13]V.S. Nechaev, *Reshaiushchii istochnik boevoi moshchi*, (series: Resheniia XXVII S"ezda KPSS— v Zhizni) (Moscow: Izdatel'stvo DOSAAF, 1987), p. 23.

[14]*Ibid.*, p. 33. Nechaev also reveals his traditionalist view of the Soviet Armed Forces in this work; on page 92 he reaffirms the Strategic Rocket Forces as the basis of Soviet military power, noting that the "tactical-technical characteristics of ballistic missiles allow for strikes on any of the aggressor's objectives, and with sufficiently high accuracy," a formulation that sounds more like 1965 than 1985.

[15]*Krasnaia Zvezda*, August 15, 1986, p. 2.

[16]Vitalii Shabanov, "Doktrina bezopasnosti i mira," *Mezhdunarodnaia Zhizn'*, October 1986, p. 23.

[17]V. A. Zubkov, "Zabota KPSS ob ukreplenii ekonomicheskikhosnov voennoi moshchi sotsialisticheskogo gosudarstva," *Voenno-Istoricheskii Zhurnal*, March 1986, p. 6.

[18]*Ibid.*, p. 7.

[19]For examples, see *Krasnaia Zvezda*, July 15, 1986, p. 3., and

G. Lukava, "Faktor vnezapnosti v agressivnoi politike imperializma," *Kommunist Vooruzhennykh Sil*, No. 11, June 1986, p. 24. In 1986, Lukava published a brief book that underscored his conservative themes, *V.I. Lenin o zashchite zavoevanii sotsializma*, (Moscow: Voenizdat, 1986).

[20]Significantly, Volkogonov did not name the offending journal, nor did he elaborate on whether "our" meant "Soviet," "Party," or "military." *XXVII S" ezd KPSS i zadachi kafedrobshchestvennykh nauk*, (Moscow: Politizdat, 1987), p. 130. The conference was entitled "The All-Union Conference of Directors of Cadres of Social Science of Higher Educational Establishments," held in Moscow Oct. 1-3, 1986. The proceedings were published in early 1987, with a printing run of 100,000. See also Thomas Nichols, "Volkogonov and Nuclear Victory," *Sovset News*, Vol. III, No. 10, September 8, 1987.

[21]*Trud*, February 22, 1987, p. 3.

[22]Valentin Varennikov, "Na strazhe i bezopasnosti narodov," *Partiinaia Zhizn'*, No. 5, March 1987, pp. 9-10. For a different interpretation of Varennikov's piece, see Eugene Rumer, "Military Follows Party Lead on Arms Control," *Radio Liberty Reports*, RL 494/87, November 30, 1987, in which he asserts that Varennikov was "assuring the Party leaders of the military's unwavering loyalty."

[23]*Ibid.*, p. 11.

[24]For the text of Gorbachev's television address to the Soviet people in the wake of the Reykjavik summit see *Pravda*, October 23, 1986, pp. 1-2. (Reproduced in Vol. 4 of Gorbachev's *Izbranne rechi...*, pp. 168-180.)

[25]Cited in Alexander Rahr, "Gorbachev Describes Himself as Head of Defense Council," *Radio Liberty Reports*, RL 87/87, March 3, 1987, p. 1. Gorbachev made the remark over *Radio Moscow* on February 28, 1987.

[26]*Sovetskaia Rossiia*, February 21, 1987, p. 1.

[27]For a detailed analysis of the article itself, see Thomas Nichols, "The Military and the New Political Thinking: Lizichev on Leninism and Defense," *Radio Liberty Reports*, RL 80/87, February 26, 1987.

[28]Aleksei Lizichev, "Oktiabr' i leninskoe uchenie o zashchite revoliutsii," *Kommunist*, No. 3, March 1987, p. 85.

[29]*Ibid.*, pp. 86-87.

[30]*Ibid.*, pp. 87-88.

[31]*Ibid.*, p. 88.

[32]Quoted in *JPRS UMA-87-002*, January 9, 1987, p. 38.

[33]For more on the new thinking, military doctrine, and the WTO, see Theodore Karasik, "Current Perspectives on the Warsaw Treaty Organization," *Current World Leaders*, Vol. 31, No. 8, December 1988, pp. 899-910.

[34]See Nikolai Ryzhkov, *Leninizm— osnova teorii i politiki perestroiki*," (Moscow: Politizdat, 1987). This Lenin's birthday

speech was published in *Izvestiia* on April 23, 1987, pp. 1-3.

[35]*Izvestiia*, May 31, 1987, p. 1.

[36]One small piece of evidence suggests Eastern European reservations about the new thinking and military affairs. In March 1987, a brief argument flared up in the English-language *Moscow News*, it should be noted, and not in the pages of *Pravda* between new thinking proponent Aleksandr Bovin and General Staff officer Iurii Lebedev. The "debate" consisted of Bovin essentially baiting the military about the usefulness of the SS-20s and implying that the military's insistence on the weapons created a pointless dilemma for Soviet diplomacy in the 1980s. Lebedev argued that the West was not serious about arms control. In any case, only Lebedev's side of the story made it to Eastern Europe, showing up in the Czechoslovak party organ *Rude Pravo* later that month. See Elizabeth Teague, "Polemics Over Euromissiles in the Soviet Press," *Radio Liberty Reports*, RL 113/87, March 20, 1987.

[37]V. Serebriannikov, "Sootnoshenie politicheskikh i voennykh sredstv v zashchite sotsializma," *Kommunist Vooruzhennykh Sil*, No. 18, September 1987. The timing and subject of the article suggests that Serebriannikov was again called in to undertake the rather thankless job of challenging Gorbachev's military critics.

[38]*Krasnaia Zvezda*, July 14, 1987, p. 3.

[39]*Krasnaia Zvezda*, September 10, 1987, p. 2.

[40]Viktor Kulikov, "Edinyi kurs, edinye tseli," *Kommunist Vooruzhennykh Sil*, No. 9, May 1987, p. 28.

[41]*Ibid.*, p. 27.

[42]*Izvestiia*, May 8, 1987, p. 2.

[43]Kulikov, *op. cit.*, p. 29.

[44]*Ibid.*

[45]*Krasnaia Zvezda*, May 9, 1987, pp. 1-2.

[46]Jan Reifenberg, "Wir reden nicht mehr davon, wie der Krieg zu gewinnen ist," *Frankfurter Allegemeine*, July 4, 1987, p. 5. This anonymous analyst was probably the military historian Daniil Proektor, who said similar things while he campaigned for the new thinking in Vienna in October 1987. If not Proektor, it was no doubt someone in a similar position at IMEMO or the Institute of USA/Canada.

[47]*Pravda*, November 28, 1985, pp. 1-2.

[48]*Pravda*, February 26, 1986, pp. 1-2.

[49]*Pravda*, March 7, 1986, pp. 1-2.

[50]*Pravda*, February 26, 1987, pp. 1-2.

[51]*Pravda*, December 8, 1988, p. 2.

[52]Yakovlev's power continues to grow. His appointment to head the Central Committee Commission on International Affairs gives him unprecedented power over foreign policy. This must also include security aspects of Soviet foreign policy as well. In addition, it is surprising that Yakovlev, who actively depicts a threat from the United States which is both "imminent and irrational," supports reasonable

sufficiency. See Aleksandr Yakovlev, *Po kraiu bezhny*, (Moscow: Progress Publishers, 1985). Dobrynin "retired" on September 30, 1988 from his position at the International Department and was appointed a foreign policy advisor to Gorbachev on October 28, 1988.

[53]Anatolii Dobrynin, "Za bez"iademyi mir, navstrechu XXI veku," *Kommunist*, No. 9, June 1986, p. 27.

[54]F. Stephen Larrabee, "Gorbachev and the Soviet Military," *Foreign Affairs*, Summer 1988, p. 1011.

[55]Iurii Lebedev and Aleksandr Podberezkin, "Voennye doktriny i mezhdunarodnaia bezopasnost'," *Kommunist*, No. 13, September 1988, pp. 110-119.

[56]Aleksandr Yakovlev, "Dostizhenie kachestvenno novogosostoianiia sovetskogo obshchestva i obshchestvenne nauku," *Kommunist*, No. 8, May 1987, p 18.

[57]*FBIS-SOV*, April 16, 1987, p. F1.

[58]*Pravda*, July 10, 1987, p. 3.

[59]Vitalii Zhurkin, Sergei Karaganov, and Andrei Kortunov, "Razumnaia dostatochnost'- ili kak razorvat' pochnyi krug," *Novoe Vremia*, No. 40, 1987, pp. 13-15. This article later appeared in *SShA*, No. 12, December 1987, and a slightly altered version was published in *Kommunist*, No. 1, January 1988, under the title of "Vyzovy bezopasnosti- starye i novye."

[60]Falin's appointment to head the International Department occurred on October 20, 1988. He made his comment while chief of APN, or Novosti. Falin's expertise on Western Europe will most likely shape the Soviet Union's outlook on security issues and ultimately contribute to the reasonable sufficiency debate. A lessening of tensions in Europe would contribute to lower defense expenditures in the WTO.

[61]An example of citizens becoming involved in the defense debate occurred on Soviet television on October 30, 1988. During a live interview at GUM (Moscow's largest department store) with representatives of the consumer goods industry, a GUM customer grabbed the microphone and said, "We will never resolve the problem of deficit goods without the demilitarization of our economy!" "RFED/RLD Daily Report," *SOVSET*, October 31, 1988.

[62]See R. Hyland Phillips and Jeffrey I. Sands, "Reasonable Sufficiency and Soviet Conventional Defense," *International Security*, Fall 1988 for a listing of the military and civilian responses to reasonable sufficiency.

[63]Soviet Foreign Ministry spokesman Gennadi Gerasimov announced Akhromeev's "retirement" due to health reasons on December 7, 1988 in New York City.

[64]*FBIS-SOV*, December 9, 1988, p. 1. The original appeared in Bulgarian in *Rabotnichesko Delo* on December 6, 1988.

[65]*Krasnaia Zvezda*, August 13, 1988, p. 2.

[66]*FBIS-SOV*, January 4, 1988, p. 1.

[67]*Ibid*.

[68]*Krasnaia Zvezda*, March 20, 1988, p. 3.

[69]*Studio Nine*, Soviet Central Television, October 15, 1988. Lobov was appointed First Deputy Chief for the WTO on January 26, 1989.

[70]*Krasnaia Zvezda*, June 14, 1988, p. 3. See also Chernavin's article in *Krasnaia Zvezda*, December 7, 1988, p. 3.

[71]It was reported in the December 28, 1988 issue of *Krasnaia Zvezda* that the General Staff Party Conference criticized Gareev. This might be related to his harsh views on reasonable sufficiency.

[72]Makmut Gareev, "Sovetskaia voennaia nauka," *Zashchita Otechestva*, No. 11, 1987.

[73]*Argumenty i Fakty*, No. 39, 1988, p. 1.

[74]*Ibid.*

[75]*Krasnaia Zvezda*, September 13, 1988, p. 3.

[76]Valentin Varennikov, "Na strazhe mira i bezopasnosti narodov," *Partiinaia Zhizn'*, No. 5, March 1987, p. 10.

[77]Kuklev is a member of Colonel General Chervov's Treaties and Legal Directorate.

[78]*Krasnaia Zvezda*, June 1, 1988, p. 3.

[79]*Krasnaia Zvezda*, December 28, 1988, p. 2.

[80]*Krasnaia Zvezda*, December 11, 1988, p. 3.

[81]*Krasnaia Zvezda*, February 23, 1989, p. 2. Moiseev's appointment was reported on December 15, 1988; his promotion from Colonel General to General occurred on February 15, 1989.

[82]*Ibid.*

[83]*Ibid.*

[84]*Krasnaia Zvezda*, January 14, 1989, p. 2.

[85]*Krasnaia Zvezda*, December 28, 1988, p. 2.

[86]*Krasnaia Zvezda*, February 23, 1989, p. 2.

[87]This viewpoint is expressed by Yazov in an article he wrote in *Die Welt*, October 21, 1988, p. 2.

[88]*Pravda*, July 27, 1987.

[89]Dmitri Yazov, *Na strazhe sotsializma i Mira*, (Moscow: Voenizdat, 1987), p. 26.

[90]Petr Lushev, "Defending the Gains of the Revolution," *International Affairs*, No. 9, 1987 p. 61.

[91]Lushev replaced Kulikov on February 2, 1989.

[92]*Moscow News*, No. 8, February 21, 1988, p. 12.

[93]L. Semeiko, "Razumnaia dostatochnost'— put' k nadezhnomumiru," *Kommunist*, No. 7, May 1989, p. 113.

[94]Semeiko, p. 114.

[95]Semeiko, p. 116.

[96]*Ibid.*

[97]Semeiko, p. 117.

[98]*Ibid.*

[99]Semeiko, p. 118.

[100]P. Skorodenko, "O voennykh doktrinakh i mezhdunarodnoi

bezopasnosti," *Vestnik PVO*, May 1989, pp. 75-77.

[101]Skorodenko, p. 76.

[102]*Krasnaia Zvezda*, February 23, 1989, p. 2.

[103]Skorodenko, p. 76.

[104]*Ibid.*

[105]One of the earliest public articulations of the idea of a professional army originated from a comment made on the Soviet television program *Vzgliad* in the fall of 1988 by journalist Artem Borovik. Soon, civilians and top military commanders began to debate the merits of a professional army with the latter, of course, opposed to such an idea. However, several middle-level officers and a number of civilian political activists expressed their support. See, for example, *Vek XX i Mir*, Nos. 9 and 10, 1988 and Nos. 1-4, 1989.

[106]*Before and After Midnight*, Soviet Central Television, July 29, 1989.

[107]*Ibid.*

[108]*Ibid.*

[109]*Ibid.*

[110]It is interesting to note that both Aushev and Akhromeev served in Afghanistan at the same time; both were awarded the Hero of the Soviet Union in 1982. See *Geroisovetskogo soiuza*, Vol. 1, (Moscow: Voenizdat, 1987), p. 87 (Aushev) and p. 93 (Akhromeev). For more on Akhromeev's service in Afghanistan, see *Krasnaia Zvezda*, July 2, 1989, p. 1. See also *TASS*, August 2, 1989, as cited in *FBIS-SOV*, August 2, 1989, p. 57.

[111]*Washington Post*, August 14, 1989, p. 15.

4

Old Soldiers Never Die: Marshal Akhromeev's Role in Soviet Defense Decision Making

Fred Wehling

When Marshal of the Soviet Union Sergei Fedorovich Akhromeev toured American military installations in July 1988, he acted in the traditional role of representative of the Soviet armed forces. However, when he spoke before the House Armed Services Committee in July 1989, he played an unprecedented and largely undefined part in the Soviet policy making process. The objectives of this chapter are, firstly, to propose an explanation for Akhromeev's abrupt retirement as Chief of the Soviet General Staff and his subsequent appointment as an advisor to the President of the Supreme Soviet and, secondly, to suggest what functions and duties he may perform in his new position. Because Kremlinology is neither exact nor a science, the conclusions of this effort are essentially speculative. Nevertheless, the information available on Akhromeev's retirement and current situation strongly suggests that he left his post as Chief of Staff because he could not continue in a position where his loyalties were divided between the Soviet military establishment and Mikhail Gorbachev's plans for perestroika (restructuring). Akhromeev's primary task in his new position, as advisor to the Soviet President, is to increase the legitimacy and effectiveness of the Supreme Soviet as an alternative center of power to the Communist Party.

This chapter begins with a summary of what is known about Akhromeev's life and career as a Soviet military officer. It outlines the views he expressed and the role he played as Chief of Staff in arms control negotiations and in formulating and promulgating the new Soviet military doctrine. Following this, it presents the case for regarding Akhromeev's retirement as the outcome of a conflict between his duties as the senior officer in the Soviet military establishment and his loyalty to a General Secretary who plans to reform that establishment. Finally, it offers a description of his probable functions as a military advisor, as a member of the newly reconstituted and more assertive Supreme Soviet, and, most importantly, as a player behind the scenes of Soviet decision making.

Akhromeev's Background and Career

By his own admission, the definitive event in Akhromeev's life was the Second World War. He was born into a peasant family on May 5, 1923, in the village of Vindrei in the Torbeevski Raion of the Mordovskaia ASSR.[1] He stated in an interview that he once hoped to attend the now-defunct Institute of History, Philosophy, and Literature in Moscow, but the pre-war situation forced another choice on him and he joined the Soviet armed forces as a cadet at the Frunze Naval College in 1940.[2] The start of the German *Barbarossa* offensive in the summer of 1941 found him as a platoon leader in a brigade of Marines. After fighting in the defense of Leningrad and serving in the Stalingrad, Southern, and Fourth Ukrainian fronts, he ended the Second World War as a captain commanding a tank battalion and a member of the Communist Party of the Soviet Union (CPSU), which he joined in 1943.[3] The war affected Akhromeev physically, mentally, and spiritually, as it influenced all Soviets of his generation. He describes the war years as the most important period in his life.[4] He was wounded six times, nearly starved to death on the Leningrad front, and counts himself fortunate to be one of the two out of every ten persons born in the same year who survived taking an active part in the fight against fascism which, as he wrote in a Victory Day article, gives "spiritual sustenance and strength" to the Soviet people to this day.[5]

After the War, Akhromeev studied at the Military Academy of Armored Troops and was graduated in 1952. He commanded a tank regiment and later a division before attending the Military Academy of the General Staff from 1964 to 1967. His subsequent service included tours of duty in the Far Eastern military region, where he was Chief of Staff and First Deputy Commander in 1972.[6] His later military career was spent primarily as a General Staff officer. He was appointed as a Deputy Chief of the General Staff and Chief of Main Operations in 1974, and in 1979 he was elevated to First Deputy Chief of Staff.[7] Akhromeev reportedly opposed the invasion of Afghanistan, as did former Chief of Staff Nikolai Ogarkov and many other General Staff officers.[8] From 1980 to 1981, Akhromeev served in Afghanistan, where he performed "difficult, front-line work" organizing operations and advising Soviet and Afghan military officers and political leaders as Chief of Staff of the Defense Ministry Operational Group.[9] His service in Afghanistan contributed to his declaration as a Hero of the Soviet Union in 1982. He became a candidate member of the CPSU Central Committee in 1981 and a full member in 1983.

Akhromeev was promoted to Marshal in 1983 and replaced Ogarkov as Chief of the General Staff in 1984. The role he played as Chief of Staff in arms control and in the formation and promulgation of Soviet military doctrine will be described in the next section of this chapter. Like his predecessors in the USSR's top military post, Akhromeev probably served as secretary of the Defense Council while he was Chief of Staff.[10] He won a great deal of respect from many quarters, in the USSR and abroad, before his sudden retirement in December 1988. The fact that his resignation was announced in New York by Foreign Ministry spokesman Genadii Gerasimov on the same day that Gorbachev declared the USSR's intention to cut half a million troops from the Soviet armed forces attests to the political significance of Akhromeev's unexpected action. His new career as advisor to the President of the Supreme Soviet began almost immediately after his "retirement." Akhromeev has served in the Supreme Soviet since 1984, when he became the deputy for the Beltski Okrug of the Moldavian SSR and a member of the Commission on Foreign Affairs. He was elected to the Congress of People's Deputies from the same district in March 1989 after running unopposed.[11] He was subsequently chosen as a deputy to the Supreme Soviet and was appointed to the Committee for Defense and State Security in July.[12] Akhromeev brings to the Supreme Soviet the experience of a man who has spent his entire adult life in the Soviet military and who survived the Second World War and the tumult and stagnation that followed. Little can be added to his own nutshell description of himself: *"Ia posledni iz mogikan"* ("I am the last of the Mohicans.")[13]

Akhromeev as Chief of Staff

Akhromeev played a major role in arms control and in instituting perestroika within the Soviet armed forces during his tenure as Chief of the General Staff. While he participated actively in arms control negotiations and almost certainly became involved in policy decisions regarding arms reductions, his primarily responsibility included the implementation rather than the formulation of reforms in military doctrine. His role in arms control stemmed not only from his position as Chief of Staff, but also from his extensive expertise in military science and technology. This role included three main aspects. The most important of these was his personal participation in arms limitation talks as a technical expert and military decision maker. As an authoritative representative of the Soviet military at the INF talks in Geneva, the Marshal was instrumental in the establishment of the verification regime necessary for the elimination of medium-range nuclear missiles.[14] Akhromeev's professional expertise, intellectual ability, position within the Soviet military and political power structure, and personal qualities of leadership combined to make him a very formidable negotiator. He cut a commanding figure at the Reykjavik summit, where he reportedly silenced Georgii Arbatov, a Central Committee member and the Director of the Institute of the U.S.A. and Canada, with a wave of his hand.[15]

The other aspects of Akhromeev's role in arms control were more political than technical, but his technical expertise in military matters made him a more effective political actor. The tone and content of many of his writings indicate that he served as a major advocate of Soviet positions on arms limitation in the international arena. Because he spoke from a position of professional authority, his critiques of American proposals on strategic weapons carried more weight than polemics prepared by civilian propagandists who possessed little technical knowledge of the issues involved.[16] He skillfully articulated the Soviet objection to the Strategic Defense Initiative (SDI) on the grounds that deployment of space-based systems would violate the ABM treaty.[17] His arguments are less credible, however, when he presents Soviet positions on areas outside his expertise, such as naval forces and operations, because he cannot support his statements with technical details.[18]

As useful as Akhromeev's writings for foreign consumption were for the Soviet arms control agenda, the domestic political aspects of his role in arms control policy were much more significant. Akhromeev fulfilled a crucial function as an explainer and justifier of arms control to Soviet audiences, and, in carrying out this function, he often bolstered Gorbachev's positions against dissent from some elements in the Soviet military. He supported the unilateral Soviet moratorium on nuclear weapons tests, for example, although he "admitted" that this placed the USSR at a temporary disadvantage in weapons development.[19] Some of his statements in support of the moratorium deny that the General Staff ever supported ending it, but these may also be read as admissions of and attempts to address concerns expressed from other quarters of the Soviet military establishment.[20] He likewise defended the INF treaty, arguing that the agreement eliminated a direct threat to Soviet territory despite the asymmetrical reductions in numbers of intermediate-range missiles.[21] Akhromeev's rebuttals of military-technical objections to arms control measures suggest that, as Chief of Staff, he performed a vitally important role in silencing potential opposition and building the political consensus in favor of arms reductions within the Soviet elite.

Akhromeev's political role in the arms control process was directly connected to his participation in the reform of Soviet military doctrine. His views on some points of the USSR's new defensive doctrine, particularly on the relative importance of political and military means as guarantees of security, appear to have undergone several changes while he served as Chief of Staff. Before the concept of reasonable sufficiency gained currency, Akhromeev, not surprisingly, emphasized the need for unswerving military vigilance against the threat of imperialist aggression and the need to maintain counter offensive capabilities.[22] (The "counteroffensive" in Soviet military literature is generally regarded as a code word for an offensive strategy.) By early 1987, after the new thinking gained wider acceptance, he stressed instead the importance of political means for preserving international security and the need for perestroika in the military.[23] Dale Herspring counts Akhromeev as one of the senior Soviet officers who "climbed on the perestroika bandwagon."[24]

Sometime afterward, however, Akhromeev returned to his earlier position. In December 1987, he defined the principle of defense sufficiency as the maintenance of no more forces than are required for a reliable defense.[25] This clearly distinguished this principle from the concept of reasonable sufficiency, which denotes the reduction of military potentials to levels which allow defense against an attack but preclude successful offensive operations.[26] He later specified that defense under the new Soviet defensive doctrine must be active and would include the ability to make retaliatory strikes, espousing a position reminiscent of his earlier advocacy of the counteroffensive.[27] He reaffirmed his support for the disciplinary and personal responsibility components of military perestroika in the same article. Stephen Meyer notes this change in Akhromeev's writings, and he, along with R. Hyland Phillips and Jeffrey Sands, regards the Marshal as a supporter of the continued provision of strong military means for the defense of the USSR.[28]

Akhromeev's less than wholehearted acceptance of the principle of reasonable sufficiency seems to indicate that, while he agreed with the political aspects of the defensive military doctrine, he had difficulties with some of the military aspects of the new thinking. He argued that Soviet military doctrine was always politically defensive but adherence to the principle of defensive sufficiency would allow the development of a defensive emphasis in the military-technical sphere.[29] Akhromeev's role as a key player in the politics of arms control was perfectly compatible with his views on defense sufficiency while he was Chief of Staff because, while he became a supporter of arms reductions as a means of enhancing the security of the USSR, he was never a supporter of arms reductions for their own sake. His view of arms control as a means rather than an end is best illustrated by his consistent statements that force reductions must be bilateral. Before and throughout his tenure as Chief of Staff, despite his apparent change of views on the relative importance of political and military means to security, Akhromeev emphasized that reductions in Soviet forces must depend on corresponding reductions in American or NATO forces.[30]

In principle, therefore, Akhromeev's support for arms control as a means to security, for elements of perestroika in the military dealing with increased efficiency and personal responsibility, and for maintaining a strong defense of the USSR were entirely compatible with one another. In practice, however, the views Akhromeev developed and articulated as Chief of the General Staff created a conflict between his institutional loyalty to the Soviet military establishment and his political loyalty to Gorbachev. This conflict may help explain his sudden, unexpected retirement from his position as the most senior and most politically influential military officer in the Soviet Union.

Akhromeev's Retirement

Akhromeev himself said that it was merely an unfortunate coincidence that his retirement and the plan to unilaterally reduce Soviet conventional forces by 500,000 troops were both announced on December 7, 1988.[31] Many figures in the Soviet foreign policy establishment, including Deputy Foreign Minister Viktor Karpov, Chief of the CPSU Central Committee International Department Valentin Falin, and Foreign Minister Eduard Shevardnadze, echoed the official explanation that the Marshal retired because of health problems and that speculation on the political ramifications of his departure were therefore pointless.[32] Nevertheless, considerable evidence indicates two factors which contributed to Akhromeev's decision to retire: conflict with Gorbachev over unilateral troop reductions and disagreement within the military over organizational and doctrinal reforms.

Akhromeev's repeated insistences that Soviet security interests could be enhanced only through bilateral or multilateral reductions in forces were noted earlier. Despite the official denials, several Soviet officials reportedly remarked that the timing of the Marshal's resignation was a signal of Akhromeev's opposition to unilateral cuts.[33] There is reason to believe, not surprisingly, that military discontent with the planned reductions was not limited to the Chief of Staff. Soviet generals, including First Deputy Chief of Staff Vladimir Lobov, argued that the cuts would not reduce the USSR's defensive capabilities and attempted to assuage the career concerns of the thousands of officers whom the reductions would make redundant.[34] After his retirement, Akhromeev stated that the troop reductions were "perfectly correct and justified from both political and military viewpoints."[35] It is difficult to determine whether this change of heart reflects a shift in his personal views, removal of his responsibility for representing military interests, or the necessity to fall in line with the General Secretary in his new position.

Institutional resistance by Soviet military officers very likely exacerbated Akhromeev's personal opposition to Gorbachev's plans for unilateral force reductions. There is clear evidence that institutional intransigence on other aspects of military reform existed some time before the end of 1988. In a speech at a meeting of the General Staff party *aktiv* in August 1988, Akhromeev sharply criticized the slow pace of implementation of military perestroika. With regard to the new military doctrine, Akhromeev charged that "certain commanders and staffs have not fully grasped the demands of the defensive strategy and operational art," and he accused the military establishment of blocking plans to increase democratization and personal responsibility: "On a number of points we are often in thrall to old ideas."[36]

Opposition to perestroika in the military appeared especially pronounced around the time of Akhromeev's retirement. An article by Akhromeev which circulated in the foreign press in November and December chastised the Soviet military for clinging stubbornly to its old habits:

The new thinking is not penetrating army and navy life easily-
the outdated, stereotype cliches are still exerting their influence.
In the past, we were often guided by ideas which, in the long
run, were by no means the best; ideas which sometimes
involved us in the arms race.[37]

Accounts of party meetings in the Southern Group of Forces and in the
Kiev Military District (which were attended by conservative Politburo
member Vladimir Shcherbitski) related that individual officers and the
political directorate in general were failing to implement the decisions of the
27th Party Congress and the 19th Party Conference.[38] While Akhromeev
defended vested military interests by arguing against unilateral force
reductions, he clashed with many elements of the Soviet defense establishment
by promoting doctrinal and organizational reforms. While it is not suggested
here that the Chief of Staff faced anything akin to a revolt by his subordinates,
it is not unlikely that bureaucratic resistance to perestroika in the military
made his job increasingly difficult and contributed to his decision to resign.

It therefore appears that in December 1988 Akhromeev had to resolve a
conflict in his loyalties but found himself unsupported on both sides. After he
worked long and hard to realize the arms reductions which were part of
Gorbachev's foreign policy agenda and to implement doctrinal reforms which
served the General Secretary's foreign and domestic political interests, a
scheme for unilateral force reductions was announced over his repeated
objections. At the same time, after he sought to protect military interests by
arguing against those unilateral troop cuts, a recalcitrant military establishment
blocked the organizational reforms which it was his duty to implement.
Akhromeev's reported health problems, including old war wounds and a prior
heart condition, possibly influenced his decision to resign.[39] Minor medical
complaints, however, are not likely to prompt a man to step down from the
summit of his career. Herspring suggests that Akhromeev was replaced in
order to bring in a younger man to implement military reforms as Chief of
Staff and to free the Marshal for work on arms control issues.[40] If he was in
fact deliberately replaced by Gorbachev, his ouster was not an astute political
move, as Akhromeev was one of the General Secretary's most capable allies
and was ideally placed to push for perestroika in the military as Chief of Staff.
The evidence seems to indicate that Akhromeev retired voluntarily because he
could no longer effectively carry out his professional and political tasks in the
face of bureaucratic resistance after Gorbachev undercut his position by
announcing unilateral troop reductions.

Akhromeev's New Role

Akhromeev's appointment as advisor to the President of the Supreme
Soviet placed him in a position which did not previously exist within the
Soviet political process. It was not uncommon prior to his appointment for
retired military officers, including Marshals Nikolai Ogarkov, Viktor Kulikov,

and Aleksandr Koldunov, to be placed in Communist Party posts to act as advisors to party organs on military matters.[41] Akhromeev's appointment to a new position within a reorganized Soviet government, rather than as part of the party apparat, is significant because it signals the intention to increase the legitimacy of the Supreme Soviet as a locus of political power. Very little could be known about Akhromeev's specific duties as advisor to the Soviet President at the time of this writing, and the scope of his responsibilities and influence may as yet be undetermined, but the available evidence suggests that his new position allows him to play the roles of advisor, back-channel communicator, spokesman, and governmental overseer.

A small professional staff reportedly assists Akhromeev, so it appears unlikely that he will continue to serve as an authoritative source of current military-technical data.[42] Instead, his role as advisor is more likely to involve the evaluation and advocacy of military and arms control policy options. In performing this role, he vehemently opposes the creation of a volunteer army. Akhromeev objects to ending the draft on ideological grounds and grounds of practicality, arguing that both a "professional" army or armed forces based on territorial militia would "violate socialist principles," would be too expensive, and should not be instituted as long as the danger of war exists.[43] He also expresses his belief as a lifelong military man that military service provides moral and spiritual benefits for young people.[44] Akhromeev's influence on political decisions cannot be determined, but his new post will allow him to continue to contribute his experience in military science and politics to the formulation of defense policy.

Because he will probably maintain his reputation and contacts with the defense establishment, Akhromeev will be uniquely well-placed to facilitate back-channel communications between Gorbachev and the military. He will be able to provide a direct link between the General Secretary and pro-perestroika elements in the armed forces, which could allow Gorbachev and his allies to bypass the General Staff or the Defense Ministry if necessary. Akhromeev remains in fairly close contact with Gorbachev and is often present at meetings with visiting foreign leaders.[45] If his position is an indication of membership in a "kitchen cabinet" of Gorbachev's close advisors, his functioning behind the scenes of the policy making process is likely to become his most important role in Soviet domestic politics.

The role he will most frequently play in foreign policy, by contrast, could be the very visible one of spokesman to foreign audiences. Akhromeev continues to advocate Soviet positions on arms control to the foreign press and in trips abroad.[46] As always, his statements intended for foreign consumption tend to closely parallel official Soviet proposals. He concentrates on the political rather than the technical aspects of arms reductions, but his experience and knowledge of military science still lend authority to his comments. His arguments on naval arms control and other issues outside his technical competence remain unconvincing, however.[47] Many of his meetings with foreign officials emphasize the establishment of relations between the Supreme Soviet and other national legislatures.[48] These contacts may indicate efforts to raise the status of the Supreme Soviet and to encourage both foreign governments and the Soviet public to recognize it as an actual policy making body and a political power base.

Akhromeev's participation in attempts to increase the legitimacy of the Supreme Soviet emphasizes the possibility that the most interesting role which he could play in Soviet politics centers on his membership in the Defense and State Security Committee of the Supreme Soviet. The mandate of this committee may include oversight of the implementation of perestroika in the military establishment. Akhromeev's wealth of personal experience in this area guarantees that he will be a leading figure on this committee, and he figured prominently in meetings in Moscow between committee members and a delegation from the House Armed Services Committee.[49] If the committee begins to exercise the authority to investigate elements of the armed forces, an adversary relationship may develop between it and the military establishment. If this occurs, Akhromeev may again be faced with a conflict between his professional loyalty to the military and his loyalty to an institution which Gorbachev intends to cultivate as a source of political power. The relationship between the Supreme Soviet committee and the military bureaucracy may become cordial and complementary, in which case the influence of the former Chief of Staff on Soviet defense decision making may well increase. If, however, the revitalized legislative body which he worked to strengthen becomes opposed to the traditional institution in which he built his career, Akhromeev could once again find himself in an untenable position of divided loyalties.

Speculative Conclusions

This chapter argues that Akhromeev exited from his position as Chief of Staff because the conflict between his duties as the Soviet Union's senior military officer and his loyalty to Gorbachev's program of military reforms became unresolvable. Furthermore, it suggests that Akhromeev's appointment as advisor to the President of the Supreme Soviet increased the legitimacy of the legislative organ of the Soviet government as a policy making institution and as a source of political power. In playing this new role, Akhromeev appears capable of helping Gorbachev to circumvent the party apparat and defense ministry in order to implement perestroika in the armed forces. However, he is likely to continue to confront the necessity to divide his loyalties between the General Secretary, his allies and personal advisors, and the Supreme Soviet on one hand and the Soviet military establishment and elements of the CPSU apparat on the other. The direction in which Akhromeev's new role is likely to develop will be determined by Gorbachev's success in broadening his basis of support and increasing his personal power and the political legitimacy of the Supreme Soviet.

If Gorbachev successfully consolidates his own power and expands the role of the Supreme Soviet, Akhromeev could become an increasingly important behind-the-scenes player in decision making on defense issues. He would continue to work to implement perestroika in the armed forces and to serve as an important link between the military and the General Secretary. He would probably not be promoted to higher government or party posts and may soon contemplate an honorable retirement from public life, as he reached the pinnacle of his career as a Soviet soldier when he served as Chief of Staff and he never really was a politician. If his work with the Defense and State Security Committee helps Gorbachev to gain greater control over the Soviet defense agenda, Akhromeev may finally be able to resolve the conflict between his institutional and political loyalties.

If, on the other hand, the *perestroichiki* cannot overcome the political and bureaucratic inertia which pervades every aspect of Soviet society, the reforms promulgated by Gorbachev and his supporters will not take hold within the military establishment. The Supreme Soviet would in this case become an increasingly irrelevant institution and would not provide a basis from which Akhromeev could take an active part in formulating defense and arms control policy. Akhromeev's experience might allow him to retain his membership in in the Central Committee, where he could act as an advisor on arms control issues, and he would still command respect for his past achievements and professional knowledge. His lack of an institutional power base would prevent him from becoming either a key policy maker or a major player in Soviet politics, however. If Gorbachev's military reforms do not succeed, therefore, the man who had once been the Soviet Union's most prominent soldier will probably just fade away.

Notes

[1] I. N. Shkadov, et al., (eds.), *Geroi Sovetskogo Soiuza: Kratkii biograficheskii slovar'*, (Moscow: Voenizdat, 1987), Vol. 1, p. 93.

[2] *Krasnaia Zvezda*, July 2, 1989, p. 2.

[3] *Sovetskaia Rossiia*, Jan. 14, 1989, p. 1.

[4] Interview on Budapest Television Service, *FBIS-SOV*, June 28, 1989, pp 72-74.

[5] *Sovetskaia Rossiia*, May 9, 1989, pp. 1-2.

[6] Alexander Rahr, *A Biographic Directory of 100 Leading Soviet Officials*, (3rd. ed.), (Munich: Radio Liberty Research, 1986), pp. 8-10.

[7] There are reports that Akhromeev headed the "Main Directorate for Camouflage (*Maskirovka*)" during the 1970s, but there are doubts as to whether this organization actually exists. See Rahr, 1986, and Peter Weiss, "Marshal Akhromeev: Chief of the Soviet General Staff and Arms Control Expert," *International Defense Review*, April 1988, p. 342.

[8] See the interview with General of the Army V.I. Varennikov in *Ogonek*, No. 12, March 1989, pp. 6.

[9]*Krasnaia Zvezda*, July 2, 1989, p. 2. Akhromeev said little else about his duties in Afghanistan or about the decision to commit Soviet troops to the conflict in that nation.

[10]Ellen Jones, "The Defense Council in Soviet Leadership Decisionmaking" Kennan Institute for Advanced Russian Studies Occasional Paper, No. 188 (Washington, D.C.: May 1984), pp. 45, 53.

[11]*Sovetskaia Moldaviia*, March 31, 1989, p. 1; trans. in *FBIS-SOV*, April 20, 1989, pp. 59-60. Why Akhromeev stood for election in Moldavia is not known.

[12]*Izvestiia*, July 14, 1989, pp. 2-7.

[13]*Newsweek*, July 11, 1988, p. 36.

[14]*Washington Post*, December 11, 1987, p. A29.

[15]*Newsweek*, July 11, 1988, p. 36.

[16]See, for example, *Pravda*, Oct. 19, 1985, p. 4.

[17]*Pravda*, June 4, 1985, p. 4.

[18]*APN Military Bulletin*, No. 17, September 1988, pp. 1-4.

[19]*New Times*, No. 35, September 8, 1986, pp. 4-5.

[20]Broadcast on Radio Moscow domestic service, April 14, 1986, trans. in *FBIS-SOV*, April 16, 1986, p. AA1.

[21]*Pravda*, December 16, 1987, p. 4.

[22]*Krasnaia Zvezda*, Feb. 23, 1986, p. 2. For a discussion of Akhromeev's earlier positions on this issue, see Dale Herspring, "The Soviet Military in the Aftermath of the 27th Party Congress," *Orbis*, Summer 1986, pp. 297-315.

[23]*Sovetskaia Rossiia*, Feb. 21, 1987, p. 1.

[24]Herspring, "Gorbachev, Yazov, and the Military," *Problems of Communism*, July-August 1987, p. 103.

[25]*Problemy Mira i Sotsializma*, December 1987, p. 2.

[26]Vitalii V. Zhurkin, S. Karaganov, and A. Kortunov, "O razumnoi dostatochnosti," *SShA*, No. 12, December 1987, p. 15.

[27]*Trud*, Feb. 21, 1988, pp. 1-2.

[28]Stephen M. Meyer, "The Sources and Prospects of Gorbachev's New Political Thinking," *International Security*, Fall 1988, pp. 140-141; R. Hyland Phillips and Jeffrey I. Sands, "Reasonable Sufficiency and Soviet Conventional Defense: A Research Note," *International Security*, Fall 1988, p. 168.

[29]*Trud*, Feb. 21, 1988, p. 2.

[30]*Pravda*, October 19, 1985, p. 4; *Krasnaia Zvezda*, February 23, 1986, p. 2; *Problemy Mira i Sotsializma*, No. 12, December 1987, p.2; *Trud*, February 21, 1988, p. 2. Akhromeev's emphasis on bilateral reductions is also noted by Herspring in "Marshal Akhromeev and the Future of the Soviet Armed Forces," *Survival*, November-December 1986, p. 530, and by Phillips and Sands, *op. cit.*, 1988, p. 168.

[31]Interview of Akhromeev by Iurii Tepliakov, "General Staff: Changes," *Moscow News*, No. 5, January 29, 1989, p. 5.

[32]TASS radio report, Dec. 15, 1988, transcribed in *FBIS-SOV*, December 16, 1988, p. 7, "Falin: We are Ready to Make Profound

Changes" (interview by Manfred Schell), *Die Welt* (Hamburg), January 24, 1989, p. 6, translated in *FBIS-SOV*, January 26, 1989, pp. 10-12; interview with Shevardnadze, *Le Figaro*, January 10, 1989, p. 3, translated in *FBIS-SOV*, January 12, 1989, pp. 8-11.

[33]*Washington Post*, Dec. 8, 1988, p. A34.

[34] *Krasnaia Zvezda*, December 16, 1988, p. 3; *Pravda*, December 17, 1988, p. 4.

[35]*Sovetskaia Rossiia*, January 14, 1989, p. 1.

[36]*Krasnaia Zvezda*, August 13, 1988, p. 2.

[37]*Rabotnichesko Delo*, (Sofia), December 6, 1988, p. 1, translated in *FBIS-SOV*, December 9, 1988, p.1. While this article had been previously published in *Svenska Dagbladet* (Stockholm), November 30, 1988, p. 3, the Bulgarian periodical claimed it was an "exclusive to *Narodna Armiia.*"

[38]*Krasnaia Zvezda*, December 16, 1988, p. 2; *Pravda*, December 21, 1988, p.3.

[39]*Washington Post*, December 8, 1988, p. A34.

[40]Herspring, "The Soviet Military and Change," *Survival*, July-August 1989, pp. 323.

[41]Raymond L. Garthoff, "New Thinking in Soviet Military Doctrine," *Washington Quarterly*, Summer 1988, pp. 131-158. Many of these generals were forced to resign from the Central Committee after the April 1989 plenum, however. Akhromeev's experience in arms control negotiations may be an important reason why he was one of four retired senior officers who retained their positions.

[42]He indicated in an interview that his staff numbered exactly two. See *Krasnaia Zvezda*, July 2, 1989, p. 2.

[43]Interview in *Sovetskaia Rossiia*, January 14, 1989, p. 1; interview on Budapest Television Service program "Panorama," June 28, 1989, translated in *FBIS-SOV*, June 30, 1989, pp. 72-74; Bernard E. Trainor, "Soviet Leaders Debating Shape of a Future Army," *New York Times*, July 31, 1989, p. 3.

[44]*Sovetskaia Rossiia*, May 9, 1989, pp. 1-2.

[45]See, for example, *Pravda*, May 12, 1989, p. 2.

[46]For examples of Akhromeev performing this role, see *La Repubblica*, March 11, 1989, p. 11; *Pravda* (Bratislava), May 11, 1989, p. 6; *Le Figaro*, June 13, 1989, p. 3; and *Zolnierz Wolnosci*, June 29, 1989, p. 4.

[47]*Suddeutsche Zeitung* (Munich), June 12, 1989, pp. 42-43, translated in *FBIS-SOV*, June 15, 1989, pp. 1-4.

[48]TASS report on his meeting with representatives of the Western European Union assembly, *Krasnaia Zvezda*, April 20, 1989, p. 3; *Los Angeles Times*, July 22, 1989, pp. 1, 6; interview in *Sovetskaia Rossiia*, August 3, 1989, p. 3.

[49]*Washington Post*, August 14, 1989, pp. A15-16.

5

Soviet Doctrine and Nuclear Forces into the Twenty-first Century

Daniel Goure

New conditions threaten to disrupt the strategic planning environment of the 1970s and 1980s. Foremost of these is the demise of the traditional Soviet approach to national security and military doctrine which drives military strategy, force planning, and the strategic competition. Soviet military planners and, to no lesser extent, Western Sovietologists take advantage of a stable Soviet military process to formulate and articulate doctrine by which to deal with changes in Soviet strategy and force posture. The current reformulation of Soviet military doctrine necessitates major changes in military policy. This doctrinal change could significantly alter not only Soviet assessments on the role of nuclear weapons as the premier military-strategic instrument, but also strategic force options.

Changes in Soviet views of the political or military utility of nuclear weapons probably would be sufficient to constitute a true revolution in Soviet military affairs. But other factors suggest that such a revolution is in the offing. These include widespread changes in military technology, the redefinition of alliances, the development of new centers of political and military power, and alterations in the character of domestic economic power and international trade. Other issues loom for Soviet decision makers. The possible introduction of strategic defense by either or both sides could undercut the utility of ballistic missiles creating a need for new offensive systems. Budget constraints and the apparent desire of the Soviet leadership to limit the growth in Soviet strategic forces challenge the ability of Soviet military planners.

Anticipating the evolution of the Soviet threat may allow the West to affect those changes so that they become more suited to Western views on stable military balances. If the West is to ensure its security in the next century, it is not too early to think about the character of the Soviet Armed Forces in the year 2010.

The Cycles of Soviet Force Posture Development

Soviet military theoreticians recognize two cycles in the development of their armed forces. Marxist-Leninist theory explains each long cycle in terms of changes in "objective conditions," referring to the basic economic and scientific-technical structure which dominated each historical period.[1] Because of changes in the basic structural elements of national power, each long cycle was marked by an intensive and costly struggle to create the industrial and scientific infrastructure and capacity to support force requirements dictated by the expansion in the strategic power of Soviet adversaries.

The first long cycle, extending from the late 1920s to the end of the 1940s, combined with Moscow's efforts to create a modern industrial state, witnessed the industrialization of Soviet military power. Soviet theoreticians developed a theory of warfare which they term "military art," based on the key technologies of that phase: mechanization and powered flight.[2] Soviet strategy focused on long wars consisting of a series of combined arms campaigns; victory would result not only from superior battlefield performance but also from superior economic strength. In this phase, Soviet operational art centered on the exploitation of new possibilities for maneuver by combined arms formations in the form of deep operations and encirclements of enemy forces.

The second long cycle began in the early 1950s and extended to at least the late 1970s. This cycle, characterized by the Soviets as "the Nuclear Revolution in Military Affairs," depended on three key technologies: nuclear weapons, long-range delivery systems such as ballistic missiles, and modern electronics.[3] Changes to Soviet military strategy in this period centered on the requirements for the proper application of military force in which the scale of destruction increased while the time element shrunk substantially. The nuclear strike became the focus of operational art, directed towards rapid and decisive defeat of an opponent's nuclear and strategic forces.

These long cycles in military planning were matched with cycles in Soviet national security policy. These policy cycles alternated between a focus inward (Iosif Stalin's policy during industrialization and collectivization) and a more outward focus (Nikita Khrushchev's assertive foreign policy) to exploit domestic strengths and international opportunities. The shift between inward and outward foci was influenced by Soviet assessments of strengths and weaknesses and of threats to Soviet security.

As the pace and scope of technology change and, consequently, Soviet military capabilities and those of its potential opponents increase, so does the possibility for the emergence of a new long cycle. Such a long cycle would be reflected in Soviet military planning by the formulation of a new or revised military doctrine. This altered formulation would take into account changes in international relations as well as military capabilities and national economic potentials. According to one Soviet military specialist:

> Soviet military doctrine...does not remain unchanged. It is refined and developed depending on the alignment of political forces in the world and the policy followed by the state, the status of the nation's economy, improvements in means of conducting war, and the growth in combat capabilities of the Armed Forces. However, its class essence is retained.[4]

When military doctrine begins to respond to external forces it puts pressure on military planners to change military art. Marshal Nikolai Ogarkov, in a statement seemingly directed within the Soviet military establishment, states that "military art has no right to lag behind the combat potential of the means of armed struggle, particularly at the present stage when, on the basis of scientific and technical progress, the main arms systems change practically every 10 to 12 years."[5] General Lieutenant M. Kir'ian declared that the intensification of the process of new weapons development itself became a "law-governed pattern" of military science. As a result, Soviet planners must adjust to more rapid cycles of change in Soviet military art. Kir'ian declares that, whereas at the start of the century it often took 20-30 years to integrate completely new technologies and operational concepts in the Armed Forces, the process of cyclic change was reduced twofold and now may take less than 10 years.[6] A change in the basic military-technical means around which modern Soviet military art was built could start a new long cycle, constituting a new revolution in military affairs.

The Doctrinal Context for a New Long Cycle in Military Affairs

The Western understanding of Soviet military doctrine and strategy was conditioned by the role of nuclear weapons in Moscow's external relations and national security policy. The West accepts the Soviet contention that its attainment of strategic parity in the early 1970s sharply shifted the political relationship between East and West. The United States and its allies not only had to struggle with the political effects of the changing strategic balance, but were also forced to confront the Soviet military's fundamentally different view of the role of nuclear weapons.

The focus of Soviet military doctrine in the nuclear age was the political character of the conflict between East and West. It was based on the view that the threat of war was ever present so long as the West maintained the capitalist system. Only a great, more certain threat of its own destruction would deter the West from initiating counterrevolutionary military action if it saw a possibility to alter the class struggle by military action against the socialist community and the USSR. While Soviet doctrinal writings of this period did not advocate preventive war, they did direct Soviet military planners to develop a strategy which could respond to the failure of deterrence by destroying hostile forces, defeating opposing political-military coalitions, and limiting damage to the Soviet Union. Doctrine also required that Soviet military planners develop the capability to control escalation and ensure that, should homeland exchanges become inevitable, the USSR could dominate the course and outcome of the unfolding conflict.

The Soviets concluded that their political objectives and views on war dictated this control of the "initial period" of any conflict. It required that the Soviet Union be able to destroy hostile offensive forces before the enemy employed them. As a result, the Soviets required forces which were responsive and reliable and able to reach and destroy distant targets. In theory, the ballistic missile assists the Soviets in this objective.

The "design" case which drove Soviet strategic and force planning always tended towards pre-emptive nuclear action in response to strategic indicators of impending attack. If successful in their effort to "outguess" their opponent, and if the appropriate means were available, the Soviets hoped for a pre-emptive counterforce operation which could substantially limit damage to the USSR.[7] A counterforce strategy also raised the prospects for limitations in the enemy's ability to strike Soviet targets. Deterrence could be achieved by threat of objective rather than punitive retaliation.

In sum, Soviet military planners saw pre-emptive attack on the enemy's nuclear forces as the the most effective way of vitiating an enemy's first strike. The value of pre-emption, according to Soviet military theory, was that it could make victory inevitable by establishing a favorable correlation of military forces. Coupled with air and missile defense operations, the pre-emptive strike held out an opportunity for the Soviet Union to deny enemy objectives and achieve its own, including the limitation of damage to critical war-waging assests.[8] Almost twenty years ago, two authors, writing in the classified military journal *Voennaia Mysl'*, argued that the most effective posture for defeating an opponent intent on a surprise counterforce attack was one which combined "powerful and numerous means of destruction maintained in high readiness" and "well-developed anti-missile and anti-air defense which can reliably repulse any aerospace attack."[9]

Although the means for pre-emptive counterforce operations were not available in the 1960s, the Soviets set about to create the desired force structure. In developing it, they addressed the fact that the temporal dimension of a future war contracted while its spatial scope expanded greatly. Moreover, and this was critical to the Soviet view of strategic operations, a world war could encompass virtually the entire expanse of the homelands of the warring sides. As a result, Soviet military theory argued that the objective of nuclear weapon strikes in a future war would not only be to beat the enemy's armed forces, but also the disruption and destruction of administrative-political and military-industrial centers.[10] The problem for Soviet strategic planners was how to prevent the destruction of the critical targets in the homeland in the course of such a war. This could be achieved, according to Soviet military art, by the proper deployment of strategic offensive forces. According to one Soviet military theoretician of the late 1960s:

> In the past, in armies of developed states, the main military equipment was identical. Now they have two types of weapons: nuclear and conventional. Additionally, an army can start a war with a limited employment of nuclear weapons or with a non-nuclear variant. As a consequence of this the qualitative determination of the combat capabilities of the armed forces of the sides has become more complex. First and foremost it depends on the presence and distribution of nuclear weapons among the various branches of the armed forces and the combat arms, on the power of available nuclear warheads, the capabilities of their carriers, and the effectiveness of the systems of air defense and the control of troops.[11]

By the early 1970s, the Soviet leadership could reasonably conclude that they were achieving their strategic goals and were in a position to reap the political benefits resulting from their improved strategic posture. Indeed, many Soviet political and strategic analysts asserted that the signing of the SALT I agreement and the apparent U.S. global pull-back of the mid-1970s articulated in the Guam Doctrine, but more importantly demonstrated in the withdrawal from South Vietnam, signified the correctness of the Soviet political-military strategy.[12]

However, in the late 1970s or early 1980s, this policy disintegrated. The Soviets recognized that their influence over the character of the strategic competition and the pace of military technological innovation was limited, at best. Senior Soviet military leaders began to question the continued viability of the Soviet emphasis on offensive nuclear power in its military doctrine and strategy. The Soviets interpreted PD 59 and its formulation of U.S. countervailing strategy as signaling U.S. intent to circumvent the Soviet counterforce deterrent. Moscow viewed the modernization program as providing Washington with the ability to conduct nuclear war-waging, in particular the destruction of critical Soviet military and leadership targets. The history of the INF deployment process marked a dual failure for Moscow. On the political level the Soviets were unable to influence NATO nations to reject deployment. On the military level they were confronted by the potential for a new strategic threat, one which promised to recouple NATO to U.S. central strategic systems. The introduction of the INF proved the danger to Moscow and NATO-WTO (Warsaw Treaty Organization) that conflict would rapidly lead to strikes against the Soviet homeland. Soviet military analysts warned that the INF put the United States in the position of being able to conduct homeland strikes on the Soviet Union while relying on the threat posed by U.S. strategic counterforce capabilities to deter Soviet response in kind or escalation.

In addition, Soviet domestic economic and scientific-technical limitations became increasingly apparent. In the early 1980s the Soviet economy was in a no-growth mode or even in an actual state of decline which resulted in a marked slowdown in the rate of growth in military spending. What concerned Soviet military leaders was that this slowdown came precisely at the time at which they were beginning to see entirely new arenas of competition emerging from the military scientific-technological revolution.[13]

External conditions were propitious for a change in Soviet military doctrine; this led to a change in Soviet national security policy in order to address the problems of domestic stagnation and economic inefficiency. This combination of doubts regarding the continued viability of the existing, nuclear-oriented military doctrine, advances in military technologies, the failures of Soviet policy in the late Brezhnev period, and domestic imperatives combined to set the stage for a new long cycle in Soviet military development.

Soviet Military Doctrine in a Period of Flux

Recent Soviet military writings show a change in view on the character of a possible strategic nuclear war. The writings of the period from 1965 to the late 1970s emphasized superiority in the initial conduct of nuclear strikes and the role which such superiority would serve in enabling the Soviet Union to dominate the course and outcome of a future conflict. Later writings suggest a decidedly less optimistic view with respect to the outcome of initial offensive operations. Strategic war, according to leading Soviet strategic thinkers, was becoming increasing complex. The Soviet Union could not hope to control the course and outcome of such a war, particularly if it involved nuclear weapons use, simply by the expedient use of massive offensive operations.

According to one such commentator, G. Negrasov, in 1977: "The time has come when existing weapons systems, one might say, have exhausted themselves, and are only being quantitatively increased. At the same time, the possibility of creating new weapons systems based on new physical principles has arisen."[14] Although it had brought about strategic parity by the mid-1980s the continual production of nuclear weapons by itself was seen by Soviet leaders as providing no enduring advantages. Marshal Ogarkov made a number of statements about the paradox which existed between the continual acquisition of nuclear weapons and their inability to achieve decisive military results against another nuclear-armed opponent.[15] In one such statement he appeared to indicate that the Soviets began to recognize the limits to their nuclear-oriented strategy and force posture:

> In the 1950s and 60s, when there were few nuclear weapons,
> they were seen as means of sharply increasing the troops
> firepower....Later, in the 1970s and 80s, the rapid increase in the

numbers of nuclear weapons, development of long-range and highly accurate delivery to targets, and their widespread distribution...led to a basic review of the role of this weapon.[16]

General Makmut Gareev criticized earlier Soviet military theory for its excessive emphasis on the role of mass nuclear strikes as the only determinant of victory in a strategic nuclear war. He argued that war must be viewed as a series of strategic operations. Success could not be determined by a single action, even if it were a massive nuclear counterforce strike. Gareev emphasized that no set of advantages, nor superior numbers, nor weight of attack, nor a better strategy, could guarantee complete success. Soviet military planners would have to be satisfied with a series of partial victories leading, hopefully if somewhat unpredictably, to overall victory:

> Regardless of the fact that the main, most powerful means of waging war are in the hands of the superior military commands and their employment can have a decisive influence both on the course of the war as a whole and on the conduct of military operations, the principle of a partial victory has still not lost its importance.[17]

Moreover, Gareev and others argued that the evolution of strategic nuclear forces made it increasingly likely that, regardless of the success of initial actions, a strategic nuclear war was likely to be protracted:

> The experience of war shows that under modern-day conditions it has become significantly more complicated to achieve the aims of a war than previously. Modern armies possess colossal viability which is completely linked to the overall state of a nation. Even after the complete destruction of the enemy, the shattered troops still have behind them an economically and politically sound rear.[18]

What appears to lie at the heart of the Soviet drive to reevaluate national security policy is a recognition that increases in nuclear forces, particularly ballistic missiles, reached the point of diminishing returns. Marshal Ogarkov, in his 1985 book, applied the Marxist dialectical principle of "negation of the negation." He argued that the Soviet strategy to exploit nuclear revolution in military affairs was a tremendous success, insofar as Moscow attained a capability to employ massive numbers of nuclear weapons. However, he went on, there was a point of diminishing returns beyond which the acquisition of more nuclear weapons was counterproductive. In other words, he argued that more is not better and may be worse.[19]

Earlier, Ogarkov set the stage for this 1985 thesis by arguing that a single-minded emphasis on strategic offensive forces failed to take into account the natural dialectic tension between offense and defense. He suggested that the offense-dominated approach to military strategy might change as offensive and defensive technologies continue to be modernized over time:

> The experience of past wars convincingly demonstrates that the appearance of new offensive weapons has always inevitably led to the creation of means to counter them....This applies fully also to nuclear missile weapons whose creation and rapid development forces military-scientific thought and practice to actively develop means of countering them. In their turn, the appearance of means of defense against weapons of mass destruction caused improvements in means of nuclear missile attack. All this confirms the conclusion that the constant struggle between means of attack and defense is one of the main sources of development of military affairs as a whole.[20]

Some recent Soviet military analyses suggest the emergence of a new long cycle during the last decade. This third cycle is based on what the Soviets describe as an ongoing "scientific-technical revolution." This revolution is the product of technological advances in such areas as micro-electronics, computers, and power supplies. The relationship between advances in science and technology and Soviet military science was outlined by Kir'ian: "Basic qualitative changes are taking place under the influence of scientific and technical progress and by the further development of productive forces. These changes are affecting the instruments of combat, the organization and preparation of combat personnel, and the means of conducting war and military activities."[21] A recent analysis of Soviet military thought by three U.S. experts notes that "evidence has been accumulating that the Soviets believe that the objective requirements for yet another revolutionary turn in military affairs have been created."[22] The Soviets do not hint at whether or not they believe that this new revolution in military technology will favor the offense or the defense.

In the early 1980s, Soviet military writings began to emphasize the need to exploit a new set of technologies which could radically alter military affairs. Marshal Ogarkov, while declaring that "an acceleration was taking place in the development of military equipment and weapons...which in turn is affecting the pace of development of military affairs as a whole," noted three specific areas of future technology development: strategic weapons, troops control processes and systems, and aerospace systems.[23] In his 1984 May Day speech Ogarkov went even farther, declaring that "...the rapid development of science and technology in recent years creates real preconditions for the emergence in the very near future of even more destructive and previously unknown types of weapons based on new physical principles."[24] The term "weapons based on new physical principles" refers to systems that employ or exploit new forms of energy and destructive power.

Soviet military analyses focus on the potential for advanced technologies to act as force multipliers, possibly serving to negate a quantitatively superior strategic force. In particular, the Soviets note the importance of new means of reconnaissance, computers and artificial intelligence in surveillance, highly accurate weapon systems, and weapons capable of penetrating the difficult frontiers of the combat environment of outer space and the oceans. These systems also contribute to what the Soviets termed the battle for the "first salvo" and fire superiority over the enemy.

The Soviets are concerned about the potential impacts of these new technologies on the theater battlefield. Former CINC (Commander in Chief) of the WTO Marshal Kulikov provided a list of possible new types of weapons systems in his 1984 May Day speech:

> Accelerator, laser and radio frequency weapons, and high explosive ammunition are being created. Reconnaissance and strike systems are being equipped with highly effective intelligence systems, and high-accuracy terminally-guided warheads. Matters are moving towards a situation where conventional weapons approach nuclear weapons in terms of effectiveness and uses. Space is being militarized.[25]

Advanced conventional munitions are changing the character of non-nuclear conflicts and opening the prospects for destruction equal to that of controlled nuclear exchanges. Minister of Defense Dmitri Yazov claims that long-range, precision-guided conventional munitions could be used against nuclear power plants and other installations creating widespread damage similar to nuclear weapons.[26] One pair of Soviets argued that the U.S. and NATO allies could employ these new weapons for missions previously met by nuclear weapons. Another concern is that advanced conventional weapons with strategic potential might be used during a non-nuclear conflict to radically alter the nuclear balance and create conditions whereby one side could achieve a first strike advantage or otherwise deny the other the capability to employ it nuclear arsenal.[27]

The Soviets are also apparently concerned that the introduction of these new technologies can undercut Soviet efforts to solidify the stability of the East-West military balance. Moreover, the speed with which such systems might be introduced raises uncertainty about the Soviets' ability to predict and plan for the evolution of scientific-technical revolution in military affairs. Colonel V. Chernyshev warns that the new NATO conventional arms programs threaten to undermine strategic stability. He declares that "...certain NATO circles are striving for the speediest introduction of the most modern achievements of the scientific and technical revolution into conventional weapons systems. This would lead to a new, still more dangerous stage in the development of conventional weapons and the armed forces."[28]

Development of advanced technologies of the types mentioned by Soviet military theoreticians will require costly improvements to the Soviet Union's military-industrial sector. The importance of economic restructuring and the intensification of scientific-technical progress for the future of Soviet defensive capabilities was underscored by Soviet General Secretary Mikhail Gorbachev at the 27th Congress of the Communist Party of the Soviet Union (CPSU).[29] Other Soviet leaders made the point even more bluntly, arguing that Soviet national security is becoming critically dependent on the ability of the Soviet economy to produce advanced weapons systems. Among the priorities set by the Soviets as part of the "intensification of scientific-technical progress," in the service of military construction, according to Major General M. Iasukov, are machine construction, electronics, nuclear industry, laser technology, and information systems.[30]

Addressing the forces which press towards a new scientific-technical revolution in military affairs requires time and resources. As a result, the Soviets introduced new political and military doctrinal concepts which appear directed at providing both the breathing space and resource base for long-term modernization of the Soviet state and military nation.

New Thinking

A reassessment is currently underway within the top Soviet political-military leadership on issues of military strategy, force sizing and character, and defense budgets. "New thinking" (*novoe myshlenie*) is evident in the high level policy debate which Soviet spokesmen argue as a new comprehensive approach to Soviet security policy.

The new thinking is an effort to redefine the national security environment in which the Soviet state will exist. It signals a change in the Soviet leadership's assessments of the nature and extent of national security threats and the relationship between domestic stability and development and external policy. Such an important shift could have a profound effect on the character of Soviet military strategy and force acquisition policy and on the share of national resources devoted to the military.

At the heart of the Soviet argument about the new thinking and the case for a new concept of Soviet national security is the contention that the character of the world political system, in general, and that of world capitalism led by the United States, in particular, changed in the last fifteen to twenty years. The slogan which Gorbachev articulates, and which is employed in innumerable subsequent commentaries, is that the modern world is interdependent and that security for one must mean security for all. One recent editorial in *Kommunist* captured the essence of Gorbachev's thesis:

Historical development has brought mankind to a period in which the agenda of international life incorporates the problem of the development of a diverse, integrated world with a new spirit unparalleled in the past. And this spirit rests on the fact that a world community united by number is similar and common interest...is being formed. The most important...is averting a nuclear catastrophe. Such interests are above any differences, contradictions, and class antagonism.[31]

Kommunist presented a modified version of this argument, referring to the hostile class nature of capitalism as the source of continuing danger of nuclear war and warning of the need to maintain a class focus in the analysis of mutual East-West security interest. The journal asserted that the need for a common response to the danger of nuclear war would never outweigh the basic class conflict that divides East and West. At best, leading capitalist elements hostile to socialism would be required to modify their policies to account for the need to pursue their interest without reliance on the threat of force:

The class struggle was and remains the pivot of social development in societies divided into classes. Nevertheless, the appearance of weapons of mass destruction has put an objective limit to class confrontation in the international arena. This naturally does not mean that the class analysis of the reasons for the nuclear threat created by militaristic circles in the ruling class of the leading capitalist countries should be abandoned. Nor does it mean an acknowledgment of any kind of convergence on the part of the different social systems.[32]

New thinking theorists argue that the change in the form of struggle between capitalism and socialism is made inevitable by the absence of militaristic alternatives as outlets for capitalist antipathy towards socialism. In the nuclear age, they argue, there can be no meaningful resort to the use of force to solve the historical class conflict between East and West. Indeed, some Soviet civilian commentators declare that Clausewitz's oft-cited dictum that "war is a continuation of politics" is no longer true in the nuclear age. According to Daniil Proektor, the presence of nuclear weapons in the hands of the superpowers fundamentally changed the relationship of war and politics and eliminated the choice of war:

Here Clausewitz has become outdated. In contemporary politics, involving the proliferation of nuclear weapons, there is no such choice (between war and politics). Also, there is not and cannot be a political objective, such that its successful attainment could give rise to the idea to start a nuclear war and to risk the future of humankind.[33]

General Volkogonov extends this argument by assessing that while war could no longer be viewed as a continuation of any reasonable or proper national security policy, war, even nuclear war, could still be a continuation of a flawed policy. He implies that for capitalist nations, which inherently tend to pursue flawed policies, war could remain an instrument of policy:

> Nuclear weapons have outgrown the purpose for which they were created. The fundamental new level of military technology has added a new dimension to war itself. In truth, nuclear war has reached a limit, a frontier, a threshold. From this perspective, Clausewitz is hopelessly outdated.[34]

An essential element of the argument put forward by Gorbachev and his allies is the assertion that capitalism is becoming a less threatening competitor to the USSR. Starting with this thesis, Gorbachev could argue that the USSR can afford to enter into arms control agreements (such as the INF treaty). After "rehabilitating" capitalism, Gorbachev could operate from a strong position in arguing for reductions in defense expenditures and for tolerance of disruptions and even reductions in internal controls and stability in the pursuit of social and economic reforms.

The new thinking in the area of military affairs is defined as a restructuring of international relations that will result in a reduced prospect for East-West conflict and, consequently, engender a reduction in military forces. This is because a qualitatively new situation exists, in which the objectives of any political dispute are dwarfed by the risk inherent in confrontation between nuclear-armed adversaries. Security, it is argued, cannot be assured unilaterally, through the attainment of military-technical superiority or a superior correlation of military forces. As a result, the Soviets argue, the new thinking must be extended to include a common framework for the resolution of regional and local political disputes.[35]

The basic framework of the new thinking is not new; many of the concepts currently articulated were introduced by the Brezhnev regime in the late 1970s and early 1980s. In his oft-cited speech at Tula in January 1977, Brezhnev publicly eschewed a policy of nuclear superiority and a first strike nuclear strategy. Nevertheless, the current discussion of the new thinking is distinct from that which occurred under Brezhnev. Soviet writings on East-West relations from the late 1970s to 1985 stressed the threat from the West and the need for vigilance and enhanced Soviet military security. The new thinking advocates appear to argue, in contrast, that the threat is not as severe as was described and that realistic forces among imperialism's ruling circles are basically in accord with the Soviet Union's view of the requirements for security.

Sufficiency and a Defensive Doctrine

The concept of sufficiency is also not new. Soviet spokesmen always assert that their policy is to maintain only the level of forces and weapons necessary to defend the Soviet state and its allies. However, the debate within the Soviet leadership is over the criterion for judging military sufficiency. Civilian analysts from the Institute of USA and Canada and IMEMO, who were invited into the debate by the top Party leadership, use the term "reasonable sufficiency" (*razumnaia dostatochnost'*) which is a code word for restricting military budgets. Many within the military argue that sufficiency should be judged by what is necessary or essential to meet the threat, using the phrase "necessary sufficiency." General Volkogonov, for example, argues that so long as the threat of war exists, it is necessary to use the military to enforce Soviet security and "maintain the military balance of power." He goes on to say that:

> We would like to do this with a reduced level of armaments and we have already taken steps in this direction, but, to be able to maintain the strategic balance, we must make use of the new scientific and technological achievements and, relying on the principle of sufficiency, we cannot afford to lag behind our potential enemies. Thus, life itself, including history, logic, and dialectics, forces us to increase the technical standard of our armed forces.[36]

Former Deputy Chief of the General Staff and now CINC of the Ground Forces General Valentin Varennikov argues that "the development of the Soviet Armed Forces is limited to essential defensive adequacy and to the strengthening of strategic military parity."[37] However, he defines "essential defensive adequacy" as that sufficient to deny the West, and the U.S. in particular, the capability for waging nuclear war under conditions of a surprise, pre-emptive attack. Thus, the General concludes by defining the requirements of Soviet defense as follows:

> In general, all of the preparations of our Armed Forces involve the ability to take responsive, protective measures. At the same time, we are not forgetting the lessons of history. We remember that imperialism is a treacherous and ruthless enemy. If it senses weakness, it will stop at nothing. It is necessary, therefore, today as never before to maintain the Army and the Navy at the highest level of combat readiness.[38]

A senior Soviet arms control and foreign policy expert, who is now Chairman of the Soviet of Union, Evgenii Primakov, defines sufficiency in the context of new thinking, saying:

What characterizes sufficiency? The Soviet Union proceeds
from the fact that in the arms sphere it is determined primarily
by the requirements of defense against aggression.[39]

A similar comment was made by the head of the Main Political
Administration, General Aleksei Lizichev, who appears to move away from
the General Secretary's position and more to the military's line:

And today, expenditures on defense, the number of personnel in
the Army and Navy, the quantity and quality of weapons and
military equipment are defined exclusively by the demands of
the Fatherland and the collective defense of the gains of
socialism. In our country, nothing more is being done than is
necessary.[40]

Against these arguments by the military, a small set of Soviet political
analysts began to develop a different view of sufficiency and to take the
almost unprecedented step of arguing military doctrine. An article in the
January 1988 issue of *Kommunist* suggests that the existing parity between the
two sides does not serve the interests of the Soviet Union, but rather continues
to stimulate an arms race. It argues that so long as the USSR can maintain a
survivable capability to inflict unacceptable damage, it is secure.[41] Moreover,
it also argues that strategic parity and a capability to inflict unacceptable
damage on the U.S. and its allies changed qualitatively the nature of the
capitalist threat; the West no longer desires to pursue a confrontational
strategy with the USSR. In essence the authors reject the standard view of the
importance of the correlation of forces and, by implication, the parity principle
as a basis for assessing the sufficiency of the Soviet military posture.

Other civilian analysts are less willing to develop a definition of
defense sufficiency, which does not take into account the specific level and
character of the threats to Soviet security. In a roundtable discussion among a
group of Soviet foreign affairs and defense experts, one analyst noted that
reasonable sufficiency must be a mutual concept, in the sense that Soviet
reductions must compel the opponent to reduce its military forces. The
difficulty of managing such a two-sided process led this analyst to conclude
that "we must not make attempts to determine what is reasonable sufficiency
apart from a general phrase that *reasonable sufficiency is the minimum effort
to ensure our security.*[42] (emphasis added)

Some Soviet military planners might agree with the civilians who argue
that the current Soviet military strategy and force posture is too burdensome in
resource and economic terms. This would create conditions in which goals
will exceed capabilities or priority missions will not be adequately addressed.
Given the character of modern, especially nuclear, war there are requirements
for the near-instantaneous readiness of the Armed Forces and for a capability
to mobilize the nation rapidly. These requirements prove to be difficult and
costly.[43]

The reformulated WTO military doctrine reflects the new thinking. However, this is not a true military doctrine about military policy and the guiding principles for development of strategy and forces. Rather, it is a political formulation which asserts the primacy of changes in political relations between the two sides as a basis for resolving their military competition. This doctrinal statement asserted that the WTO's goal was no longer a reliable defense of the socialist community but, instead, the prevention of wars of any kind.[44] In the interest of attaining this objective, the WTO advocated the reduction of forces on both sides, strategic as well as those in the theater, to the lowest possible level of strategic equilibrium.[45]

The issue of sufficiency re-emerges with respect to what level of forces are consistent with Soviet national security objectives. One of the leading Soviet civilian theorists on new political and military strategies, A. Kokoshin, argues that the key to the problem of the arms race and to a stable balance of power is the struggle between offense and defense. While this is not novel, Kokoshin's conclusion is that the problem of the arms race is a product not of the defense but of the offense with continual efforts by military and scientific experts to find new ways of overcoming the defense. He argues that instability is a product of the increasing destructiveness of offensive systems and their increased cost. Kokoshin makes reference to the offense-defense dialectic citing Marshal Ogarkov. He argues that even the destabilizing aspect of the offense-defense dynamic could be mitigated if efforts were made to ensure the non-offensive character of strategic and theater forces:

> In examining the cyclic alternation of the prevalence of either offense or defense in major wars on the European continent, including World War II, one cannot fail to note the presence of one stable, long term trend that seemingly permeates all these phases; namely, there was a constant increase in the destructive capability of the weapons used and a growth in the interest of combat operations in the depth of operations and the territorial area encompassed by military events. There was also an increase in resources used for warfare and in the level of their mobilization and military-economic strain that each state experienced during a war.[46]

Kokoshin took his argument even farther in another piece, arguing that, given the destructiveness of nuclear weapons, a stable strategic balance can be achieved at extremely low levels of forces, so long as both sides can ensure the survivability of their retaliatory capability.[47] He asserts that the existing strategic nuclear arsenals could be reduced by 95 percent, leaving both sides with a small number (600) of strategic nuclear weapons. It is interesting to note that Kokoshin's article produced an immediate and stormy debate in the Soviet civilian press. Several articles published criticized his analysis of a stable strategic balance. They argued, not unlike Western analysts, that at extremely low levels of Soviet forces, other factors such as the French and

British nuclear deterrents and even advanced, long-range conventional weapons could upset Kokoshin's notional equilibrium.[48]

Some Soviet civilian analysts cite the examples of defensive operation during the Great Patriotic War, particularly the battle of Kursk, to show the value of a defensive doctrine, at least with respect to conventional conflicts. Kokoshin and retired Soviet military analyst V. Larionov assert that Kursk demonstrated the potential superiority of the defensive over the offensive. Moreover, the authors claim that the greatest significance of the battle was that it marked a change in Soviet military art, a situation in which the side with quantitative superiority chose to conduct a defensive rather than an offensive operation. They conclude by arguing, in contradiction to established Soviet military thought, that the increasingly lethal modern weaponry, while not completely negating the utility of the offensive, demonstrates the potential superiority of the capabilities of the defensive.[49]

They fail to note, however, that the plan formulated by the Soviet commander, Marshal Zhukov, viewed the Soviet defensive operations as a temporary maneuver, conducted not for the purpose of defending Soviet territory but to create the conditions for the planned offensive intended to drive the German Army from the Ukraine.[50] In contrast to civilian "innovative thinkers," Soviet military leaders indicate that they did not abandon the idea of the offensive or the goal of the destruction of the enemy as part of their wartime strategy. This should not come as a surprise. There is no contradiction in Soviet military thought between a defensive doctrine and an offensive strategy. The onus of war initiation, and of an offensive doctrine, rests with the leaders of the capitalist world. Once having crossed the line from peace to war Soviet military doctrine specifies the requirement to both defend the Soviet Union and the socialist community and rebuff the aggressor. While defensive operations may be required, so too are offensive ones. Indeed, it can be argued that the Soviet Union would have to undertake offensive operations to prevent the aggressor from posing a future threat to world socialism. Thus, Minister of Defense Yazov asserts that "Soviet military doctrine regards defense as the main type of military operation for repelling aggression." He goes on to say that "it is impossible to route an aggressor with defense alone, however. After an attack has been repelled, the troops and naval forces must be able to conduct a decisive offensive." Yazov resolves the seeming contradiction between these two statements by a legalic sleight-of-hand to confuse military actions with political intent:

> The Soviet Armed Forces used a combination of defense and offense to rout the aggressor during the civil war and the Great Patriotic War. This in no way contradicts the defensive nature of Soviet military doctrine, since, I would stress once again, it was an issue of offensive actions against an aggressor which had attacked our country.[51]

Two Soviet colonels, writing in *Voenno-Istoricheski Zhurnal* on army defensive operations during the Great Patriotic War, argue that the defense was a temporary form of combat action dictated by unfavorable circumstances or inferior forces. They note that "the counterattack was the decisive form for destroying the attacking opponent." They illustrate that the experience in the War with "active defense" had deep significance for the current defensive doctrine of the WTO.[52]

General Gareev takes a similar approach in addressing the new Soviet military doctrine. He states that Soviet military doctrine is defensive because it is drawn from the political principles of the Soviet state which, at least by assertion, are defensive and non-aggressive. However, if the USSR was confronted by aggression, Gareev asserts that the Soviet Armed Forces would undertake those operations necessary both to defend the Soviet homeland and to deal the opponent an annihilating responsive strike. Defense and offense are operationally linked:

> In correspondence with the defensive character of military doctrine, military art starts from the premise that at the start of the war in the repulse of enemy aggression, the basic form of combat action, it is impossible to achieve the full destruction of the enemy by defense alone. For this reason, in the course of the war [following the repulse of the enemy aggression] the basic form of combat action will be by the transition in the counteroffensive to decisive counteroffensive actions in conjunction with defense, depending on the circumstances.[53]

This discussion does not mean that the Soviets dismiss the possibility of strategic nuclear war involving pre-emptive counterforce strikes or abandon the desire to prevail in such a conflict. Rather, they debate the likely character and scope of such a conflict in order to define the military strategy and force posture with which to pursue their strategic objectives. In a recent work by senior Soviet military theoreticians from the General Staff Academy, it was argued that war did not cease to be an instrument of policy and that such a war, unleashed by imperialism, would still constitute a political struggle conducted by military means. This collective work goes on to argue that in the event of such a war the central means to be employed would be long-range strike systems.[54] Finally the authors point out that nothing in the current strategic situation or military balance negates the concept of offensive action in a strategic conflict. Rather, they assert, the offensive is the proper and most direct route to the solution of military and political conflicts:

> Extremely important in this connection is the Leninist instruction that the socialist state conducts and will only conduct defensive wars. *However, these wars are defensive only in their political goals, but not in the means of their conduct....The offensive is the fundamental type of military activity, and this*

goal is the full and total destruction of the opponent.[55] (emphasis added)

The debate regarding sufficiency and its operational and force posture implications is likely to continue. If, as some Soviets allege, strategic nuclear offensive forces no longer hold the promise of a reduction in the opponent's retaliatory potential, even if employed in a first strike, and the scientific-technical revolution threatens to render irrelevant, or at least complicate, Soviet military strategy and force acquisition planning, then radical changes in the current Soviet approach to strategic forces and their uses may be in the offing. Certainly, the implementation of proposed START reductions would alter the character of the strategic offensive force posture (but not necessarily its effectiveness). Moreover, the discussion of defensive actions as the centerpiece of Soviet military doctrine might suggest an increasing Soviet interest in strategic defenses, even a preference for enhancement of existing limited strategic defensive over offensive forces. In either case, the Soviet strategic force posture that will exist over the next thirty years will undoubtedly look substantially different from what it is today. Moreover, the missions and tactics for strategic nuclear forces may change even more substantially.

Doctrinal Alternatives for the 1990s

The Soviet strategic leadership is in the midst of a major doctrinal debate. The cleavages within the leadership do not appear to conform to traditional civil-military divisions. Instead, there appear to be three basic positions emerging from this debate, which can be termed "reformers," "modernists," and "conservatives." Each group represents a different combination of views with respect to the nature of the military-strategic problem, sources of solutions, role of technology, and force requirements.

Civilian analysts, generally but not exclusively associated with the foreign policy research institutes of the Soviet Academy of Sciences, are reformers. They emphasize the primacy of politics over military and technical issues in the formulation of doctrine and arms control policy. They can be distinguished from modernists insofar as they seek to establish a stable balance between East and West based on an understanding of weapons technologies and forces, using the leverage created by the attainment of a stable military environment to achieve political accommodations. Other contributors to the reformist camp come from Party and government institutions and research institutes of the Armed Forces.

However, this group is not united. The Soviets themselves acknowledge a split among the civilians over the basis for the formulation of national security and arms control policies. Alexei Arbatov, in a series of articles reviewing the Soviet civilian debate on arms control, identifies two schools of Soviet political scientists which he calls the "politicians" and the "technocrats." The first school argues that weapons may impact upon policy, but the latter drives the former. By implication, the "politicians" would hold that a change in the definition of the threat and the character of relations between the two sides would drive changes in military doctrine and arms control initiatives and result in a policy-mandated military balance. The latter group, which would appear to include Arbatov himself, argues that only by achieving a stable military balance, eliminating first strike and arms race instabilities, and thereby reducing the level of anxiety and mistrust that blocks political accommodations can a stable political relationship be achieved.[56]

In addition to members of the Soviet foreign policy establishment such as Politburo Member and Chairman of the CPSU Central Committee Commission for International Affairs Aleksandr Yakovlev and Central Committee Department Chief Valentin Falin, the civilian reformers include a strong cadre of political scientists such as Kokoshin, Primakov, Deputy Director of the Institute of Western Europe Vitalii Zhurkin, as well as some retired military officers employed by civilian research establishments such as General Mil'shtein and Colonels Semeiko and Larionov. They are in the forefront of efforts to redefine Soviet military concepts, including the review and critique of Soviet military thought, and in the development of alternative policies and arms control proposals.

The Soviet military tends to divide between modernists and conservatives. The former include "retired" senior serving officers such as Marshals Ogarkov and Akhromeev, some defense industry leaders, and most of the new military leadership including Yazov. The latter include a block of serving officers, members of the MPA, some defense industry personnel, and some members of the military's higher academies.

Many within the Soviet military resent the intrusion in their traditional domain. Their concern surfaced publicly in a recent article in *Kommunist* by Major General Lebedev. While noting the need to address new views of national security and to review Soviet military theory, he directly criticizes the participation in it of "unqualified amateurs":

> In our view, one cannot avoid noting that the peace offensive taken by the USSR and its allies in recent years has been so dynamic and on such a scale that foreign policy and military thinking in the Soviet Union as in the West has only been able to record what is happening without being able to subject it to an in-depth analysis, thus lagging behind political practice. This exact situation seems to have arisen around the initiative put forward by the Warsaw Pact members in May of last year, at a time when this major action was not appropriately developed or supported by the public information media and the scientific community. The discussions held last year within scientific and public circles in the USSR demonstrates the inadequate training

of political scientists on questions of military doctrine, an inclination to draw rash conclusions at times, and a lack of professionalism which is vital to the analysis of military-political problems. Let us repeat that this is explainable partly by the poor quality of specialized training, and partly by the fact that some of the people drawn into the recent discussions...had only a very vague notion of the subject under discussion.[57]

It is difficult to judge the contribution of the civilian analysts and commentators to the Soviet debate on doctrine. Much of their work, particularly their more extensive efforts such as those in arms control and against SDI, appears directed at Western audiences. The military and the scientific-technical and industrial establishments still retain responsibility for definitions of force posture and weapons systems requirements and for the development of strategies and targeting policies. The military, including newly appointed leaders such as Yazov, Chief of the General Staff Mikhail Moiseev, CINC of the PVO Ivan Tretiak, and others, appears to take a restrained approach to the issues of new thinking, sufficiency, and the defensive doctrine. It is likely that while civilian analysts will carry some weight in the public posturing around doctrinal issues, particularly as they relate to defense expenditures, the military will continue to dominate the formulation of doctrine and force requirements.

National Security Policy

Reformers and modernists view the problem of national security policy as one of making the USSR competitive with the West. They both appear to agree on the need to establish Soviet national security interests as an integral part of the system and rule of international relations. For both it is a matter of developing economic strength to sustain a new foreign policy and the development of a force posture based on widespread exploitation of advanced military technologies. Both these positions provide a major role for arms control as a means of freeing resources and restraining the pace and character of the arms race.

The reformers go farther than the other two groups in arguing that national security policy should reflect the importance of politics and economics over military capabilities. Their argument is that politics must lead military strategy and that the acquisition of strategic forces must be directed towards fulfilling the political objectives of the state. Major General Kirshin of the Military History Institute accuses the past leadership of mistaking military power for political leverage. He declares that "the expansion of nuclear potential, the creation of new types of weapons of mass destruction has lost political and strategic sense." He further goes on to declare that a paradox was created in which the nuclear strategies of states contributed to political impotence. Nuclear weapons could not guarantee security; only politics could provide the basis for a lasting peace.[58]

The conservatives disagree with the other two positions in two major respects: on the nature of the capitalist threat and on the extent to which the Soviet Union can safely enter into arms reduction agreements. They hold that the only basis for reductions are the principles of parity and necessary sufficiency, based on a worst-case assessment of the capitalist threat. The conservatives resist efforts to reduce the role of the Armed Forces in Soviet foreign policy.

Where the modernists split with the reformers and side with the conservatives is on unilateral Soviet reductions in the Armed Forces. Moreover, both modernists and conservatives probably see the necessity for a higher ceiling on defense expenditures than would the reformers in order to meet the requirements for matching Western defense programs and maintaining the necessary levels of military R&D.

Lebedev's attack against the civilian reformers illustrates what appears to be the modernist-conservative argument. He declares that the potential to change military doctrines and force postures unilaterally is limited. He urges a more realistic approach to changing doctrine and forces, reflecting a continuing threat from the West. He goes on to declare the Soviets could not establish unilaterally a defensive doctrine and force posture:

> Even if the socialist states already had a purely defensive doctrine and armed force structure and possessed only defensive weapons and systems [which it is not possible to clearly delineate], it would be impossible to guarantee that there would not be a war. It is important for the other side, the United States and NATO, to take analogous steps.[59]

Western analysts speculate that the modernists' positions accept the need for the shift in investment priorities advocated by the reformers in exchange for a substantial improvement in future military economic and military-technical potentials. While this may be true in the short term, the modernists are still oriented outward, judging the requirements for new forces and capabilities in terms of the external threat. Hence, any failure on Gorbachev's part to secure a significant reduction in the strategic threat would probably result in a fundamental split between reformers and modernists on the requirements of Soviet national security.

The Character of Future Wars

Reformers argue that the presence of a survivable retaliatory capability on both sides makes war between the superpowers unthinkable. They favor reductions in virtually all areas as a means of increasing the restraints on conflict initiation and arms competitions. They also argue that the most likely causes for a nuclear war would be an accident or an escalation between the superpowers' main allies. This position is propounded by civilian analysts, such as Kokoshin and Larionov, who argue the possibility for a purely defensive doctrine, based on a radically different force structure.[60]

Modernists argue that conventional or theater war is of vital importance. They maintain that the possibility of a war between the WTO and NATO continues to exist. The likelihood of escalation beyond the theater is not necessarily great; wars may remain limited, if one side possesses the means to enforce escalation control. This means that the modernists view a theater war as one which would follow traditional Soviet doctrinal precepts: rapid operations intended to seize the initiative and paralyze the opponent. Nuclear operations, including intercontinental strikes, are possible but not necessary or decisive. Reformers and modernists appear to agree that prevention of war is a suitable doctrinal goal.

Conservatives make the case that nuclear war remains viable. They insist that the United States seeks strategic superiority and the capability to conduct offensive, including pre-emptive, nuclear operations against the USSR. For them it is the ultimate level of war. They argue that because the West may yet attempt to defeat socialism by escalating to nuclear war, there continues to be a requirement to seize the initiative and control the course of war, regardless of its level.

Conservatives and modernists appear to agree that offensive actions will be necessary in any future war. Military advocates of modernization such as Yazov and Gareev argue, in opposition to the civilian reformers, that while an initial defensive phase is plausible, only decisive action will rout the aggressor. For example, General Serebriannikov, identified by Kokoshin as an opponent of the "defensive doctrine," asserts that defense can only be a temporary phase and that the offensive is the decisive means of routing an aggressor and ending the conflict.[61] Conservatives, not surprisingly, appear to downplay the significance of the new WTO defensive doctrine, arguing that a defensive posture actually results in an intensification of the long-standing Soviet military requirement for combat readiness, often a code word for a pre-emptive response capability. Marshal Kulikov, the former CINC of the WTO, interpreted the new defensive doctrine in just such a manner:

> The emphasis of the Warsaw Pact's military doctrine on defense requires the allied states to realize all the necessary possibilities for preventing war. This means that the aggressor has strategic advantages because it can at its own discretion select an advantageous time, means, and method of attack, and take advantage of the factor of surprise. Steps must be taken, therefore, to neutralize the enemy's advantages. In other words, the defensive nature of our doctrine does not reduce the requirements set for combat readiness of the armies and navies of the fraternal nations: on the contrary, it increases those requirements.[62]

Deterrence Requirements

Reformers assert that the nature of capitalism has changed sufficiently to warrant a review of Soviet assumptions about the requirements for deterrence. For them, the U.S. strategic deterrent is of increasing irrelevance as a restraint on Soviet policy, and, hence, the Soviet Union does not require a matching deterrent capability in all instances. Moreover, they argue that the Soviet military buildup damaged the USSR's effort to discredit the Western view of the Soviet threat. They also dismiss the relevance of the independent European nuclear forces to deterrence of the strategic threat, at least at high levels of forces. The objective of the reformist position is to neutralize the Western capability to contain Soviet pursuit of its national interests without eliminating the utility of central strategic systems to deter direct attack.

Modernists and conservatives both hold that the West is still deterred by Soviet military capabilities. Modernists agree with the reformers that deterrence of a strategic nuclear war is most important but appear to doubt the certainty of deterrence at the theater level. Modernists also assert the need for Soviet capabilities to intervene in regional conflicts in order to deter Western involvement. Conservatives argue that the inherently hostile and militaristic nature of capitalism means that Soviet strategic forces must be directed at deterring capitalist efforts to find a military solution to the political competition. Deterrence can be maintained only by a large Soviet nuclear posture. They hold that strategic parity itself justifies the maintenance of a large and varied nuclear arsenal.

Roles for Nuclear Forces

The future role of nuclear forces in Soviet national security policy is a major source of contention between the three schools. A recent survey of current Soviet literature on the problem of politics and nuclear war in the journal *Kommunist Vooruzhennykh Sil* noted the broad range of opinion expressed, particularly by those who would be classed as reformers. They criticize the lack of consideration of such basic issues as the relationship between preparations for war and state politics, the placement of thresholds limiting nuclear use as an exercise in politics, and the role of politics in decisions of nuclear weapons use.[63]

Reformers are supporters, even formulators, of the new thinking. In the main, they reject the possibility of nuclear war as an instrument of policy and hence tend to devalue the role of nuclear forces. They argue that the emphasis on nuclear weapons in Soviet national security policy is proven counterproductive. The reformers assert that the pursuit of nuclear power, while effective up to a point (such as the historic achievement of parity with the United States in the early 1970s), does not provide a basis for ensuring Soviet security. They strongly reject the classic dictum that "war is a continuation of politics" by other means, at least as it applies to nuclear war.[64]

Hence, they assert, there can be no such thing as a rational nuclear warfighting policy nor a reasonable definition of nuclear sufficiency, and, therefore, they argue that there are enough nuclear weapons. Some adherents to this position even argue that a minimum deterrent position is possible so long as parity is maintained.

Modernists view deterrence more classically as the product of war waging capabilities. They do not accept the notion of a winnable, all-out nuclear war, but neither do they reject the effort to establish full capable nuclear forces. Modernists, epitomized by Marshal Ogarkov, want a balanced force posture. The Ogarkov line is not anti-nuclear but rather pro-conventional; he parallels the position taken by those in the military who opposed Khrushchev nuclear monomania and advocated instead a spectrum of capabilities. They also argue quality over quantity. The modernists' position treats nuclear weapons as a means of escalation control enabling conventional forces to dominate the theater level of war.

Ogarkov and others in the modernists camp argue that Soviet military thought and force development paid insufficient attention to the implications of advanced non-nuclear weapons for Soviet national security and arms control policy. Among those asserting this view is Deputy Defense Minister V.M. Shabanov. In a number of articles he calls attention to the explosive growth in capability of advanced conventional weapons, the potential destructiveness of non-nuclear warfare, and the threat of escalation created by so-called "nuclear equivalent" conventional weapons. Recently he suggests the need to focus attention on conventional arms control as a means of limiting Western advanced weapons programs.[65]

The conservatives argue that nuclear forces provide the necessary leverage for Soviet political doctrine. Their position argues that nuclear weapons hold the key to modern warfare. However, they see some potential for restraint below the strategic threshold. Moreover, they adhere to the position that quantity counts, particularly in modern warfare. Conservatives argue that more and varied nuclear firepower, more speed, and greater reach are necessary to a war waging and deterrent posture.

Desired Force Postures

Reformers want a force posture sizable enough to deter attack and sustain Soviet national security policy. They do not view military power as the *sine qua non* of Soviet state power. Instead, they desire modern forces with a demonstrated equivalence to those of the United States. Their themes are essential equivalence and sufficiency in that existing Soviet strategic capabilities are more than sufficient for expected contingencies. They accept significant force reduction in all areas. The modernists desire a robust and balanced posture. They are willing to see a "fire-break" between theater nuclear and strategic forces emerging out of reduction in theater range missiles. If anything, they want an expansion of theater level forces. But, they also want continued modernization of the Soviet strategic offensive.

The conservatives are opposed to both unilateral cuts and to an emphasis on non-nuclear and defensive actions. They argue that there is a level below which Soviet strategic forces may not be reduced without unacceptable risks to national security and the ability to implement war plans. The conservative position emphasizes more and better nuclear forces; conventional forces are secondary in their eyes.

The Role of Technology

Reformers tend to see technology as creating problems, particularly under conditions of Soviet internal turmoil and change. They recognize the need to take advantage of technological opportunities but do not desire a technological race with the West. Reformers consistently criticize past Soviet national security policy for its overemphasis on technology as a solution to what they see as political problems. They do not reject the idea of a modern Soviet military but do dispute the importance of superiority, either quantitative or qualitative.

The modernists believe such a race and competition is inevitable and want the USSR to win that race. Indeed, their position is that a technological competition is already underway. Both modernists and reformers are concerned that advanced technology might allow the West to reestablish a position of strategic superiority. The modernists are at odds with the reformers over requirements for rapid introduction of advanced military technology. Many senior Soviet military officers, including Minister of Defense Yazov, argue that the meaning of perestroika (restructuring) for the military is to make more efficient and effective use of the new weapons. They see perestroika as an opportunity to improve existing force posture. Chief of Staff of the WTO Colonel General V. Lobov declares that the introduction of a new means of war places tremendous pressure on the Armed Forces to improve military readiness while moving to a new force posture.[66]

The conservatives believe that technology should not be pursued for its own sake. Moreover, they do not believe that new weapons technology alters the fundamental nature of warfare in the nuclear age nor that it invalidates the role of strategic nuclear forces. They hold that the Soviet Union needs perceptual equivalence in high-technology weaponry but not necessarily absolute equivalence.

Framing Soviet Strategic Weapons Acquisition Choices

All three positions accord with the pressing Soviet need for more effective defense spending; however, they each emphasize different criteria for selection of investment priorities. The reformist position on meeting the challenge of a new long cycle in military affairs can be summarized as "less, possibly better, definitely later." They contend that changing international circumstances should be the test for the scale and scope of reorganization and modernization of the Soviet Armed Forces. The modernist position is "maybe less, definitely better, and now." They focus on enhancing Soviet military power but argue that the basis for this enhancement and for the potential use of Soviet armed might are different, largely as a result of technological change. The conservative position is "more, maybe better, but now." They reject the ideas that the basis for evaluation of requirements for military power changes significantly and that forces based on advanced technology are still the mainstays of modern warfare. The answer to the question of how much to spend and on what will be determined, in large part, by which position's view on the nature and evolution becomes official policy. While the reformers' position appears to be in the ascendancy now, failure to make progress on arms control and thereby prove the correctness of the reformers' view of capitalism could result in a return to the more conservative view.

Participants in the current Soviet doctrinal debate know that, barring radical moves by either superpower towards strategic arms reductions or the introduction of qualitatively new forms of strategic defense (such as SDI), the character of Soviet strategic forces is already set for the 1990s. The Soviets are committed to modernization programs involving all aspects of the Soviet strategic defenses. The character and timing of these programs suggest that Soviet military planners in the early 1970s anticipated many of the changes in the threat to the Soviet homeland, assessed the resulting changes in the mission structure for Soviet strategic forces and in particular the targeting requirements for offensive nuclear forces, and proposed an appropriate set of systems requirements. As a result, the systems available to be deployed in the 1990s are, in many respects, potentially highly effective responses to these changes. The current Soviet strategic modernization program is a realization of the long-term Soviet acquisition strategy set down in the early 1960s for the attainment of a secure strategic deterrent and a meaningful nuclear war waging capability.[67] Changes in Soviet military strategy did not lead to the abandonment of Soviet interests in perfecting their strategic posture but merely levied new requirements such as those for forces useful for fighting controlled nuclear conflicts, for exercising control over near-Earth space, and for establishing a secure strategic reserve force.

Adherents to all three Soviet positions recognize that the means of targeting, weapons delivery, and target destruction will continue to change over the next decade. For this reason it is possible to envision the beginnings of a movement towards a Soviet strategic offensive force posture which does not rely nearly so much on the ICBM. There is reason to believe that the Soviets may already recognize this change, downgrading the role of the ICBM as the decisive war waging instrument and according greater value to the SLBM and strategic bomber forces.[68] A recent book on the Soviet Armed Forces called the Strategic Rocket Forces (SRF) "the leading link," a characterization which is a far cry from earlier descriptions of the SRF as the decisive force in Soviet military strategy, capable of determining both the course and outcome of a strategic conflict.[69]

The 1990s, then, should be viewed as a transitional period for Soviet strategic forces. Old doctrines, strategic and acquisition policies, and force postures will be replaced by new ones influenced by the introduction of new and innovative technologies and by changes in political relations between superpowers and members of alliances. Given competing budget priorities and Gorbachev's commitment to modernize the Soviet economy, the Soviet military-industrial leadership may not possess the resources to alter the character of the Soviet strategic force posture in line with these new trends. The costs of technology development programs and learning curves involved must affect the decision to alter a well-established acquisition style and force posture. It may be that the 1990s are a decade in which the Soviet decision makers will temporize, choosing to emphasize investment in and reliance on capabilities and technologies which are well known and for which the costs are established, rather than taking the risks involved in pursuing radical alternative strategies and force postures. Viewed in this manner, the Soviet arms control strategy may be one of attempting to hold back the inevitable movement towards new forms and means of strategic conflict, to temporize in the face of internal difficulties.

Conclusion

Each of the three positions presented above represents a different doctrinal-strategic solution to the challenges confronting Soviet national security. The reformers believe that war is unlikely. Hence, there is no need for Soviet military doctrine to treat nuclear escalation as a given in the event of an East-West conflict. The reformers also include a defensive approach to meeting aggression and eschew the requirement to resolve a conflict with the absolute defeat of the aggressor. They assert that nuclear deterrence is the key to stability. At the same time, they reject any effort at replacing nuclear deterrence with defensive deterrence as the term is used in the West. The essence of the reformers' military doctrine is conflict management and not preparation for a strategic nuclear war. This perspective supports an emphasis on arms control. The reformers are also more inclined to define sufficiency in a restrictive manner and possibly to unilaterally reduce the missions of the Soviet Armed Forces. The targeting requirements for Soviet strategic forces could thereby be reduced, enabling the strategic nuclear forces to maintain a high-confidence assured destruction threat but not a capability to prevail in a nuclear war.

The modernist view focuses on the prospects for controlled conflicts and even protracted, non-nuclear wars as the basis for planning purposes. The issues for the modernists are control and restraint. Reduced strategic nuclear forces might be acceptable under this position so long as the Soviet Armed Forces are capable of prevailing in the theater. Appropriate forces are required to enable the Soviet Union to achieve its military objectives in war rapidly and with a minimum of collateral damage. Pursuit of this doctrinal approach requires the capability to enforce a broad conventional-nuclear firebreak both politically and by means of conventional pre-emption of in-theater nuclear forces. The modernists emphasize the rapid introduction of the new technologies, a high technology competition, although they would prefer to see it conducted along a Soviet timeline.

The modernist position is agnostic with respect to arms control. This position incorporates sufficiency criteria as a way of rationalizing defense spending but not if it interferes with the attainment of the necessary war waging capabilities. Thus, they would not agree with the reformers on a defensive military doctrine. The idea of protracted wars would increase the importance of defense mobilization and secure the Soviet strategic rear from attack. This might lead to a requirement for some level of defense against ballistic missiles, as well as robust air defense.

The conservatives' position is that the current doctrine is still valid or, at least, can still work. The conservatives emphasize the need for superior warfighting capability at all levels. The scope and character of the threat from the West warrants a spectrum of Soviet capabilities. Because escalation control is unlikely, the emphasis in Soviet military planning should be on strategic nuclear forces. A future nuclear war would be intense, although the conservatives share the views of the modernists that it could be protracted. Therefore, the emphasis would be on capabilities: the maintenance of large and redundant reserve forces, even at high costs. The conservative view would reject a transition to a mutually defended environment, since they see it as enabling the West to circumvent the Soviet strategic offensive deterrent.

At present, it might appear that a modernist-reformist coalition is in the ascendancy. The INF treaty, signed in 1988, coupled with Gorbachev's December 7, 1988, announcement of a unilateral troop cut, took place over intense and public protests from many military officers. This signals the rejection of traditional conservative views of the need for maximum military power.

However, Marshal Akhromeev's resignation as Chief of the General Staff may indicate broader dissatisfaction with Gorbachev's decision. In his last public statement prior to his change of status, Akhromeev struck a decidedly conservative note. He warned that the military would require the most modern means if it were to be able to accomplish its missions with fewer forces:

The defense orientation in the structure of the Armed Forces is combined with the new means of maintaining military potential at a level that guarantees our country's reliable security under conditions of the possible reduction in both nuclear and conventional armaments. Under these circumstances, the combat effectiveness and the quality of the arms and equipment deployed in the Army and Navy assume decisive importance, since they permit us to cope with our military tasks with a smaller range of military weapons and equipment.[70]

This type of comment is typical of those made by high-ranking military leaders. Akhromeev's final statement and similar commentaries by senior officers, typified by Lebedev's critique of the current arms control "euphoria," suggest that the military is pressing for a more restrained approach to reformulating Soviet national security policy. The weight of experience, time, and circumstances is on their side. As noted before, the current Soviet force posture will change only slowly over time. A START agreement will only partially change the character of Soviet strategic forces and their missions. Indeed, it may well be that the Soviet military already developed the long-range acquisition strategy and operational plans to accompany such an agreement. If so, then the Soviet arms control process may strengthen the hand of the military, in general, and the modernists, in particular.

The modernists probably possess the strongest case. They are the only ones to speak to the full range of Soviet national security concerns. The need for a strong defense remains, they argue, despite progress in arms control. Also, by placing the onus for further changes in Soviet forces on the U.S. and NATO, they challenge Gorbachev and the reformers to provide the evidence to support a radical change in Soviet military concepts and practice. Even the most extreme advocates of new thinking and sufficiency do not assert that the threat to Soviet security has disappeared. Hence, the modernists can rightly claim the need for strength.

The modernists can support military reforms and changes in the manner in which doctrinal principles are articulated while at the same time holding out for the capability to prevail in the event of war. This is the gist of the arguments put forward by Yazov, Gareev, and others on defensive doctrine. They say that defense is fine, in principle, but should war come it must be fought to a successful conclusion. Asserting this, they can argue for the necessary "counterattack" capability which could, albeit incidentally, provide leverage in the event of Soviet first use. This capability can be more moderate than that advocated by conservatives because different operational concepts and a different mix of technologies will be applied. The presentation of a reasonable position with respect to both sufficiency and necessity allows the modernists the advantage of having a foot in both of the other camps.

Some changes in Soviet military doctrine, strategy, and the associated nuclear force posture is already in evidence. However, what is not occurring is a revolution, either political or doctrinal. The new military leadership is committed to a qualitative buildup of Soviet forces, even if that puts them in opposition to the Gorbachev program. What the future is most likely to bring is a revamped Soviet military machine directed by a new cadre of modernist officers. While modifications in the existing Soviet force structure are likely and some elements, such as the surface Navy, may even be cut back, the modernists will push for an upgrading of the Soviet Armed Forces. Gorbachev may find it necessary, perhaps even desirable, to support a leaner, meaner, and possibly almost as costly military machine.

Notes

[1]See S.S. Lotoski, (et al.), *Istoriia voin i voennogo iskusstva*, (Moscow: Voenizdat, 1970) and S.A. Tyushkevich, (et al.), *Sovetskie voennie sili*, (Moscow: Voenizdat, 1978).

[2]The Soviet concept of military art encompasses three levels of military operations: strategy, operational art, and tactics. See Harriet Fast Scott and William F. Scott, *The Armed Forces of the USSR*, (Boulder, CO: Westview Press, 1982), pp. 70-72.

[3]N.A. Lomov, *Nauchno-tekhnicheski progress i revolutsiia v voennom dele*, (Moscow: Voenizdat, 1973), p. 23.

[4]Franklyn Griffiths, "The Sources of American Conduct: Soviet Perspectives and Their Policy Implications," *International Security*, Fall 1984, pp. 92-123.

[5]N.V. Ogarkov, "Na strazhe mirnogo truda," *Kommunist*, No. 10, May 1981, p. 85.

[6]M.M. Kir'ian, *Voenno-tekhnicheski progress i vooruzhennie sili SSR*, (Moscow: Voenizdat, 1982), p. 330.

[7]William T. Lee and Richard F. Starr, *Soviet Military Policy Since World War II*, (Stanford, CA: Stanford University Press, 1986), Chapters Five and Six.

[8]See, for example, V.D. Sokolovski, *Voennaia strategiia*, (Moscow: Voenizdat, 1962, 1963, 1968).

[9]N. Vasendin and N. Kuznetsov, "Modern Warfare and Surprise Attack," *Voennaia Mysl'*, No. 6, June 1968, in FPD 0015/69, January 16, 1969, p. 22.

[10]Sokolovski, *op. cit.*, 1968, p. 360.

[11]I. Anureev, "Determining the Correlation of Forces in Terms of Nuclear Weapons," *Voennaia Mysl'*, No. 7, July 1968, in FPD 0112/68, August 11, 1968, p. 38.

[12]Georgi Arbatov, (ed.), *Doktrin Niksona*, (Moscow: Nauka, 1972), p. 67.

[13]John Hines, Phillip Petersen, and Notra Trulock III, "Soviet Military Theory 1945-2000: Implications for NATO," *Washington Quarterly*, Fall 1986, pp. 124-125.

[14]*FBIS-SOV*, February 17, 1977, p. AA 2.

[15]*Krasnaia Zvezda*, May 4, 1984, p. 2.

[16]N.V. Ogarkov, *Istoriia uchit bditelnost'*, (Moscow: Voenizdat, 1985), p. 89.

[17]M.A. Gareev, *M.V. Frunze: voenni teorik*, (Moscow: Voenizdat, 1985), pp. 330-331.

[18]*Ibid.*

[19]Ogarkov, *op. cit.*, p. 89.

[20]N.V. Ogarkov, *Vsegda v gotovnosti k zashchite otechestva*, (Moscow: Voenizdat, 1982), p. 36.

[21]M.M. Kir'ian, *Sovetskaia voennaia entsiklopediia*, (Moscow: Voenizdat, 1979), p. 82.

[22]Hines, Petersen, and Trulock, *op. cit.*, p. 118.

[23]Ogarkov, "Na strazhe...," *op. cit.*, p. 86.

[24]*Krasnaia Zvezda*, May 9, 1984, p. 2.

[25]*Krasnaia Zvezda*, May 9, 1984, p. 1.

[26]*Krasnaia Zvezda*, February 23, 1988, pp. 2-3; D. Yazov, *Na strazhe sotsializma i mir*, (Moscow: Voenizdat, 1987), p. 50.

[27]S. Davidov and V. Chervanobab, *Energiia, ekonomika, tekhnika, ekologiia*, No. 7, July 1987, pp. 43-48.

[28]*Krasnaia Zvezda*, March 15, 1988, p. 3.

[29]*Kommunist*, No. 4, 1986, pp. 1-22.

[30]*Krasnaia Zvezda*, December 3, 1986, p. 2.

[31]*MEMO*, No. 10, October 10, 1987, p. 104.

[32]*Kommunist*, No. 18, December 1987, p. 6.

[33]D. Proektor, "O politike, Klauzevitse i pobede," *Mezhdunarodnaia Zhizn*, April 1988, p. 82.

[34]D. Volkogonov, "Armiia novogo mira," *Aziia i Afrika Segodniia*, January 1988, No. 1, p. 23.

[35]See, for example, Evgenii Primakov, *Pravda*, July 10, 1987, p. 3.

[36]*FBIS-SOV*, February 20, 1988, p. 89.

[37]V. Varennikov, "Na strazhe mira i bezopasnosti narodov," *Partinaia Zhizn*, No. 5, March 1987, p. 9.

[38]*Ibid.*, p. 11.

[39]*Pravda*, July 10, 1987, p. 3.

[40]A. Lizichev, "Oktiabr' i leninskoe uchenie o zashchite revolutsii," *Kommunist*, No. 3, 1987, p. 90.

[41]V. Zhurkin, S. Karaganov, and A. Kortunov, "Vyzovy bezopasnosti: starye i novye,"*Kommunist*, No. 1, January 1988, pp. 42-50.

[42]*Vek i Mir*, No. 12, December 1987, pp. 77-78.

[43]See, for example, Marshal Akhromeev's interview in *Sovetskaia Rossiia*, February 21, 1987, p. 1.

[44]*Pravda*, July 27, 1987, p. 5.

[45]*Krasnaia Zvezda*, September 28, 1987, p. 4.

[46]A. Kokoshin, "Razvitie voennogo dela i sokrashchenie

vooruzhennykh sil i obychnykh vooruzhenii," *MEMO*, No. 1, January 1987, p. 25.

[47]A. Kokoshin, "Sokrashchenie iademykh vooruzhenii i strategicheskaia stabil'nost'," *SShA*, February 1988, pp. 3-12.

[48]See, for example, S. Viborkov, A. Gusenkov, and V. Leontiev, "Ne vse prosto v evrope," *Mezhdunarodnaia Zhizn*, No. 2, February 1988, pp. 29-37. For a defense of Kokoshin, see A. Arbatov, "Glubokoe sokrashchenie strategicheskikh vooruzhenii," *MEMO*, No. 4 and 5, April and May 1988, pp. 23-33 and 18-30.

[49]A. Kokoshin and V. Larionov, "Kurskaia bitva v svete sovremennii obornitel'noi doktriny," *MEMO*, No. 8, August 1987, pp. 32-40.

[50]*Soviet Military Review*, No. 12, December 1987, p. 57-59.

[51]Yazov, "Na strazhe...," *op. cit.*, p. 33.

[52]*Voenno-Istoricheski Zhurnal*, No. 2, February 1988, p. 75.

[53]Gareev, "Sovetskaia voennia...," *op. cit.*, p. 36.

[54]A.S. Milovidov, (ed.), *Voenno-teoreticheskoe nasledie V.I. Lenin i problemi sovremennoi voini*, (Moscow: Voenizdat, 1987), p. 249.

[55]*Ibid.*

[56]A. Arbatov, "Glubokoe...," *op. cit.*, pp. 23-33.

[57]I. Lebedev and A. Podberezhkin, "Voennye doktriny i mezhdunarodnaia bezopasnost'," *Kommunist*, No. 13, September 1988, p. 112.

[58]I. Kirshin, "Politika i voennaia strategiia v iademyi vek," *MEMO*, No. 10, November 1988, pp. 35-44.

[59]Lebedev and Podberezhkin, *op. cit.*, p. 116.

[60]Kokoshin and Larionov, *op. cit.*, pp. 38-40.

[61]V.V. Serebriannikov, "Bezopasnost' gosudarstva v iademyi vek," *Kommunist Vooruzhennykh Sil*, No. 9, May 1988, pp. 32-39.

[62]*Agitator*, No. 1, January 1988, p. 23.

[63]A. Pavlov and V. Liashenko, "Sootnoshenie voiny i politiki: diskussii i problemy," *Kommunist Vooruzhennykh Sil*, No. 21, November 1988, pp. 23-30.

[64]See, for example, *Krasnaia Zvezda*, June 17, 1987, p. 3; *Izvestiia*, August 13, 1987, p. 5.

[65]V.M. Shabanov, "Doktrina bezopasnosti i mira," *Mezhdunarodnaia Zhizn*, No. 10, October 1988, pp. 22-26.

[66]V. Lobov, "Vysokoe kachestvo: glavnyi kriterii boevoi podgotovki," *Kommunist Vooruzhennykh Sil*, No. 1, January 1989, pp. 12-18.

[67]Lee and Starr, *op. cit.*, pp. 183-187.

[68]Daniel Goure, "C3 for the New Soviet Nuclear Forces," *Signal*, December 1986, pp. 61-63.

[69]A. Babakov, *Vooruzhenie sili SSR posle voini*, (Moscow: Voenizdat, 1987), p. 246.

[70]Akhromeev's comments appeared in several sources including *Rabotnichesko Delo*, December 6, 1988, p. 1; translated by *FBIS-SOV*, December 9, 1988, p. 1.

6

Soviet Military Doctrine's Requirements for a Space TVD

Stephen J. Blank

Soviet President Mikhail Gorbachev, in an interview with NBC correspondent Tom Brokaw, stated that the USSR possesses a Strategic Defense Initiative (SDI) program similar to that of the United States. Ordinarily, official Soviet commentary uniformly stigmatizes the SDI as allowing an offensive first strike capability. The reconciliation of the apparent contradiction between "defensive doctrine" and Soviet attempts to establish space forces can be found in Soviet doctrinal innovations concerning the military role of space.

In 1986 an intriguing innovation in Soviet doctrine came to light when the latest edition of the *Soviet Military Encyclopedia* stated that space could constitute the area of a Soviet theater of strategic military operations (*Teatr' voennykh deistvii*: TVD).[1] This admission never appeared before and indicated that Soviet military theorists arrived at a number of important conclusions regarding the role of space in projected future conflicts. First, space would be a theater of operations among the Soviets, their allies, and belligerents. Second, such combat could have a strategic significance for the future of war by exercising a potentially decisive influence on the course and/or outcome of operations. Soviet thinkers expect future wars to be of global or near-global scope, suggesting that control of space would be decisive for operations aimed to control large sections of the Earth. Third, weapons capable of deployment from Earth or already in orbit are about or are already viable. Such weapons may be refinements of existing technologies or weapons based on physical principles such as directed energy beams. Fourth, the existence of such weapons presupposes the need to deploy organized forces in, into, or from space and would thus fall under the supervision of a TVD commander. Since such an organization is essentially a Command and Control (C2) structure, the designation of a command implies the existence of a force under it.[2] Finally, the designation of a theater also implies a process of study and decision concerning the demarcation of space into one or many theaters. The demarcation would include the corresponding main operational axes, high commands, etc., for future operations. Moreover, such a designation logically implies a program to prepare the theater according to the principles of doctrine and military art. This process of preparation involves its geographical and physical mapping, the prepositioning of necessary logistics, determination of the necessary lift capabilities, reconnaissance requirements, physical requirements for the stationing of men over a long time, and weapons requirements for the conduct of operations in the theater.

The military aspects of the Soviet space program amount to nothing less than preparation of the new space theater. But the scope of the analysis required to address this innovation far exceeds the limits of a single chapter. In previous publications, I discussed the kinds of forces from which a space theater might grow and how they might be configured.[3] The purpose of this chapter, however, is to demonstrate that the designation of space as a theater is the logical outgrowth of Soviet technological-strategic planning and analysis concerning major trends for future war. By tracing the doctrinal process in the 1980s it becomes possible to see the Soviet military's need for a space force and command and, more importantly, the need to align or integrate those forces with theater forces both on land and sea. Moreover, the creation and structure of these land, sea, air, and space forces are guided by principles and notions that are fully consistent with what Soviet military theorists term defensive doctrine.

Phillip Petersen and Notra Trulock provide a framework for arriving at such a determination on the Soviet planning process.[4] They conclude that the weapons revolution in technology led Warsaw Pact theorists to identify five basic directions of change in force developments. These five changes are the transformation of land warfare into air-land battle; the broadening requirement for mobility in all forces; the development and dissemination of the practice of combat operations within enemy formations, especially raid or OMG (operational maneuver group) operations (which are themselves combined arms or potentially air-land formations); the initiation of battle at ever greater distances; and the struggle for information and time in which the Soviet commander will seek to disrupt the enemies' decision cycle.[5] These changes will drive Soviet decisions not only about equipment, but also about the method of operations and force structures. In support of their views, Petersen and Trulock note General Vorob'ev's 1980 contention in *Voennaia Mysl'* that once both sides are equipped with qualitative new means of forces a new race will ensue between offensive and defensive means of war and the formation of new concepts of military strategy.[6]

Therefore, the Soviet determination that space will be a theater resulted from prolonged reflection about the impact of such weapons and reflects their determination to advance the role of space in Soviet military doctrine. Major General Kuznetsov referred to this when he observed that one cannot solve specific missions when formulating plans for *strategic campaigns* (emphasis added) without a proper conception of the "nature and content of the categories and of strategic objectives, strategic missions, military theaters, etc."[7]

Defensive and Technical Applications

Soviet theorists found, as a result of their investigation into the new and forthcoming generation of weapons, that the technical basis of military art and science has an increasingly deterministic effect on the nature and content of combat operations, a trend which is leading to a blurring of the line between offense and defense. The opposition between the two is manifested in the form of a "skillful combination of firepower, surprise attack, and troop mobility. Firepower is the main motive in perfecting the conduct of operations."[8] Both offense and defense will be able to and want to conduct offensive operations since both will be fully armed with long-range strike weapons. Defensive and offensive forces will likely interpenetrate in conflict. At the same time the former distance between front and rear will collapse as deep strikes occur throughout both sides. This has come about because no one side can be knocked out by a first nuclear strike; both sides will possess these new strike weapons. Already, Soviet theorists see the introduction of these weapons as favoring the defense. They altered their theories and force structures to get rid of the slower forces in return for those which can maximize troop mobility, firepower, and surprise (e.g., helicopters, airborne troops, and the equipping of their naval strike vessels with SS-N-21).[9] This move is evident in recent Soviet conventional arms control proposals for Europe, which if realized (or if a compromise along NATO's lines is accepted) would leave those forces with more airpower than tanks. This is accompanied by Soviet statements concerning the self-evident superiority of planes to tanks; a radical departure from the past.

Indeed, for the future, Soviet theorists equate success with the more frequent introduction of qualitatively superior weapons into combat. Forecasts see major, imminent change as occurring mainly in conventional weapons.[10] These weapons will introduce "a new order of magnitude" into fire capabilities which will no longer be dependent on weather or distance. Instead PGMs (precision guided munitions) will rely on their guidance systems and reconnaissance and intelligence capabilities which will allow the soldier to "program" his weapons to the target. What the fighting man or forces will need, therefore, is real-time intelligence to track mobile targets or distant stationary ones, i.e., Marshal Ogarkov's vaunted "Reconnaissance strike complex" is what is now required.[11]

The advent of such weapons led Soviet theorists, according to Petersen and Trulock, to conclude that the war's duration will probably be long and that it will embrace not just the five Eurasian TVDs on the Soviet Union's perimeter but perhaps the entire globe.[12] Owing to the capabilities of these weapons, strikes on each other's homeland or targets throughout the globe are likely. Indeed, defensive forces can pre-empt the offense and strike at enemy forces during the preparatory stages of attack. Thus, for example, General Gareev told a London audience in October 1988 that under defensive doctrine the air operation is replaced by the anti-air operation. It is, in fact, an offensive counter-air operation.[13]

The massing of forces to conduct an offensive seems a more effective way of maximizing fire as forces converge upon their objectives from widely dispersed zones, where they will have to be "masked" to escape detection. Such a stand-off operation would involve a long-range combined-arms fire operation to create an opening in the air corridors in particular, combined with possible amphibious and airborne landings supported by helicopters and comprising a large-scale air assault and the combined arms of naval infantry forces. Thus, defensive doctrine allows for the Soviets to retain a capability for alternating rapidly to one or another form of combat and maintain a viable offensive capability. Another advantage is the attractive political platform this presents to NATO, with a possible return of inhibiting or slowing its modernization. In this new Soviet conception, defense retains substantial capabilities for offensive actions and for seizing the initiative.

There are a number of requirements for defensive operations under such conditions. First, for the defense to hold and be able to move forward to conduct offensive operations, anti-missile operations (whether against conventional or nuclear missiles) and the anti-air operation become absolutely vital. Unless enemy fire capabilities are suppressed, at least in the main operational axis, Soviet assets and most importantly Command, Control, Communications, and Intelligence (C3I) are at risk. Moreover, failure to suppress enemy fire puts Soviet fire capabilities, nuclear and conventional, equally at risk. Soviet doctrine has long recognized the vital importance of accurate real-time intelligence and redundant C3I as well as a blinding and degrading of enemy C3I as a priority task for the initial period of the war.[14] In the actual theater operation air superiority becomes the *sine qua non* to conduct offensive operations. This is not only to deliver fire across the depth of the theater; mobility is impossible otherwise both on land, sea, or with air and helicopter forces.[15] Interdiction of enemy forces or their pre-emption by accurate fire strikes is impossible without accurate real-time reconnaissance; this can only be accomplished from space. Hence Soviet discussions of air superiority, whether at the strategic, operational, or tactical level, insist that it is unattainable without pre-existing or concurrent superiority in low-space. This is true even now before space-strike weapons (apart from ASAT), are operational.[16] Such remarks suggest that ASAT, air defense, and space-based reconnaissance would cooperate in the the air and anti-air operation. They are already included in combined arms units and tactically integrated with all possible Soviet formations, including OMGs.[17] Soviet sources approve of the Western idea that air superiority means penetrating air space as well.[18]

The foregoing suggests the importance of space as providing a platform for both C3I purposes of global monitoring of ships and terrestrial targets and of coordinating fire strikes against missile platforms.[19] In analyzing the impact of the weapons revolution, Petersen and Trulock cite Ogarkov's observations that these weapons extend the zone of active operations to the point that whole countries can be involved in operations, an implicitly global scope for potential targeting plans. They note that, while such possibilities do not seem likely in the near term, an accurate observation is:

> A longer term perspective which envisions widespread deployment of space-based reconnaissance and target location systems directly linked in real-time to long-range strike means might consider such a scenario more feasible. The Soviets apparently see no contradictions in the objective of extending the depth of conventional fire destruction throughout the theater, and eventually, into the strategic rear of the homelands.[20]

As Soviet theorists increasingly realize, the advent of these new weapons gives them and their opponents the capability to conduct simultaneous fire over the enemy's entire depth, a primary objective of Soviet deep strike theories.[21] Accordingly, fire strikes by combined arms "artillery" of all sorts can simultaneously eliminate or suppress tactical, operational, or strategic objectives. But here too accurate real-time reconnaissance and intelligence is essential. The American technological lead, exemplified by the SDI program, constitutes a major danger to the Soviets in this arena, apart from its projected capability against strategic weapons systems. The danger is reinforced by the projection of SDI to a European defense initiative, with the possible participation of Israel and Japan. The emplacement of SDI and its related technological spin-offs would virtually eliminate Soviet capability to "look over the horizon" to obtain any kind of reliable intelligence and conduct correlation of forces analysis or achieve a working reconnaissance-strike complex capability. In addition, a functioning Western SDI would also negate both Soviet ASAT and satellites.[22] At the tactical, operational, or theater level, SDI would blind Soviet forces to fire strikes coming from enormous distances, and it would possess its own space-strike missions and fulfill an American or Western version of the reconnaissance-strike complex while eliminating the Soviet capability along such lines.[23] As Petersen and Trulock note:

> One trend of concern to the Soviets, for example, is the potential application of electromagnetic gun technologies to theater warfare, not only in anti-tactical missile roles, but also against armored targets. The direct linkage of space-based reconnaissance to fire systems capable of ranges deep in the enemy's defensive depths, including even homelands, in real time to produce the true reconnaissance-strike systems seems to represent the Soviet vision of warfare in the post-2000 forecast.[24]

Application of Historical Analyses

Study of the great Soviet offensives of World War II by both Western and Soviet commanders and analysts demonstrates that after 1942 Soviet commanders felt the need to link air and ground reconnaissance, fire superiority, troop mobility, overcoming of the enemy's air defense, adequate and redundant C3, the operational objective of breaching enemy defenses, and widening the breach to allow penetration by mobile groups.[25] Additionally, these Soviet documents asserted that the experience of these offensives substantiated the requirement of the strict subordination of the mobile groups, regular shock forces, and air assets to a centralized command formation, subordinate to the military council of the front.[26]

Therefore, in the 1960's, when the TVD concept returned, it based itself on wartime experiences. It underwent a series of refinements and changes in force structure to the point where the flexible mission and theater-tailored combined arms forces stressed mobility and firepower. Not only is the space TVD a C3 formation for troops and the result of a doctrinal reassessment, it also is a combined arms force for ultimate escalation dominance. In other words, the Soviet Union is determined to post where it can, in tandem with ground, sea, and air forces, implement strategic (not to mention tactical or operational) influence upon the course of combat, influence enemy decision making, launch fire strikes, and defensively pre-empt offensive and enemy fire strikes. Tactically such forces will also seek to provide the real-time intelligence without which the Soviet Armed Forces would be brought to a standstill.

At this tactical level one can also see that the operative norms which govern the actual conduct and planning of operations at all levels impose the same kind of demanding C3I requirements that the theater operations or global ones do, albeit in proportionate ratios. Contemporary analysts insist that the crucial battle is over time. Accordingly, an important operative norm to the success of the operation is the timely introduction of appropriate forces or echelons into battle. The work to be done here must fall within the time norms given to the commander as a set drill for the operation to succeed.[27]

During World War II, the higher the level of command, the higher the average length of time needed to prepare an offensive. Thus, at the level of the reinforced battalion, the lowest level combined unit to be committed in a theater operation, the time element is relatively demanding. But for a successful, planned operation within the ever shrinking parameters of time, the commander must absolutely possess accurate real-time reconnaissance and intelligence about the targets. This demand is made ever more urgent by the fact, pointed out by Admiral Chernavin below, that the time frame for what once used to be a tactical engagement is now allotted to the strategic operation.

Inaccurate or laggard target acquisition processes compromise the offensive from the start. Moreover, artillery's efficiency also falls off sharply against ill-defined targets.[28] Since modern warfare increasingly depends upon such real-time target acquisition integrated with precision guided munitions, inaccurate target acquisition leads to the breakdown of the unit's mission and the failure to achieve its temporal norms. These considerations also preclude or severely limit the possibility of infiltrating an enemy's decision cycle. Failure to conduct proper reconnaissance also renders commanders vulnerable to tactical deception and camouflage.[29]

Commanders engaged in preparing operations must also undertake an analysis of the correlation of forces, which Soviet doctrine insists must be scientific, not guesswork. This analysis provides a concept which at every level governs the deployment of attacking forces, their echelon, and fire support. If that correlation is more favorable than assumed, the enemy's artillery must be suppressed before tanks and infantry combat vehicles are brought up to the front lines. This requirement, in turn, drives Soviet logistics connected with artillery support. The more fire support needed to take a position, coupled with a stretched logistics network, the less dispersed and vulnerable the forces become. Even at the tactical level the emerging picture is one in which defense can or must pre-empt by offensive means. This involves prompt, accurate target acquisition and calculated fire strikes.

H.F. Stoeckli's work in this area provides two conclusions. First, under the fluid conditions of today's battlefield when Moscow expects interpenetration of troops in both offensive and defensive operations and demands forward advance norms of 40 km/day, a weapons system that undercuts this time norm and gets inside the command and control cycle poses a threat to the entire stability of the system. Such a system is the emerging complex of NATO's proposed reconnaissance-strike systems. Here, target acquisition and weapons impact takes place within minutes.[30] Secondly, if adequate drills cannot be organized to coordinate the combined arms of the battalion, the practicality of combined arms battalions (the basic building block of the land forces), is undermined.[31] Repeated instances of failure to coordinate air strikes and ground offensives due to the advent of Stingers in 1986-87, for example, were a major reason why Moscow abandoned offensives in Afghanistan.[32]

From the foregoing it is clear that changes at the tactical level of the battallion and the overall changes in weapons are driving changes in C3I and force structures in order to conduct successful offensives. These are enhanced by the need for mobility, first strike (conventional) capability, real-time intelligence to be integrated with that capability, and, lastly, the capability to move and strike with surprise at the tactical and/or operational level. Such trends are pushing Soviet doctrine concerning land-air (or air-land) battle to the occupation of space and the necessary C3I and strike capabilities towards implementation. The question, however, remains whether or not Western understanding of Soviet thinking as to the need for a TVD in space is solidly anchored in Soviet doctrinal methodology. Are the driving forces identified by Petersen and Trulock the ones that the Soviets themselves have pointed to or relied upon in organizing a theater command and force structure?

The Naval Argument

A recent book, *Voenno-morskoi flot: rol', perspectikvy razvitiia, ispol'zovanie*, lays out the Soviet forecasting process. It is the acuity of that process and its doctrinal correlates that has largely enabled Moscow to make up its technological deficit and to compete strategically with the West. Forecasting, they contend, is the determination of future probability data about the directions and trends in the development of the military, its equipment, military art at home and abroad (or in friendly and enemy coalitions), and on the course and outcome of the armed struggle and the war as a whole.[33] The results of military forecasting predetermine strategic decisions on naval arms development, plans, and programs. Forecasts are the basis for drawing up these program documents and are thus intimately tied to the planning process outlined by Petersen and Trulock. As a rule they precede planning and creates the scientific data base for it. Forecasts are used to increase the scientific level and validity of planning.[34] For example, in his preface to the work, the late Admiral of the Fleet of the Soviet Union S.G. Gorshkov stated that the present conditions of naval warfare demand the most rational combination of weapons capabilities, offensive and defensive alike, in combined arms operations, joined by automated control and target designation equipment. Therefore, the naval planner cannot limit himself to forecasting the development of individual weapons systems and their platforms. Instead:

> In order to meet today's demands, a forecast must encompass the development of weapon systems, the means for controlling them, and means for global surveillance over vast areas which are adequate for the increased ranges of modern weapons. In other words, now it is necessary to have a comprehensive forecast of combat equipment development that takes into account the world military-political situation, economic and scientific-technical capabilities for creating arms, the military capabilities for creating arms, the military objectives for which weapons and combat equipment are being created, the conditions under which they will be employed, as well as the methods of their combat employment.[35]

The book does more than substantiate trends in naval development and the employment of the Soviet Navy in warfare. Because it is oriented towards the future requirements of the navy, its methodology is explicitly general. The book's forecasts are based on the "modeling of operations by forces and means for achieving a certain level of mission accomplishment and for determining the requirements for forces and resources to this end."[36]

The conclusion of this work is to make the anti-air and missile operations the first strategic priority of the naval forces. This mission mandates heavy space sensors and target acquisition requirements, along with control for the saturation of U.S. and NATO airspace with missiles to pre-empt Western naval artillery and missiles. Ultimately, it makes clear that space strike weapons and lasers will emerge with revolutionary consequences. In short, a space forces requirement is explicitly embraced here.[37] The strategic ASW task, as well, must become a national mission requiring a strategic combined arms force, like the PVO (Air Defense Forces), to focus naval, missile, and air assets on the anti-sea based missile defense.

Some analysts reacted to this message with incredulity, overlooking its conformity with Soviet ideas of defensive operations as outlined by Petersen and Trulock. As Theodore Neely and Steven Kime point out, this thinking is not an idiosyncracy of Admiral Gorshkov.[38] The book reflects trends increasingly apparent in the West as well as the East, as the Soviet Union reacts to American maritime strategy and both sides incorporate technological advances.

Western accounts expect naval scenarios, e.g., among rival submarines, that resemble the Soviet view that offense and defense will be increasingly interpenetrated and that victory goes to the side better able to integrate target acquisition, fire, and mobility. There is also every indication that present Soviet force developments derive from a need to master these technological breakthroughs as well as to defend against American threat most recently codified in the Maritime Strategy.[39]

The adoption of this strategy and the deployment of a corresponding force by the U.S. Navy demanded a Soviet riposte. And Moscow's analysts saw in that strategy and its sequels a strategy of "ship-to-shore" fire strikes plus strategic ASW used by combined arms fire strikes against Soviet SSBNs leading to blockade, horizontal escalation, and thus the risk of global nuclear war. Since the Maritime Strategy was introduced as Soviet apprehensions about SDI peaked, Soviet planners probably assumed that both programs were part of an integrated strategy of deploying and moving towards the high-tech reconnaissance-strike concept at sea. The requirements for antimissile and anti-aerospace operations to counter the United States came increasingly to represent a combined arms force, operating in a naval or even oceanic TVD.

In a series of articles in 1986-1987, CINC of the Soviet Navy Vladimir Chernavin addressed these issues. He commented that the revolution in weaponry made it possible for surprise strikes to come from maneuvers. Technical reconnaissance development made it difficult to hide operations at sea, making surprise all the more important and elusive at the strategic level if not at the tactical or operational level. The increased precision of weapons and their ranges made it more difficult to stop an enemy's fire strikes. The

Soviet commander resolved this problem by defining a mission which depended to a large degree on the timeliness of target detection and destruction.[40]

Achieving such a reconnaissance-strike capability today demands greater attention. Chernavin noted that time constraints in combat will normally be extreme, and radio-electronic means of C3 as flagship command posts may be suddenly destroyed by a surprise strike from enormous distances. Indeed, experience shows that C3 assets are the first to be targeted. During combat involving massive use of radio-electronic combat a senior commander may find himself cut off from his subordinates, a situation requiring initiative from the latter to fulfill the mission. He observed that it is "impossible to provide incentives for deviating from the plan on the off-chance that it may work out. But if there is a creative approach that is supported by well-thought out conclusions that were verified ahead of time in training [then they should be implemented]."[41]

In an earlier article, Chernavin wrote that shrinking time frames force commanders to achieve strategic tasks within the time previously allowed for tactical tasks in a limited zone. Today, under present operating conditions, where strategic operations may take place over enormous distances, the C3I requirements become urgent. The combined arms assets Chernavin finds most useful for both the tactical and operational engagement are missile weapons, both nuclear or conventional. The strike from distant sea is becoming the dominant form of force employment since it maximizes the armed forces' combined arms potential and dynamism; exactly what the TVD structure is supposed to achieve. Accordingly, he demanded a more effective use of space resources to enhance C3I, reconnaissance, and maneuverability. Space weapons will also help along with air and air defense platforms to surprise enemies at a great distance by striking pre-emptively.[42]

Chernavin's conclusions echo those of Gorshkov and the contributors found within *Voenno-morskoi*. The qualitative changes in weaponry, they assert, brought about a situation where even light, short-range naval strike forces can conduct strategic missions, a factor in increasing the prominence of the oceanic sector in the battle.[43] In effect, given the requirement for space-based C3I and later strike forces, this is an implicit call for a space-based TVD.[44]

Since the TVD is the basis upon which the Soviet military attempts to have a combined arms force to maximize its potential synergies in an operation and is also the basis for combat C3I, the combined arms ASW mission fits in along with the strategic antimissile operation; it too is a combined arms operation and formation. This is not so much a strategy for global nuclear war as a sea-denial strategy. The Soviet military would use the same methods of integrated reconnaissance-strike complexes, with heavy use of space assets, to prevent the U.S. Navy from reaching those forward-based positions astride the GIUK gap while deterring the threat of strikes against counterforce or countervalue targets.

By holding U.S. Navy missile platforms at risk and by building the Kirov guided missile destroyer to combine battle management, air, and air defense operations, the Soviets are moving to implement a sea-denial strategy which they believe will negate the maritime strategy and force the United States to discuss naval disarmament. At the same time, Soviet SLBMs are being upgraded, along with space links and possible pre-emptive deployment in the Arctic or Hudson Bay to target the MX in its boost phase.[45] In effect, such a deployment would constitute the Soviet Navy's submarine forces as the first echelon of a layered air and missile defense system that would be ground- and sea-based but use space for monitoring. Such a concept would validate the claim found within Gorshkov's book that it is the first echelon of a layered ABM defense.[46] As a combined ground- and naval-based system with air assets and space C3I for global monitoring, this will convert the anti-air (PVO), anti-submarine, and anti-missile forces into linked strategic combined arms along with their strategic missiles and general purpose forces. Moreover, their emerging fleet force structure will be perfectly consonant with the defensive doctrine, whose purpose is as much to prevent war as it is to win.

As Petersen and Trulock and Neely and Kime note, Soviet spokesmen claim that even under defensive doctrine they will need to master offensive techniques and operations to win.[47] Kime and Neely probably state correctly that Soviet doctrine, strategy, and force requirements outlined in this chapter in no way contradict those stated under the defensive doctrine. Certainly, such a threatened first strike by Soviet forces to pre-empt U.S. "offensives" would deter any commander from striking with nuclear weapons. They note that the necessary missile and space forces of new technologies constitute an active world-wide defense. Like its air-land counterpart, it emphasizes surprise and the initial period of operations against enemy C3I and missile platforms wherever they may be, since this tends to negate U.S. concepts such as horizontal deterrence or escalation:

> Philosophically it can be viewed as a world-wide version of the combined arms counter-air operation in the theater that has been widely described in the West.[48]

Since this statement, General Gareev stated that under defensive doctrine the air operation is replaced by the offensive anti-air operation. Soviet discussions of the air and anti-air operations explicitly call for recognizing space as a theater of possible strategic military operations, not just an arena for C3I functions.

This development is backed by other authoritative Soviet statements. In 1985, Major General Vorob'ev cited the weapons revolution currently underway and noted that as these weapons are improved, refined, and perfected, they will expand the spatial and vertical dimension of warfare to the point where first low space and then higher altitudes become a theater of war.[49]

Nine months later, Colonel General Dolnikov cited Western sources concerning the need to penetrate enemy airspace to obtain real air superiority. He noted that one can also create numerical supremacy in the air more easily by increasing the defensive forces. To overcome enemy air defenses, which are after all missiles and artillery projectiles of all arms, the electronic warfare (EW) radar aircraft can reduce their advantage and greatly simplify air combat over a large radius.[50]

By the same token, Soviet air defenses increased all arms at the tactical level by 1984, fully mobile and integrated with every level of command. At the same time, Lieutenant General V. Rabchevski identified air defense as a combined arms operation whose essential components are troop and air surveillance along with control and anti-air fire complexes.[51] This integration of air and missile defense, along the lines suggested by both Petersen and Trulock on the one hand and the authors found in Gorshkov's book on the other, can already be seen in the September 1988 missions of the Soviet Pacific Fleet:

> These exercises can be directly linked with three Soviet fleet missions: area defense of SSBN operating areas, anti-carrier warfare (ACW) and defense of the homeland missions. The last two are often combined into a single large-scale exercise in which air, surface, and sub-surface units simulate detection, localization, and attacks against a carrier battle group.[52]

These deployments currently underway represent the culmination to date of a thirty-year effort to conduct all arms strategic ASW from great distances.[53] In 1967 Army General Batitski noted that the changing employment of strategic nuclear weapons provided for unified air-space operations in which air, ballistic missiles, and space weapons could be used, giving rise to a corresponding need to repulse them "with the coordinate forces of anti-missile, anti-aircraft, and anti-space defenses."[54] Colonel E. Kalugin was equally explicit the next year:

> It is sufficient to say that the very concept of "air defense" in our time has been given a new meaning and is now regarded not as the traditional anti-aircraft defense, but as air and space defense, which involves the struggle against aerodynamic, ballistic, and space means.[55]

A Chinese analysis of developments in space written in December 1985 claimed outright that in 1964 the Soviet Union established its Space Defense Command under the PVO.[56] And, since former President Reagan's 1983 announcement of the SDI, numerous Soviet articles concerning laser weapons claim the destruction of all types of ballistic and cruise missiles. If deployed offensively, they could launch space to space, air, or surface attacks. Either way or in tandem their development would revolutionize warfare because they were the most advanced forms of weapons since the introduction of nuclear weapons.[57]

Conclusions

The foregoing analysis demonstrates that the planning process outlined by Petersen and Trulock harmonizes with the forecast and doctrinal process argued by Gorshkov and others. That process, they both observe, is a general one and substantiates both force acquisition and deployment demands as well as missions and mission requirements on the one hand and the requirements for balanced naval disarmament on the other. The strategy they outline is a quintessential one of sea-denial and deterrence by denial and pre-emption which mandates a command and forces structure (a TVD in space) to optimize its possibilities and combined arms synergies. The same holds true for the air-land battle: space is a combined arms force TVD that ties together emerging force and mission requirements.

At the same time existing and incoming force programs represent an almost complete fulfillment of forecasts made almost thirty years ago concerning strategic and force structure needs of the Soviet military. These programs are fully coherent with defensive doctrine and "reasonable sufficiency" to the degree that they not only deter American initiatives and strategies, but enable Moscow to move from palpable inferiority strategically and conventionally then to parity. The Soviets now master the ability to understand the requirements of war and its prevention at any time, as well as the forces they need to fulfill them. This serves to remind Western observers that Soviet concepts of defensive doctrine and reasonable sufficiency are rather different than what the Soviets often claim.

More to the point, through out this period the military-political and military-technical sides of the process are linked. Thus, Gorshkov's authors give political considerations as well as technical ones to demonstrate why the West will not attain the superiority of which it dreams:

> Thus, a statistical analysis of the length of life-cycle phases of ships and ship weapon systems provides a basis for the development of the enemy's navy will not change substantially if the military-political situation does not undergo radical changes during the forecasting period.[58]

No more explicit military-political rationale for new thinking and defensive doctrine could be given.

Gorshkov's authors note that "Western military ideologists" believe that technological racing can deprive an enemy of the will to resist; in short, that the United States has a technological war strategy. This entails constant acceleration of the rate of technological change and of arms developments and creation by effective management methods.[59] It would be more than a little ironic if the United States lost out in space because the Soviet military thought better and harder about advancement into new frontiers while the U.S. military concentrated on design elegance. At the same time, Americans blind themselves to the political art of operations and misread both Soviet doctrinal requirements and the political and military dimensions of defensive doctrine. In that case, Soviet doctrine will defeat American scientific hubris. Moreover, Soviet writing about doctrine and force structuring years ago logically entailed requirements for a space TVD and its ominous portents are increasingly visible for all to see.

Notes

[1]*Voennyi Entsiklopedicheskii Slovar*, (Moscow: Voennoe Izdatel'stvo, 1986), p. 732 and also p. 564 which stresses the peacetime preparation of the theater.

[2]Stephen Blank, John H. Lobengeir, Kevin D. Stubbs, Richard E. Thomas, *The Soviet Theater of War (TV)*, (College Station, TX: Center for Strategic Technology, Texas Engineering Experiment Station, Texas A&M University, 1988), pp. 12-13, 23-25.

[3]*Ibid.*, and Stephen Blank, "Developing Soviet Strategy for Space," presented at the annual convention of the International Studies Association, London, March 29, 1989.

[4]Phillip A. Petersen and Notra Trulock III, "Soviet Views on the Changing Context of Military Planning," *Journal of Soviet Military Studies*, No. 4, December 1988, pp. 451-485.

[5]*Ibid.*, pp. 480-481.

[6]*Ibid.*

[7]*Ibid.*, p. 458.

[8]*Ibid.*, p. 483.

[9]Derek da Cunha, "Soviet Naval Capabilities in the Pacific in the 1990's," in Ross Babbage (ed.), *The Soviets in the Pacific in the 1990's*, (Rushcutters Bay, Australia: Brassey's Australia, 1989), pp. 54-55.

[10]Petersen and Trulock, *op. cit.*, p. 369.

[11]William P. Baxter, "Ground Forces," in David R. Jones (ed.), *Soviet Armed Forces Review Annual, 1984-1985*, (Gulf Breeze, Florida: Academic International Press, 1986), p. 105.

[12]Petersen and Trulock, *op. cit.*, pp. 478-479.

[13]*Ibid.*

[14]I. Anureev, "Determining the Correlation of Forces in Terms of Nuclear Weapons," *Voennaia Mysl'*, June 1967, pp. 164-168.

[15]Blank, *op. cit.*, pp. 8-13.

[16]*Ibid.*

[17]*Ibid.*, and William Odom, "Trends in the Balance of Military Power Between East and West," *Adelphi Papers*, No. 189, Summer 1984, p. 16.

[18]G. Dolnikov, "Fighters for Air Supremacy," *Soviet Military Review*, May-June 1986, p. 76.

[19]Phillip A. Peterson and John Hines, "The Soviet Air and Anti-Air Operation," *Air University Review*, March-April 1985, pp. 36-54.

[20]Petersen and Trulock, *op. cit.*, pp. 479-480.

[21]*Ibid.*

[22]Blank, *op. cit.*, pp. 18-20.

[23]Petersen and Trulock, *op. cit.*, p. 472.

[24]*Ibid.*

[25]See, for example, Richard N. Armstrong, "Battlefield Agility: The Soviet Legacy," *Journal of Soviet Military Studies*, No. 4, December 1988, pp. 486-513.

[26]Richard N. Armstrong, "Action of the Mobile Groups of the 5th Tank Army in the Penetration," *Journal of Soviet Military Studies*, No. 4, December 1988, p. 564.

[27]H.F. Stoeckli, *Soviet Tactical Planning: Organizing the Attack at Battalion Level*, Soviet Studies Research Centre, RMA Sandhurst, January 1987, p. 1.

[28]*Ibid.*, pp. 2-3.

[29]*Ibid.*, p 10.

[30]*Ibid.*, pp. 21.

[31]*Ibid.*

[32]Stephen Blank, "Soviet Forces in Afghanistan: Unlearning the Lessons of Vietnam," forthcoming in an Air University Press publication on low intensity conflict.

[33]S.G. Gorshkov (ed.), *Voenno-morskoi flot: rol' , perspectikvy razvitiia, ispol'zovanie*, (Moscow: Voennoe Izdatel'stvo, 1988), p. 49.

[34]*Ibid.*, pp. 61-62.

[35]*Ibid.*, pp. 12-27.

[36]*Ibid.*, p. 14. This makes it an invitation to arms control since the forecast shows that the USSR can negate the American technological drive.

[37]*Ibid.*, pp. 16-42.

[38]Theodore A. Neely and Steven F. Kime, "Perestroika, Doctrinal Change, and the Soviet Navy," *Strategic Review*, Fall 1988, p. 54.

[39]David Alan Rosenberg, "It Is Hardly Possible to Imagine Anything Worse: Soviet Thoughts on the Maritime Strategy," *Naval War College Review*, Summer, 1988, pp. 86-87.

[40]William H.J. Manthorpe Jr., "The Soviet View," *Proceedings of the U.S. Naval Institute*, August 1987, pp. 129-130.

[41]*Ibid.*, p. 130.

[42]V.N. Chernavin, "O nekotrykh kategoriiakh voenno-Morskogo istusstva v sovremennykh usloviakh," *Morskoi Sbornik*, September 1986, pp. 26-33.

[43]Gorshkov, *op. cit.*, p. 25.

[44]*Ibid.*, pp. 27-42.

[45]*Ibid.*, pp. 99-100, 124, 221, and Kevin D. Stubbs, Rob E. Gest, Richard E. Thomas, "Surface-Based Layered Defense by the Soviet Navy," (College Station, TX: Center for Strategic Technology, Texas Engineering Experiment Station, Texas A&M University, March 1987).

[46]Gorshkov, *op. cit.*, p. 221.

[47]Neely and Kime, *op. cit.*, p. 49, Petersen and Trulock, *op. cit.*, pp. 463, 479-480.

[48]Neely and Kime, *op. cit.*, pp. 49, 53.

[49]*Krasnaia Zvezda*, September 15, 1985, p. 3.

[50]Dolnikov, *op. cit.*, p. 76.

[51]V. Rabchevski, "Some Trends in the Development of Troops Air Defense Tactics," *Soviet Press*, No. 5, September-October 1985. Translated from *Vestnik protivovozdushnoi oborony*, No. 4, 1984, pp. 413-416.

[52]*Jane's Defense Weekly*, July 8, 1989, pp. 34-35.

[53]Raymond A. Robinson, "Incoming Ballistic Missiles at Sea," *Proceedings of the U.S. Naval Institute*, June 1987, p. 67.

[54]P. Batitski, "Development of the Tactics and Operational Art of the Country's Air Defense Troops," *Voennaia Mysl'*, October 1967, pp. 28-41, as cited in Blank, et al., *op. cit.*, p. 65.

[55]E. Kalugin, "The Nature of Combat Operations of Air Defense Troops," *Voennaia Mysl'*, January 1968, pp. 35-40, as cited in Blank, et al., *op. cit.*, p. 65.

[56]Sa Benwang, "A Qualitative Escalation in the Superpower Arms Race," *Peking Review*, No. 49, December 9, 1985, pp. 15-16.

[57]*Ibid.*

[58]Gorshkov, *op. cit.*, p. 55.

[59]*Ibid.*

7

Perestroika and Soviet Military Personnel

Patrick Cronin

Until recently the Armed Forces of the USSR held an enviable position within Soviet society. Carefully censored history books were replete with lengthy accounts of the selfless, heroic soldier or sailor, standing sentry over the motherland during the Civil War, the Great Patriotic War, and the Cold War that followed. In the postwar years, the Soviet Union's superpowerdom was one-dimensional, a derivative of the power of the sword rather than the power of the purse or the word. As a result, many Soviet leaders openly coveted the military mantle. Paradoxically, despite his ruthless purges of the military leadership in the 1930s, Stalin's favorite apparel was a marshal's dress uniform. According to one of Stalin's biographers: "When he...donned it the General Secretary gazed at himself in the mirror with satisfaction: the severity of the uniform with the splash of gold epaulets suited his ideas of aesthetic perfection."[1] Likewise, "Marshal of the Soviet Union" Leonid Brezhnev often appeared publicly in a military uniform bristling with combat medals. The Soviet military, although tightly monitored by political commissars, has enjoyed a position of privilege within Soviet society, most tangibly demonstrated in the tremendous resources devoted to defense by the postwar Communist leadership.

Since his ascension to power in 1985, Mikhail Gorbachev has ushered in a wave of "new thinking" manifested in a troika of reforms including restructuring (*perestroika*) of the Soviet economy, democratization (*demokratizatsiia*) of Soviet society, and openness (*glasnost*) in the Soviet press. Each of these reforms is eroding the military's elite ranking in Soviet society and transforming the future character of the Soviet Armed Forces and its personnel. In effect, Gorbachev has put the military on notice that the halcyon days of squandering the national treasury and siphoning off the brightest of Russian youth have ended. Despite an outward veneer of cooperation, the military high command seems to be girding its loins for a long, drawn-out clash with the civilian leadership in order to preserve the position of the Armed Forces.

This chapter examines the broad impact of Gorbachev's perestroika program on Soviet military personnel. Gorbachev's vision of "what is to be done" to reform his country's stagnant economy and society is a radical departure from the policies of his predecessors. Yet elements of his reform program lack a clear destination or a plausible means of getting there. Given the nebulous character of the "new thinking" in the Soviet Union, attempts to make conclusive judgments about the likely outcome of the reforms are fraught with pitfalls. Nevertheless, the Soviet perestroika program is effecting tumultuous changes within the Soviet Armed Forces under Gorbachev.

Since the dawn of the nuclear age, the great powers have avoided direct confrontation. Now, declares Gorbachev, the concept of war between them has actually become an anachronism. In his words: "Clausewitz's dictum that war is the continuation of policy only by different means...has grown hopelessly out of date. It now belongs to the libraries."[2] In place of military force, Gorbachev heralds the need to base international "universal ethical norms,"[3] to elevate the importance of economic security, and to substitute multilateral diplomacy for the bipolar East-West contest. Perestroika in the Armed Forces is affecting Soviet military personnel in several ways, from troop reductions and the conversion of defense industries to a renewed emphasis on officer training and education, a growing apathy among draft-aged Soviet youth, and a debate over whether to end or radically modify conscription.

The Primacy of Economic Security

Poignantly illustrated by the Red Army's retreat from Afghanistan, the Soviet Union is embarked on a drive for a quiescent international environment in which rubles and energy can be channelled into critical domestic reforms. The USSR's "overriding priority" in external affairs, asserts Soviet Foreign Minister Eduard Shevardnadze, is to ensure "through political means peaceful and totally favorable conditions for carrying out [domestic] transformations."[4] The Soviet Union is capitalizing on an alleged trend toward global demilitarization, toward "an increasing shift in efforts to ensure security from the sphere of military-political solutions to the sphere of political cooperation."[5] Indicating that the Cold War is subsiding, Shevardnadze asks rhetorically: "Should we not conclude that the rivalry between the two systems can no longer be viewed as the leading tendency of the modern age?"[6] Most significant with regard to the Armed Forces is the implication of this "new thinking" that the military ought to absorb fewer raw materials, troops, and money. Instead, claims Shevardnadze, "Qualitative parameters must become foremost."[7] But of course, elements of that outdated Cold War world order still remain, and the litmus test of the "new thinking" may be the question of whether Gorbachev ultimately will have to resort to military force to defend it. Apparently the General Secretary is attempting in his reforms to discredit the "Brezhnev doctrine," which has justified Soviet military intervention into neighboring satellite states in the name of defending socialism. While some

Soviet officials maintain that the doctrine itself is a Western fabrication, some civilian reformers have implicitly recognized its existence by declaring it moribund.[8] Contemporary criticism in the Soviet press can hardly be considered a reliable reflection of government policy, but it is significant that military misadventures, such as the Soviet-led invasion of Czechoslovakia in 1968, are now being singled out for condemnation.[9] Meanwhile, the Warsaw Pact is being challenged by the Communist Party's waning power in Poland and by official talk in Budapest about a neutral, nonaligned Hungary. No one can confidently predict whether or not the Kremlin will eventually opt to use force to save the integrity of the Eastern alliance. At a minimum, Gorbachev has obviously raised the threshold at which Eastern European crises trigger Soviet military intervention.

Surely the Soviet high command would object strenuously if it interpreted the "new thinking" to be declaring military force completely anachronistic. But, in finessing this issue, the Gorbachev regime declares itself adamantly in favor of defense, at least in terms of maintaining qualitative parity with the West. According to Shevardnadze, "Ability, not numbers, reliance on quality, not solely on quantity, general development and high level of the scientific and technological infrastructure, not size of armament and contingents. This is what guarantees the reliable defense and security of a country." He continues: "Under no circumstance will we allow military superiority over us."[10] However incompatible this seems to be with other Soviet pronouncements, it is this kind of staunch support for qualitative improvements in defense that has won support for perestroika from the generals. In fact, it would seem that the military leadership is more interested in a *peredyshka* than a *perekhod*, i.e., a "breathing space" or respite rather than a true transformation. The generals hope that at the end of Gorbachev's perestroika rainbow lies a "meaner but leaner" fighting force. Hence, the political and military authorities are in harmony over the need for qualitative improvements in the military.[11]

Illustrative of the military's interest in a "leaner but meaner" force is the Soviet initiative to scrap the majority of its old ships and submarines in at least the Pacific Fleet.[12] The rationale for such a cut was laid out in advance by discussion in the press over the cost-effectiveness of maintaining older classes of combatants. Maintenance of an "old ship," argued one Pacific Fleet officer, requires a great deal of money "with almost no benefit to combat readiness."[13] To support this contention, several examples were offered. There was the *Admiral Oktiabrski*, a large antisubmarine combatant that after seven years in repair still had inoperable guns and missiles. Then there was the 1950s vintage destroyer that, in order to go through the motions of demonstrating combat readiness, had to be towed in order to conduct gunnery practice. Coupled with the fact that such an old ship might have no electrical appliances in the galley, no mess hall, no laundry facilities, and "cabins the size of clothes closets," it is easy to see why morale might be sagging and why such ships might be dubbed "a burden to the fleet."[14] In brief, the Soviet

Navy, like the other armed services, might fare better by resorting to a smaller but more capable force, retiring obsolete platforms, and enhancing training.[15]

The extent to which quantitative factors are to be de-emphasized, however, is likely to lead to an ever-widening civil-military schism. By accentuating the primacy of economics, Gorbachev seems to be paving the way for extreme reductions that many military leaders are unlikely to countenance. In fact, Gorbachev appears to have embraced the popular thesis of Western historian Paul Kennedy, who argues that great powers lose their greatness when they no longer have a sufficient economic foundation on which to base their security; that is, power derives more from productive potential than military wherewithal and military burdens can in fact undermine that economic base.[16] The "new thinking" rejects the traditional postulate that "the more a state arms itself, the more reliably it makes itself secure."[17] A central lesson of World War II, posits Shevardnadze, is "that any advantage enjoyed by the aggressor can be reduced to nought if the state possesses a developed industrial and scientific and technological base."[18] The Foreign Minister further asserts that the USSR's unbridled military buildup during the Brezhnev era, coupled with a breakdown in the Soviet Union's industrial base, has proved counterproductive to the national interest. Whether it was in Europe, where SS-20 intermediate-range ballistic missile deployments helped to unify the Western alliance in opposition to the Soviet Union, or in Afghanistan, where the mighty Soviet military suffered a humiliating stalemate at the hands of ill-equipped and arguing tribal groups, military force seems to be losing its utility. Far from being a zero-sum bipolar contest, then, East-West competition in the Third World has garnered neither side a meaningful advantage. In the words of Shevardnadze, the "map of the world has changed...only...in minor details." He adds that "even if the force is superior, more often than not it does not give the aggressor the planned result, and in instances it becomes a sort of boomerang which strikes its own positions."[19]

Arms Control: Duet for One?

By relegating military power to an ancillary position in world politics, Gorbachev has set the stage for a dramatic demobilization of the armed forces. In this respect, Gorbachev is pursuing limitations on the whole gamut of armaments: strategic nuclear, both offensive and defensive; chemical; conventional; confidence and security building measures; and nuclear testing. While Gorbachev would like an accord in any of these areas in order to spur momentum for his over-arching program, his acute need to reorient military spending to the civilian sector has laid special stress on conventional force reductions. Thus, in July 1987, the Warsaw Treaty Organization announced a three-phased conventional disarmament scheme that envisions the elimination of: (1) each side's asymmetrical advantages in specific classes of conventional arms; (2) 25 percent of each side's troops and their organic arms; and (3) offensive military doctrines and postures. In addition, geographical buffer zones between East and West are to be erected in order to hedge against the possibility of a surprise attack.[20]

Because arms control can be a cumbersome, tedious process, Gorbachev has resorted to commencing an arms control duet without a Western companion. In spite of the fact that there was no certainty that the West would reciprocate, or perhaps because of it, Gorbachev unilaterally began thinning out Soviet Armed Forces.[21] The far-reaching Warsaw Pact proposal provided a portent of what was to follow. On December 7, 1988, Gorbachev captured the headlines by his announcement of the USSR's intention to cut from the Soviet Armed Forces by the end of 1990: (1) half a million men, including 100,000 officers; (2) 10,000 tanks worldwide, including six tank divisions (5,000 tanks) in the German Democratic Republic, Czechoslovakia, and Hungary; (3) one air-assault brigade and all assault-landing bridging formations forward deployed in Eastern Europe; (4) nearly one-fifth of all Soviet armament production; and (5) the level of defense spending, by 14.2 percent. All told, Moscow would reduce its troop strength by 12 percent, including approximately 240,000 from Eastern Europe and the western USSR, 200,000 Army and Navy personnel in the Far East, and 60,000 personnel in the southern USSR.[22] These bold initiatives were followed soon thereafter by parallel reductions in the Armed Forces of the other Warsaw Pact nations. Altogether, Soviet and East European force reductions in Europe alone will amount to nearly 300,000 troops, 12,000 tanks, 9,130 artillery systems, and 930 combat aircraft.[23]

Beyond quantities, Gorbachev has rejected Western charges that the USSR is "merely getting rid of obsolete tanks." The General Secretary has declared that the Soviet Union will be withdrawing 5,300 of the "most modern" tanks from East Europe. He added that half of the 10,000 tanks to be withdrawn would be "physically liquidated and the remainder will be converted into tractors for civilian needs and training vehicles."[24] At this writing, it remains to be seen exactly which tank models will be demobilized and how they will be cannibalized. Undoubtedly many military leaders would prefer to scrap the oldest hardware, just as they might also wish to prevent the USSR from meeting its self-imposed timetable. However, the cuts announced are unprecedented in their scope.

Military Opposition to Unilateralism

Despite Gorbachev's apparent attempt to implement the basic precepts of the 1987 Warsaw Pact proposal and to address NATO's longstanding concern about its relative inferiority in conventional forces, the December 7, 1988, gambit startled most Western observers. If the cuts were implemented, some Western experts concluded, the USSR's ability to launch a deep offensive on short notice would be sharply diminished.[25] The unilateral cuts, representing significant reductions and coming on the heels of a widespread debate over the meaning of reasonable sufficiency, led many Western observers to conclude that they had to have been imposed from above on a reluctant military high command. These Western analysts further detected a civil-military rift over the cuts in the fact that the retirement of Marshal Sergei Akhromeev was revealed on the eve of Gorbachev's December 1988 announcement. It did not take a great deal of imagination to sense military opposition to unilateralism when the Soviet press was soon replete with references to Khrushchev's ouster (which was in part triggered by radical reductions in the military) and rumors of a possible military coup against Gorbachev.[26]

While it is impossible to know whether a military coup was or is in the realm of possibility, it seems that the extent of the civil-military rift was overdrawn in the early months after the unilateral arms reduction announcement. In the first place, a crucial piece of evidence, Akhromeev's resignation, is open to alternate interpretations. Akhromeev himself vehemently denies that his departure was linked to the unilateral reductions, contending that the "so-called resistance is a complete lie"[27] and noting of certain Westerners that "even on the absolutely white canvas they always try to find some sort of spots."[28] Instead, Akhromeev contends that his retirement was prompted by his flagging health and the fact that he was "burned out" by arduous, 15-hour work days.[29] If Akhromeev is to be believed, the General Staff was intricately involved in the decision to make unilateral cuts from June of 1988:

> According to some propagandists in the West, if the USSR decides to reduce its Armed Forces, the military leadership must be against it. As if we, the military, do not understand objective needs or are not participating...in perestroika....And the reduction of our Armed Forces by 500,000 people is...a result of a major study conducted jointly with the military. Naturally, from the very beginning the General Staff leadership took part in this work.[30]

Akhromeev's contention aside, surely what most affronted the General Staff about the reductions was not the fact that they occurred, but that they occurred unilaterally. Akhromeev seems to rationalize the unilateral cuts by maintaining that Western public opinion will force NATO to follow suit.[31] The most "hawkish" Soviet generals would probably have found the reductions palatable, even desirable, had they been contingent upon commensurate reductions in the West.[32] At least since the 1970s, when Marshal N.V. Ogarkov was Chief of the General Staff, Soviet military leaders have debated the need for shoring up qualitative aspects of military power, such as high technology, readiness, and training. Because they affect the periphery and not the core of the Soviet Armed Forces, the unilateral reductions announced by Gorbachev are consonant with the Soviet military's interest in qualitative parameters. As for Akhromeev's resignation, as Dale Herspring argues, General G.A. Moiseev's replacement of Marshal

Akhromeev as Chief of the General Staff should probably be viewed as an opportunity to usher in a younger general to implement the reductions while concomitantly permitting Akhromeev to focus on arms control issues from his new post at the Supreme Soviet.[33]

Thus, the political and military leadership seem to have reached a general consensus on the need for qualitative improvements in the Armed Forces. Where they are most at odds, however, is on the subject of the magnitude of the quantitative military reductions.[34] In this regard, the military is concerned that Gorbachev's December 1988 announcement presaged additional resorts to unilateralism.

Conversion: From Plutonium to Strawberries

Soviet military leaders have emphasized that their proclaimed shift to nonoffensive military doctrine[35] based on the principle of reasonable sufficiency is permitting the conversion of much of the defense industry into civilian enterprises. The rationale for this shift is justified in historical terms. Suggesting that defensive forces can be stronger than offensive forces, for instance, General Moiseev notes that in the summer of 1942, when Germany approached Stalingrad, "after bleeding the enemy in defensive battle the Soviet forces inflicted an unprecedented defeat in the course of a counterattack." Then the Wehrmacht made its final attempt to seize the strategic initiative in the summer of 1943 in the Kursk region: "The [defensive] Soviet Armed Forces inflicted irreplaceable losses."[36] Moiseev argues that it is this emphasis upon the principle of reasonable sufficiency that is permitting "a systematic conversion of the defense complex." "By 1995," he continues, "60 percent of the total volume of production will be converted over. Many factories, design offices, and their related knowledge are engaged in the production of consumer goods and machinery, equipment, and other goods for agriculture, light industry, and the food industry."[37] It is planned to produce 7.5 percent of the total output of consumer goods at the USSR's military enterprises in 1989 alone.[38]

Two conversions that are taking place already have been highly publicized in the Soviet press. The first concerns the closing of three of the USSR's oldest plutonium production facilities, with two more scheduled to be shut down in 1990.[39] In the aftermath of the Chernobyl disaster, there undoubtedly were keen pressures to close these obsolete plants in the southern Ural mountains regardless of conversion. The three reactors are part of the first Soviet industrial nuclear power unit, commissioned in 1948. Nuclear waste had been routinely dumped into the Techa River "until it was ruined and filth was discovered as far away as the Arctic Ocean."[40] Furthermore, they were the site of a serious nuclear accident in 1957, when a "cloud of dangerous substances" spread over the area.[41] The incident was kept under tight secrecy because, "we were frenzied rushing ahead toward the summits of communism and tried not to notice those who fell by the wayside. We pretended that the race was proceeding successfully."[42] But such a horrible event can no longer be kept secret, because people should not be treated like "automatons." "People brought up on lies have simply ceased believing even the most probable things."[43] Economic activity resumed on 80 percent of the contaminated area in 1978, while the remaining 20 percent continues as a restricted-area "nature preserve."[44] Regardless of the various objective reasons for closing down these plants, then, the publicity given to the conversion of these plants, located in an area previously declared top secret, is obviously intended to give momentum to the conversion process. At least within one plant, the reactor's radioactive metal components are to be entombed in perpetuity, and the plant itself will be converted to manufacture fiber-optic cables for the "twenty-first century."[45]

A second milestone in the path toward conversion is the use of military transport aviation (VTA) to support the national economy. Approximately 60 aircraft will haul 50,000 tons of food and other cargo, mostly to remote areas of the Far North and the Far East. About 70 percent of the profit will be pumped into the state budget, with the remaining 30 percent used to cover expenses and to provide material incentives to the airmen. But once again, there may be less philanthropic reasons for this conversion. As the general in charge of VTA explains, "We burn thousands of tons of fuel transporting air. Why not take cargo?" And so military transport aircraft have begun to haul strawberries and other freight for the civil sector.[46] While some civilian officials predict a smooth transition from military to civil production,[47] most reformers and military officers agree that there are numerous obstacles. Some of the most critical barbs are aimed at those who see conversion as a ready nostrum to cure all the ills of Soviet society:

It would seem that it is just one step from modern combat equipment to equipment of a deeply civil purpose. But that is merely an illusion. A whole range of special measures have to be conducted in order to create new equipment for civilian purposes on the basis of military equipment. And the people who are now speaking so much about conversion consider that, as soon as the military industrial complex and the branches in that complex restructure, celestial manna will pour down on us from the sky. No, unfortunately this will not happen.[48]

Others counsel on the need for conversion to occur slowly in order not to disrupt the USSR's ability to make first-rate military hardware. Defense must come "first and foremost," said one Communist Party official, for "[i]t is impermissible for anybody to leave the country defenseless. We must understand...that we can buy bread and we can buy various machines, but nowhere can we purchase tanks. And not only are we able to make them, but we must make them the best in the world."[49] Even proponents of conversion recognize the enormous requirement for new capital investment to reequip production facilities and create new ones. But as two commentators remark,

"Disarmament, like arms, costs a good deal."[50] These supporters of conversion argue the need for introducing cost-accounting methods and competition:

> It is no secret that the difficulties arising in conversion are largely associated with the general shortcomings in defense building. These are the monopoly position of client and supplier, the absence of competition in the solution of various tasks, and the dominance enjoyed by the cost-based mechanism in mutual relations between industry's defense sectors and the Defense Ministry.[51]

Whatever the methods employed, however, critics and proponents of conversion agree that the transition cannot be accomplished quickly.

A Leaner Officer Corps

The decision to reduce Soviet military personnel by 500,000 men includes roughly 400,000 conscripts, whose departure will not greatly affect continuity in the Armed Forces. But the reduction of some 100,000 officers has opened up a Pandora's box of problems, from determining whom to demobilize to deciding where they will work and live. To be sure, even in the military's eyes there is a positive side to the officer reduction. The first and obvious benefit is the potential for economic savings. In this regard, favorable comparisons have been made with Khrushchev's military reforms:

> The reduction in strength of the Armed Forces during the "Khrushchev thaw," for example, made it possible to set up 100 house-building combines and to double age-old pensions....The recently announced reduction in the Armed Forces will make it possible to release hundreds of millions of rubles for purposes of social development. But why is it that the Soviet legislator becomes aware of such millions or, perhaps, billions, only when such funds are being released and not when they are being appropriated for military purposes?[52]

Another less direct benefit of the troop trimming is the possibility of reducing the problems of "formalism" (i.e., overly centralized and impersonal decision-making) and favoritism by forcing closer scrutiny upon the officer selection and rotation processes. For instance, some feel that the officer cuts could help to curtail the unnecessary transfer of officers to equivalent positions or that they might help to crack the old boys' network that allows one-third of the officer corps to serve only in the plusher western military districts.[53] Juxtaposed with these putative advantages, however, is a stark image of thousands of unemployed and homeless veterans. The Soviet press is filled with questions about where the professional military men will live and work after they are released from the military. Some of the

Gorbachev-minded civilian reformers seem to be genuinely concerned with the welfare of these officers. Much is being made over the preparations to give each officer being considered for demobilization a fair hearing[54] and to provide housing and job retraining.[55] While the military also seems to be concerned about the welfare of "demobbed" officers, its motivations are more suspect. Widely expressed military warnings about not repeating the mistakes made by Khrushchev, when he demobilized 1.2 million military personnel, seem to suggest a tacit signaling to the political leadership that it should take care not to go too far. First Deputy Chief Colonel-General Lobov has underscored the importance of minimizing any adverse effects from a sudden dislocation of troops. After all, he argues, Gorbachev would not want to repeat a situation in which "many former frontline officers found themselves literally in the street."[56] After all, if the military is already complaining about the dislocations caused by 500,000 troops, then there is sure to be resistance to any large reductions that accompany a possible CFE (Conventional Forces in Europe) accord.[57]

Renewed Emphasis on Training

Another characteristic of Gorbachev's military reforms relates to the renewed emphasis on training. The officer corps comprises numerous incompetent or otherwise undesirable men, according to many Soviet press accounts. Many members of the military apparently would like to use Gorbachev's de-emphasis on quantity of forces to improve their quality and to weed out those unproductive soldiers and place them in the reserve. In addition, the renewed interest in better training is bringing about a revolution in the higher military schools. Some schools are to be shut down, and all others are to revamp their curricula to improve technical training and to make military schools well-rounded universities with liberal arts. In addition, women may be admitted to raise academic standards.

Military officials concede that within the vast Soviet officer corps there are some plainly incompetent or undesirable people. "It is no secret," comments one high-ranking official, "that we have people that do not meet today's high requirements; they bring discredit on the Soviet officer's uniform."[58] Similarly, Marshal Akhromeev observes that while there have always been incompetent military officers (hence the "blunders" of World War II), "We've got shortcomings today, too. Not all top officers, commanders, and political organs are ready to control troops at war and in peacetime."[59] Junior officers coming directly out of higher military schools are being criticized for a lack of skills.[60] At some schools, instructors sometimes even lack "a good knowledge of Russian."[61] A second problem with the officer corps concerns corruption, drug addiction, and racism. Yazov further charges that a general lack of discipline is fueling interethnic tensions within the military. But even if the military is the source of the problem, it is also the best hope for a solution, for "the events in Armenia and Azerbaijan and in the republics of the Soviet Baltic region confirm the danger of underestimating internationalist education,"[62] that is, national service is one of the best means of assimilating the hundred-plus nationalities that comprise the USSR.

Officer incompetence and corruption is being blamed first and foremost on the higher military education system. Faced with a shrinking 18-year-old cohort of ethnic Russians and widespread criticism in the wake of the Afghanistan intervention, it is easy to see why the military is suddenly hard-pressed to recruit good officer candidates. In fact, applications for higher military schools have recently fallen off sharply. While there are still an average of 2.5 candidates per opening and 18 applicants per opening at the airborne assault school, some schools, such as those in the Baltic republics and Georgia, appear to lack any competition for admission.[63] At least three schools will be closed: the Ordzhonikidze Higher Missile Defense School and the Borisoglebsk and Saratov Higher Pilot Training Schools.[64] But the decline in officer quality cannot all be blamed on developments since the initiation of glasnost'; it is clear that the military's senior leadership is discontent with the latest crop of young officers. Defense Minister Yazov contends that:

> There are numerous instances of military VUZ [Higher Military School] graduates being irresolute when making troop command decisions, being insufficiently confident in their mastery of weapons and equipment, lacking firm habits in the organization of practical work on the personnel's political, military, and moral education, and frequently being unable to work efficiently in conditions of democratization and glasnost.[65]

Yazov calls for a host of reforms, including reorganizing the higher military schools, improving instruction through stricter certification of teachers, and modifying the curriculum. Especially important here is the task of "broadening the military cadres' engineering horizons and computer literacy."[66] Moreover, more realistic training is critical to perestroika, according to Yazov, because it "is one of the key sources for enhancing the Armed Forces' qualitative condition while incurring virtually no additional material costs."[67] In addition, Yazov wants to improve the leadership of the military schools, who are guilty of formalism, of "sham efficiency and unnecessary paperwork."[68] Finally, the schools need to focus on indoctrination, especially with regard to teaching officers how to operate within a system of "socialist pluralism" and to uphold "the officer's honor, dignity, and nobility, which are an officer's compass in his service and his life."[69]

In a more scathing review of officer education, one officer has called for a complete transformation of the higher military schools to conform with the "new thinking." Harking back to a 1909 text, *The Higher Military School*, Colonel V. Kovalevski notes that the book argues that the Russian defeats at Tsushima and Port Arthur four years earlier were the result of shortcomings in the higher military schools. He concludes that "there is a dire need for a well-thought out concept of restructuring the higher military school."[70] The schools churn out mass-produced officers who are incompetent and abuse their privileges and have poor integrity because they lack "a true education and intellectual sophistication." Unlike Yazov, the officer declares that "knowledge of military science alone is insufficient; there is an increasing need for an intellectual type of officer."[71] And the "bitter truth is that the present day military VUZ is not quite in a position to produce such an officer."[72] To create truly intellectual officers, Colonel Kovalevski advocates the following ambitious measures:

> Part of the solution lies in effecting a complete renewal of the material and technical base and instituting comprehensive computerization of the educational process, even though this task constitutes the epitome of difficulty. Probably even more difficult would be the conversion of the VUZ, especially the academy, into a unique Armed Forces university, which would offer lectures on literature, art, ethics, military courtesy, aesthetics, military rhetoric, design, ergonomics, and ecology; all of which would occupy a position of equality with other subjects. In this university, lecture halls would be the scene of seminars led by public figures and statesmen, famous military leaders, outstanding scientists, artists, and writers....More than a center of education and science, it would be a true seat of culture. This is the only kind of VUZ that can train cadre that will be capable of the new political thinking and possess the wherewithal to function successfully under the conditions attending democratization of military service and assure a high state of combat readiness on the basis of quality factors and cadre born of perestroika.[73]

He adds that there is even "merit in taking up the problem of possible admission of women to a number of academies and officers' schools. Why cannot our military VUZ's train women to become specialists in communications, administrative and support activities, financial service, and military law, thus making it possible to enhance the process of selecting men for admission to academies and officers' schools by attracting the most talented and worthy candidates?"[74] Yet another sign that the state of military education in the Soviet Union is poor is the high drop-out rate of conscripts allowed to attend higher military schools. Under new rules, first-term conscripts up to the age of 23 with a secondary education are accepted at military schools and institutes regardless of their specialty. But the number of these cadets who quit is high, a fact that is attributed to their "disinclination to study and lack of discipline resulting from their attitude toward their future career."[75] The high drop-out rate is leading to ever-more-careful screening of applicants. From now on, "only those who have erred in selecting a career and express a desire to change it soberly assessing their abilities toward service will be removed from the VUZs."[76] In a hint at how difficult it might be to reform military education, however, there is the case of the 15- and 16-year-old students who boycotted classes at the Petropavlovsk-Kamchatka Navigation School because they were losing their exemption from active military service. Previously these merchant sailors were excused from active duty on the grounds that their military preparation (about four months' worth) qualified them upon graduation to be commissioned ensigns (junior-lieutenants) in the naval reserves. But the navy did not want to waste its money on reservists with "notoriously limited capabilities," incapable of understanding modern standards.[77] Hence, even in those instances where the military genuinely favors reform, countervailing tendencies within Soviet society may retard any movement toward change.

The Assault on Conscription

One of the most amazing aspects of the current debate over restructuring the Soviet Armed Forces concerns whether to modify, if not eliminate, universal military service. Various proposals center on the notion of adopting a smaller, volunteer army, a conscripted territorial-militia, or a combined cadre-militia system. The ongoing debate again has the political and military leaderships at loggerheads. On the one hand, reformers see moving away from a large, conscripted force as freeing up human resources for the civilian sector, being more in line with defensive defense concepts, and being more democratic. On the other hand, most senior military officials see moves to tinker with conscription as threatening to undermine further the military's power and prestige and exacerbating the already vexing recruiting problem. Even though the military leadership is participating in a fairly open debate on the subject, its conspicuous distaste for banning conscription suggests that the likelihood of this occurring within the next few years must be considered remote.

Nonetheless, among the radical proposals for replacing conscription, the most realistic alternative is a compromise cadre-militia system, which would entail "a relatively small, high-tech equipped, professionally trained and manned, predominantly volunteer cadre military organization, supported by a broad network of territorial-militia formations."[78] Here history is again invoked. In discussing the problems associated with the current system, some critics contend that the professional army was really an aberration, forced upon the USSR by the fascist threat in the West. In the 1920s the Armed Forces were demobilized from a peak figure of 5.5 million men to roughly one-tenth that figure; until World War II, Soviet Armed Forces hovered just around half a million men. Although some, notably Trotski, sought a territorial militia system, the military feared that exclusive reliance upon this type of force would erode military professionalism.[79] Hence, a compromise was struck in favor of a cadre-militia system, in which the "army was based essentially on a territorial-militia system and only a portion of it was regular."[80] Gradually, however, the regular army grew in proportion to the militia, and by 1936 the cadre assumed more than three-fourths of all divisions.[81] In 1939, the Eighteenth Party Congress abolished the territorial militia system.[82] Proponents of changing the current mass army offer various arguments. Surprisingly few put forward the intuitively obvious case that ending conscription would save human if not financial resources. Almost all advocates of reform argue that moving away from universal service is logical in light of the more tranquil international environment. Similarly, abandoning large-standing armies in peacetime would reinforce the doctrine of reasonable sufficiency and defensive defense. Others opt for a volunteer force or a cadre-militia system. But perhaps the most intriguing argument in favor of adopting a different system revolves around the general emphasis on qualitative factors. The reformer Savinkin truly advocates a leaner but meaner military, contending that a cadre-militia force would have been more potent against the Nazis than Stalin's mass conscript army.[83]

On the other hand, Soviet military officials have myriad reasons why they oppose any move toward a professional army. First, the threat of war has not vanished,[84] and only mass conscription provides an adequate pool of reserves in the event of war with the West.[85] Indeed, Deputy Chief of the Main Political Directorate General G.A. Stafanovski asserts, "in spite of our country's peace initiatives, the United States has not abandoned a single one of its military programs."[86] Secondly, the expense of moving toward an all-volunteer force is exorbitant. Akhromeev has flatly stated that an all-volunteer army would cost more than the current force,[87] and General Moiseev initially voiced the opinion that a hired army would cost at least five to eight times as much as a conscripted one.[88] In the words of one officer, "at this point the state cannot afford to maintain a professional army. I will not give away any secrets if I say that the enlisted men and noncommissioned officers in the volunteer U.S. Army today receive more than our officers and generals do."[89] Thirdly, some military officials claim that the military already comprises elements of a volunteer, professional army and navy: "Pilots and a considerable portion of the sailors and missile men, and all the officers, ensigns, and warrant officers are professionals."[90] Conceding that professional military men fight better than short-term soldiers and sailors, General Moiseev claims that more than one-third of the current Armed Forces is made up of long-term professionals.[91] Finally, some, such as Lieutenant Colonel A. Savinkin, reject the concept of a purely professional army on the grounds that "such an army will be cut off from the people."[92] Related to this is the already mentioned notion that conscription is needed to provide a "national university," to provide a countervailing force against the problems associated with a multi-ethnic state. Some fear the decentralization that would accompany a move toward a national-territorial military system, such as that suggested by many in the Baltic republics. Asks one officer: "But what will be the result of separating our army into "national" barracks? Will it not become "a tower of Babel," where each speaks in his own tongue, and does not understand the other?"[93] In short, regardless of the remarkably open discussion on the subject, there are too many obstacles in the way of ending conscription. The fact that nearly all senior Soviet military leaders are on the record opposed to such a radical departure from the past suggests that Gorbachev would have to expend much of his political capital and efforts if he is serious about ending universal service in the near future. While undoubtedly the Soviet leader would like to free up manpower for the civilian economy, the exorbitant costs of attempting such a move are likely to preclude its occurrence in the foreseeable future. To be sure, this pessimistic judgment does not mean that the present system will not change. In fact, as one officer sums up the debate, "Changes will inevitably touch both the numerical strength of the army and the conditions of serving in it."[94]

Soviet Youth's Disenchantment with the Military

Although historical analogies often can be more misleading than illuminating, the widespread disaffection of Soviet youth toward the military is reminiscent of the latter part of the Vietnam War years in the U.S. While criticism of the military hails from all corners of Soviet society, the younger generation is singularly estranged from, even repulsed by, the Armed Forces. Hunger strikes, boycotts, and other protests of military preparation classes have been reported in numerous major cities, from Leningrad and Riga to Irkutskand Tashkent.[95] For example, two students at the Kiev Medical Institute unwittingly ignited a major protest after they were thrown into the brig for the heinous indiscretion of slinging their military jackets over their shoulders and not wearing their caps. This prompted fellow students to stage a hunger strike, which in turn grew into a belligerent rally aimed at the crude military training of the medical students. These students were castigated for attempting to take advantage of Gorbachev's liberal reforms. As one officer carped: "The process of democratization and glasnost is seen by some as giving them carte blanche. Some people's common sense changes when emotions are given free rein."[96]

Several months prior to this incident, physics students at Kiev State University had won important concessions from the school and state after setting up a picket line in front of the military classrooms. As a result, students who had prior military experience were exempted from drill exercises and other portions of the preparatory work, which is currently mandatory in all but the freshman year of undergraduate university education.[97]

One of the most contentious issues regarding military personnel concerned the tussle over the decision to grant an early discharge into the reserves to 176,000 students whose education had been disrupted by the draft. During hearings on his reappointment, Defense Minister Yazov implored delegates of the Supreme Soviet that an early discharge of so many highly educated young men would strike a severe blow to combat readiness. "Understandably," the Defense Minister said, "these are highly rated specialists and junior commanders, in point of fact the best part of the Army."[98] Yazov's plea fell on deaf ears, however, as only five members of the Supreme Soviet voted to support Yazov and another three abstained. While the debate demonstrates a loss of prestige by Yazov, who was widely viewed as a "new thinker" only two years earlier, it also implies that the political leadership may have been concerned with the possible further alienation of Soviet youth.

If Soviet youth are less than enamored with the idea of two years of required service in the army, the prospect of a three-year tour at sea is anathema to them. Some of those drafted into the navy pretend to be drug users or alcoholics in order to avoid sea duty.[99] The incentives for conscripts in the naval service are virtually nil: the token pay increase is more than offset by the 90 percent chance that they will not be permitted to take the theoretically permissible two leaves during the three-year tour of service. Some view the extra year of service as a violation of the Soviet Constitution. In any case, few young men can countenance the idea that their friends will have completed their compulsory military requirement a year ahead of them.[100]

Summary and Conclusion

A major goal of perestroika is to invigorate the Soviet economy. The years of stagnation under Brezhnev and the bankruptcy of the model of central planning have led to a widely felt fear of imminent economic collapse; in Gorbachev's own words, a "pre-crisis situation." Gorbachev himself initially may not have appreciated the magnitude of the challenge facing the Soviet Union, but in view of current realities at home, his regime has gradually redefined what constitutes national security. Economic and political means of attaining foreign policy objectives have recently been elevated above the historically favored military instrument of Soviet power. "For today more than ever before," Foreign Minister Eduard Shevardnadze has declared, "the capacity of the Armed Forces to fulfill their missions depends directly and chiefly on a strong economy and highly developed scientific potential."[101]

Without a sound economic base at home, the Armed Forces of the Soviet Union can achieve nothing but hollow victories abroad. Questioning the very utility of military force, the "new thinking" offers a robust rationale for scaling back the military through a variety of means, including asymmetrical and unilateral measures.[102] For the military, restructuring chiefly implies a drastic cut in resources, aimed at slimming down the corpulent military bureaucracy. Gorbachev's unilateral reduction of Soviet troops by half a million men, coupled with the prospect of further troop cuts through an agreement on Conventional Forces in Europe, is placing an emphasis upon officer training and a corresponding overhaul of higher military education in the Soviet Union. Most interesting for outside observers, glasnost has provided a window for those in the West and East to witness an unprecedented debate within the USSR over the possibility of abandoning compulsory military service. While there are severe obstacles preventing the adoption of a military force based on either all-volunteer, professional, or territorial militia principles, Gorbachev is revising doctrine and training to conform with "nonoffensive defense" concepts. At the same time, the "new thinking" attempts to convert portions of the military-industrial complex into civil-industrial facilities.

A central contention of this chapter is that the political and military leadership seem to have reached a general consensus on the need for qualitative improvements in the Armed Forces. Where they are most at odds, however, is on the subject of the magnitude of the quantitative military reductions. If the military seems supportive of perestroika thus far, it is largely because it recognizes that there is little alternative: the USSR must reform in order to maintain qualitative parity in the technological arms race with the West. The high command is willing, in some cases even eager, to accept a leaner military, so long as it is also a meaner one; i.e., modernized, efficient, and well-trained. But if Gorbachev is intent on carving into the marrow, and not just the excess fat, of the military leviathan, then future reductions in the size of the Armed Forces and the defense budget are likely to incur the ever-growing ire of Gorbachev's generals and admirals. The political and military leadership may be in agreement over the need for qualitative improvements throughout Soviet society, but they appear to be headed for an inescapable crisis over the extent to which the Armed Forces can sacrifice quantitative factors.

Notes

[1]Dmitrii Volkogonov, "Triumf i tragediia: politicheskii portret I. V. Stalina," *Oktiabr*, (October, November, December 1988).

[2]Mikhail Gorbachev, *Perestroika*, (New York: Harper & Row, Perennial Library, 1988), p. 127.

[3]*Ibid*.

[4]Report by E.A. Shevardnadze on July 25, 1988, to a conference of the USSR Ministry of Foreign Affairs on "The 19th All-Union CPSU Conference: Foreign Policy and Diplomacy," *International Affairs*, (Moscow), October 1988, p. 1.

[5]*Ibid*.

[6]*Ibid*., p. 16.

[7]*Ibid*., p. 17.

[8]For instance, see the statement of Leonid Yagodovski in *Yomiuri Shimbun*, June 27, 1989.

[9]*Izvestiia*, September 15, 1989.

[10]Shevardnadze, *op. cit*., pp. 16-17.

[11]In short, many elements of the Ogarkov school of thought appear to be extant. For a persuasive overview of this argument, see Edward L. Warner, III, "New Thinking and Old Realities in Soviet Defense Policy," *Survival*, January-February 1989, p. 23.

[12]See statement by Rear Admiral B. Pekedov, chief of the

Political Department of the Pacific Fleet: "I can confidently say that the majority of old ships will be scrapped in the next few years" in *Krasnaia Zvezda*, April 16, 1989, p. 4.

[13]*Ibid.*

[14]*Ibid.*

[15]See Captain 2nd Rank S. Turchenko interview with Admiral of the Fleet I. Kapitanets in *Krasnaia Zvezda*, August 15, 1989. p. 2.

[16]Paul Kennedy, *The Rise and Fall of the Great Powers*, (New York: Random House, 1987).

[17]*Ibid.*, p. 14.

[18]Shevardnadze, *op. cit.*, p. 16.

[19]*Ibid.*, p. 17.

[20]*Pravda*, July 16, 1988, p. 1.

[21]Supporting the notion that the Soviet regime feels it can spur the West to curtail military spending by taking independent actions, Shevardnadze has said repeatedly that "unilateral actions presuppose reciprocal multilateral restraint." See, *inter alia*, *TASS*, January 19, 1989.

[22]See "Restructuring in the USSR Armed Forces: Toward Reasonable Sufficiency," *Bratislava Pravda*, February 23, 1989, in *FBIS-SOV*, March 2, 1989, and "Lebedev Briefs Press on Troop Reductions," *TASS*, December 22, 1988, in *FBIS-SOV*, December 23, 1988.

[23]*Izvestiia*, February 28, 1989, pp. 1-3.

[24]Gorbachev made the comment during an January 18, 1989, meeting with members of the Trilateral Commission. Similarly, General Lebedev has said that only modern tank models would be cut. See *Ibid.*

[25]*New York Times*, January 26, 1989, p. 1.

[26]*Wall Street Journal*, September 13, 1989, p. 1.

[27]Interview with Sergei Akhromeev by Ezio Mauro, *La Repubblica*, March 11, 1989, p. 11, in *FBIS-SOV* March 15, 1989, pp. 1-3.

[28]*Moskovskie Novosti*, No. 5, January 29, 1989.

[29]*Ibid.*

[30]*Ibid.*

[31]*Ibid.*

[32]See, for example, the comments of Manki Ponomarev about public concern over unilateralism in *Krasnaia Zvezda*, August 25, 1989, p. 2.

[33]Dale R. Herspring, "The Soviet Military and Change," *Survival*, July-August 1989, pp. 321-338.

[34]In one article in the military press calling for the preservation of qualitative parity with the West, it is also stressed that "equilibrium is maintained mainly through military aspects of security....Thus military-strategic parity is an objective necessity, not a historical error. Consequently the important thing is not for us to abandon it and for it to

disappear." In this view, parity can be achieved at lower and lower levels, but only if the West cooperates. See *Krasnaia Zvezda*, January 3, 1989.

[35]In tandem with this alleged shift to defensive defense, the Soviet Union claims its forces are training for defensive missions and reducing their out-of-area operations. In addition, one general claims that Soviet military advisers in the third world are plagued by numerous shortcomings and that Soviet foreign military assistance will be slashed under perestroika. Such cutbacks could suggest an even steeper decline in the frequency of Soviet Navy out-of-area operations. Soviet commentators have pointed to their decreased out-of-area naval operating tempo (OPTEMPO) as being indicative of their defensively oriented force posture. The general suggests that advisers in such countries as Angola, Syria, Ethiopia, and Afghanistan are lacking basic skills, such as a foreign language, to perform effectively, and even properly trained advisers are guilty of excessive reticence or haughtiness. The officer concludes that the USSR must use fewer resources to fulfill security needs. See *Krasnaia Zvezda*, October 26, 1988, p. 4.

[36]*Sovetskaia Kirgizia*, May 9, 1989, in *JPRS Military Affairs*, June 27, 1989, pp. 23-25.

[37]*Ibid.*

[38]*Krasnaia Zvezda*, June 27, 1989, p. 2.

[39]*Pravda*, July 17, 1989, p. 2.

[40]*Ibid.*

[41]*Ibid.*

[42]*Ibid.*

[43]*Ibid.*

[44]*Ibid.*

[45]*Ibid.*

[46]*Krasnaia Zvezda*, May 1, 1989, p. 2.

[47]See, for example, the interview with First Deputy Chairman of Gosplan V.I. Smyslov in *Krasnaia Zvezda*, July 26, 1989, p. 2.

[48]*Vremia*, July 27, 1989, in *FBIS-SOV*, July 28, 1989, p. 106.

[49]*Ibid.*

[50]*Krasnaia Zvezda*, June 29, 1989, p. 2.

[51]*Ibid.*

[52]Evgenii Shashkov's comments in *Kommunist*, No. 4, March 1989, pp. 110-117.

[53]*Ibid.*

[54]*Krasnaia Zvezda*, February 12, 1989, p. 4.

[55]See, for example, *Krasnaia Zvezda*, February 16, 1989, p. 1.

[56]*Krasnaia Zvezda*, February 14, 1989, p. 4.

[57]See, for example, letters to the editor in *Krasnaia Zvezda*, December 15, 1988, p. 4.

[58]V. Lelin, "The Social Sphere: Sphere of Party Influence: Proper Assignments," *Kommunist Vooruzhennykh Sil*, No. 6, March

1989, pp. 33-38

[59]*Moskovskie Novosti*, No. 5, January 29, 1989.

[60]*Morskoi Sbornik*, No. 6, June 1989, pp. 29-32.

[61]Unattributed article, "In the Turkmen SSR Ministry of Education," *Mugallymlar Gazeti*, February 3, 1989, p. 1, in *JPRS-Military Affairs*, July 13, 1989, p. 10.

[62]*Krasnaia Zvezda*, December 25, 1988, p. 2.

[63]*Krasnaia Zvezda*, August 4, 1989, pp. 1-2.

[64]*Ibid.*

[65]*Krasnaia Zvezda*, January 28, 1989, p. 1.

[66]*Ibid.* In addition, there is a general push in the Soviet Union to strengthen scientific research as a means of abetting both the economy and the military. See Mikhail Tsypkin, "Turmoil in Soviet Science," *Report on the USSR*, RFE/RL, Vol. 1, No. 29, pp. 17-20.

[67]*Ibid.*

[68]*Ibid.*

[69]*Ibid.*

[70]*Krasnaia Zvezda*, March 30, 1989, p. 4.

[71]*Ibid.*

[72]*Ibid.*

[73]*Ibid.*

[74]*Ibid.*

[75]Colonel V. I. Samoilov, senior officer with the Main Personnel Directorate of the USSR Ministry of Defense, answering questions for the editors, "At Your Request: The New Rules," *Agitator Armii Flota*, No. 10, May 1989, pp. 26-27 in *JPRS Military Affairs*, July 13, 1989, pp. 54-55.

[76]*Ibid.*

[77]*Krasnaia Zvezda*, May 14, 1989, p. 4.

[78]*Moskovskie Novosti*, No. 45, November 6, 1988.

[79]Both this historical and current debate are discussed in lucid detail by Suzanne M. Crow, "The Current Soviet Debate on a Cadre-Militia System," *Jane's Soviet Intelligence Review*, August 1989.

[80]*Voenno-istoricheski Zhurnal*, No. 2, February 1989, pp. 16-31.

[81]Crow, *op. cit.*

[82]*Ibid.*

[83]*Moskovskie Novosti*, No. 45, November 6, 1988.

[84]For example, see the essays published under the title "Poka sushchestvuet opasnost' agressii," *Kommunist Vooruzhennikh Sil*, No. 2, January 1989, pp. 18-25.

[85]For instance, see M.A. Moiseev, "Unfading Deed," *Sovetskaia Kirgizia*, May 9, 1989, p. 3, in *JPRS Military Affairs*, June 27, 1989, pp. 23-25.

[86]*Sovetskaia Kultura*, February 23, 1989.

[87]*Sovetskaia Rossiia*, January 14, 1989.

[88]*Krasnaia Zvezda*, February 10, 1989.

[89]*Ibid.*

[90]*Ibid.*

[91]*Pravitel' stvenni Vestnik*, No. 9, May 1989, p. 5.

[92]*Vek XX i Mir*, September 1988, p. 22.

[93]*Krasnaia Zvezda*, May 4, 1989.

[94]*Ibid.*

[95]Kathleen Mihalisko, "Report from Kiev University on Future of Student Military Obligations," *Report on the USSR*, RFE/RL, Vol. 1, No. 4, 1989, pp. 3-5.

[96]*Krasnaia Zvezda*, July 23, 1989.

[97]See Mihalisko, *op. cit.*

[98]*Pravda*, July 5, 1989.

[99]*Krasnaia Zvezda*, July 8, 1989.

[100]*Ibid.*

[101]Shevardnadze, *op. cit.*

[102]A. Izyumov and V. Kortunov, "Sovetski soiuz v meniaiushchemsia mire," *Mezhdunarodnaia Zhizn'*, July 1988, pp. 53-64.

8

Changes in Soviet Military Thinking: How Do They Add Up and What Do They Mean for Western Security?

Paula J. Dobriansky and David B. Rivkin, Jr.

For over four years, changes, or lack thereof, in Soviet military thinking under Mikhail Gorbachev have been a subject of lively speculation among Western analysts.[1] Indeed, the matter has been preoccupying not only professional Sovietologists: it has been injected into the broader context of Western defense debates and has been discussed at length by many a journalist and pundit. Almost immediately, roughly two schools of thought about Soviet military developments emerged.

The first school is pessimistic. It posits that most of the new Soviet doctrinal themes have been promulgated either to mislead the West or, even if genuine, would not have a lasting positive impact on Soviet military posture. Consequently, the proponents of this viewpoint anticipate that, sooner or later, Moscow will revert to its old evil ways.

In contrast, the second school is notably optimistic, both about the sincerity of Soviet doctrinal innovations and about their prospects for permanently transforming the nature of Soviet military policies. The net result being envisioned by the advocates of this position is a more benign Soviet Union, presenting less of a security threat to Western interests. However, the reality of changes in Soviet military thinking and of their implications for Western security is far too complex to fit snugly in either of these two simplistic paradigms.

To be sure, there is no doubt that, a decade from now, Soviet military forces and associated war plans will be quite different from those that Moscow has today. Thus, the ongoing changes in Soviet military thinking are very real indeed. What is far less clear, however, is precisely what the Soviet military will look like in the year 2000 and beyond. The reason for this is that, regular uncertainties attendant to any exercise in futurology aside, there are presently numerous contradictory and competing tendencies evident in Soviet military affairs. This, in turn, makes an assessment of these developments and of their implications for U.S. policy an exceedingly difficult enterprise.

Causes of Change in Soviet Military Policy

How Real are the Changes?

What is the proof that serious changes in Soviet military thinking are underway? Since the evidence comes largely in the form of Soviet writings and statements, a natural question arises: Do they reflect accurately what is taking place in the Soviet military establishment? Or perhaps this is all a clever Soviet ruse to deceive the West and lull it into a false sense of complacency? After all, despite all of Gorbachev's declarations and arms control proposals, so far, there has been continued growth in Soviet defense spending and military production. Thus, for example, such major ticket items as the Soviet submarine construction and carrier programs have not been cut back. In fact, according to public U.S. intelligence estimates, the growth rate of Soviet military spending in the last two years doubled as compared with the 1981-1986 period (the present rate is three percent). Nor has there been much reassuring change in the Soviet force structure and weapons production "which would reflect [Gorbachev's] soft smile and the smooth words, the acknowledgement of the mistakes of history or the inspiring words for the future."[2]

Two additional key questions often posed by Western skeptics are how durable is Gorbachev's tenure and how likely is it that Soviet reforms would survive without Gorbachev? The short answer to the former question is that it is difficult to surmise the extent of Gorbachev's longevity. By all accounts, he appears firmly in control of the Soviet state, and his reshuffling of the military and the KGB, restructuring of the Central Committee apparatus, purge of the so-called "dead soul" members of the Central Committee, and, last but not least, the forced portfolio switching of such prominent Politburo members as Egor Ligachev and the firing of *all* remaining members of Brezhnev's Politburo indicate Gorbachev's strong bureaucratic skills and self-confidence. On the other hand, the Yeltsin affair manifests limitations on Gorbachev's power, and, even more fundamentally, Gorbachev's own pet reforms, glasnost, perestroika, and *demokratisatsiva* (democratization), make it more difficult for him to eliminate political opponents. The fate of Gorbachev's reforms without Gorbachev being present to guide them is also difficult to predict. All in all, we simply lack an ability to estimate reliably the future Soviet political and bureaucratic landscape, and, for that matter, so does Gorbachev himself.

These uncertainties prompt legitimate concerns. Yet, at the end of the day, there is no denying the serious nature of the ongoing transformation of the Soviet military. To begin with, doctrinal writings are taken very seriously in the Soviet system. For instance, historically, the Soviet procurement of weapons systems and their deployment has not been a random process. Rather, they proceed according to an elaborate set of doctrinal guidelines. As noted by William Odom:

Most states do not build military forces randomly, or just to be in fashion, or purely because of bureaucratic momentum. They build toward some mission, to meet some threat, in accordance with some doctrinal rationale.... The Soviet Union has been very advanced in working out new rationales for force development. Its unclassified military literature is among the richest in the world, which is indicative of the existence of an even more extensive classified analysis.[3]

The Soviets also devote considerable attention to the analysis of war as a phenomenon.[4]

It should be noted, however, that, while Soviet doctrinal guidance determines the overall thrust of Soviet force posture development, interpreting Soviet pronouncements is no easy matter. The Soviets frequently use esoteric or ambiguous terms in describing their doctrinal intentions. Furthermore, the enunciation of doctrinal requirements often significantly precedes the time the corresponding force posture elements are fully fielded. For example, in the early 1960s, Soviet writings discussed the need for sizable nuclear forces, capable of defeating NATO and the U.S. in a global war. Moscow did not, however, acquire capabilities to implement this doctrinal guidance until well into the 1970s. All of this suggests that the Soviet military doctrine ought to be interpreted with care.

Still, given the importance of doctrinal prescriptions, for Moscow to present deliberately misleading information to the Soviet elites, just in order to trick the West, would be quite out of character. This is all the more true because, despite the secretive nature of the Soviet system, it would be impossible for Moscow to deliver one set of doctrinal messages in open channels, while proffering completely different guidelines *sotto voce*. And, to the best of our knowledge, a Soviet deception on such a grand scale never has been attempted. Moreover, even a cursory examination of the ongoing Soviet doctrinal debates reveals the seriousness and even passion displayed by numerous Soviet participants. It is difficult to believe that a staged debate can feature these attributes.

Past Revolutions in Military Affairs Revisited

Moreover, the notion that major changes in Soviet military thinking are underway is not, in itself, surprising. The Soviets themselves have always stressed that their military planning is not ageless and is subject to constant review and revision. In addition to perpetual fine-tuning of Soviet military doctrine, it, from time to time, has undergone a more fundamental transformation, referred to by the Soviet writers as a "revolution in military affairs."

The first such revolution occurred in the 1920s-30s and was triggered by the advent of "aviation, motorization, and chemical weapons," all of which were originally introduced in World War I but did not begin exerting decisive influence on warfare until a decade or two later. According to William Odom, the implications of this revolution were as follows:

> [emergence of] a less clear distinction between the "front" and the "rear" in war. Bombing of cities, industrial plants, and military forces deep in the rear areas could be expected. Motorized forces could conduct much deeper operations. The new weapons would also require a well- trained officer corps and a literate manpower pool for military recruitment.[5]

The second revolution took place during the 1953-1960 period. It was primarily caused by several interrelated developments in military technologies: the creation of atomic/nuclear weapons, the invention of ballistic missiles, and, last but not least, the extraordinary progress achieved in the fields of cybernetics and computers. The synergistic impact of these inventions was to usher in an era of nuclear firepower, which could be delivered accurately and promptly anywhere in the world and would reign supreme on any battlefield on which it was used. From that time on, the nature of deterrence and warfare was fundamentally transformed.

The consequences of the revolution, presided over by the Soviet Premier Nikita Khrushchev, for the Soviet military establishment were radical indeed; nothing comparable to, for example, Khrushchev's creation of the Strategic Rocket Forces (SRF) or his disestablishment of the Ground Forces as a separate service (a decision subsequently overturned by his successors) has been observed since. While a number of changes in Soviet military planning took place during the 1960s-70s, these were not comparable to Khrushchev's revolution in military affairs.

The New Revolution in the Making?

By the late 1970s, tentative signs of a major new doctrinal upheaval began to emerge. Like the revolutions of old, the new revolution in military affairs is also being prompted by a host of technological, political, and economic developments anticipated by Soviet analysts. These developments fall into roughly two major categories: external factors and internal pressures.

Under the category of external factors, Soviet analysts describe a range of changes in the external environment which heavily impact on Soviet military planning. These include such technological[6] milestones as the advent of artificial intelligence, progress in the development of systems incorporating low observable/stealth technologies, miniaturization of all categories of military hardware, creation of new conventional systems with levels of lethality approaching those heretofore vested only in nuclear weapons, increase in the range and accuracy with which firepower can be dispensed on the battlefield, and the potential introduction of weapons systems based on new physical principles. In fact, according to Soviet writers, just one type of new technology, artificial intelligence, and its pending integration into numerous aspects of military affairs alone promises to revolutionize warfare at numerous levels.

For example, at the highest level of warfare, supercomputers, incorporating artificial intelligence features, and new sensors enable political leadership to assess in extremely short time an entire global politico-military situation and make the necessary decisions.[7] As argued by G. Kochetkov, a well-known Soviet researcher, at the strategic level, artificial intelligence, when incorporated in weapons systems, leads to the emergence of super accurate and smart weapons and enables conventional weapons to destroy virtually any target. He further claims that, in the future, at the operational and tactical levels, many tasks will have to be performed so fast that human intelligence has to be "taken out of the loop," leaving decisions to computers. This trend, while militarily efficient, allegedly causes serious political problems, at least from the public relations standpoint (wars caused by a rogue computer have been a regular fixture of Hollywood productions), and *may* create highly unstable military balances. All of this, of course, is mostly futurology, and there is no reason to believe that the Soviet's ability to predict the future is invariably better than that of its Western counterparts. What is significant, however, is that Moscow takes these futurological musings seriously.

Also, obviously, not all of these changes are taking place at once. Rather, at most, they represent trends likely to evolve over the next decades. For the Soviet analysts, however, these trends are important and merit timely adjustments in Soviet military thinking.

In addition to coping with purely technological changes, the Soviets manifest considerable concern about the evolution of Western political and military thought and planning.[8] In particular, they highlight U.S. and NATO's evident emphasis on devising operational and technological counters to the Soviet theater *blitzkrieg* strategy and to Western efforts to develop "competitive strategies," designed to exploit areas of perceived Soviet weakness. Specifically, the Soviets visibly fret about such U.S. doctrinal initiatives as Airland Battle, Follow-on Forces Attack (FOFA), and Counterair-90 that appear designed to attack Soviet formations and military assets throughout Eastern Europe and Western Russia. Insofar as the standard Soviet operational approach to winning a war against NATO is heavily dependent upon the timely arrival of Soviet reinforcements and their orderly presentation against NATO defenses, these U.S. initiatives threaten the viability of Soviet strategy.

The Soviets also manifest considerable concern about the U.S. Strategic Defense Initiative (SDI).[9] At the most fundamental level, the Soviets subscribe to the view, articulated by Engels, that it is the dynamics of offense-defense struggle that shape the evolution of warfare. To be sure, Moscow also asserts that nuclear weapons impart a unique character to offense-defense interactions; allegedly, the enormous destructive power of nuclear devices renders offense supreme and the resulting strategic balance highly stable. Nevertheless, in the Soviet view, SDI constitutes a major military challenge to their strategy. The Soviets allege that the most likely path for an East-West war is through an inadvertent escalation of events arising out of a political crisis, *a la* Sarajevo. Thus, a force posture, which generates an atmosphere of mistrust and complicates the computation of military balances, makes war more likely, and the deployment of space-based strategic defenses is alleged to produce precisely such a set of negative consequences.

> With each new spiral of the arms race with the real danger of its
> exit into space, nuclear "protective scroll" is turning into a
> "death sentence" for mankind. Under the conditions of suspicion
> and fear, the possibility of unsanctioned outbreak of war would
> grow immeasurably.[10]

Soviet analysts also claim that the deployment of partially effective defenses, in conjunction with highly capable offensive forces, may create an illusion in the minds of military and even civilian decision-makers that they can win a war by delivering an effective first-strike and absorbing the retaliatory attack with their defensive forces. This insidious calculus and the "theory of victory" that it backs are alleged to generate high crisis instability. Moreover, insofar as the U.S. defense initiative promises to harness a number of key technologies with a range of promising military and civilian applications, it presents Moscow with a broad technological, scientific, and political challenge. In fact, Soviet writers posit that SDI's impact may well be felt first in the conventional, and not the strategic nuclear, arena.

To be sure, SDI and other U.S. and NATO doctrinal innovations have not been fully implemented. Moreover, they have encountered considerable bureaucratic obstacles and political opposition, both in the United States and other NATO countries, and the prospects of securing the necessary levels of budgetary and political support for them are far from certain. SDI in particular has evolved from a political and budgetary darling of the early Reagan years into a much more modest, slow, and fiscally restrained effort. These facts are well know to Soviet planners. Yet, just as in the case of their assessment of emerging technological trends, the Soviets appear to believe that, even if NATO does not put all of its bright new ideas into practice, enough changes would take place to make warfare infinitely more complicated and much more dependent on the quality of the forces involved. These developments require a major adjustment in Soviet military thinking.

Under the category of internal factors, the Soviets consider the current sorry state of the Soviet economy and society. In the economic area alone, over the last 20 years, the Soviet rate of economic growth declined from five percent to nearly zero. In the view of the new Soviet leadership, economic, demographic, and social problems threaten to undermine the hard-won Soviet superpower status and to relegate it to the ranks of a second-class power. From the military standpoint, the problem is far more serious than the simple matter of economic constraints on Soviet defense spending. Rather, it is the manifest inability of the Soviet economy to master mass production of high quality goods, establish precision manufacturing, or secure the rapid tempo of technological innovation that are the primary obstacles to the ability of the Soviet military to field new sophisticated weapons systems they require to do well on the battlefields of the 21st century. Especially disquieting to Soviet military planners is the failure of the Soviet society and educational system to provide enough highly educated, motivated, and trained personnel to man the new weapons systems. Changing demographic trends and decline in the birth rate of Russians and other Slavs in the Soviet Union further contribute to the manpower shortfall facing the Soviet military. As estimated by Western experts, over the last decade, the number of available 18-year-old Russian draftees fell by about 30 percent.

As both the Soviet military and political leaders appear to realize, these economic and manpower bottlenecks can be fixed only as a result of a fundamental restructuring of Soviet society and economy. Yet, restructuring, even under the best of circumstances, is likely to be a lengthy process. In the interim, the Soviet military can clearly benefit from the slowing down of the tempo of the technological and military competition with the West and from the related readjustment of Soviet planning and deployments to fit the new circumstances.

Moscow is also troubled by the spreading economic and political malaise in Eastern Europe which, among other things, increases the unreliability of Soviet-WTO (Warsaw Treaty Organization) allies. For example, despite the protestations of fidelity to the WTO, the advent of the first post-war non-communist government in Poland is bound to enhance Soviet anxiety about the conduct of East European militaries in an East-West war.

Soviet Military Doctrine: Old and New Themes

Khrushchev's New Look and the Nuclear Emphasis

To appreciate the nature and magnitude of the changes taking place in Soviet military thinking, it is useful to reflect briefly on the nature of the "old" Soviet military doctrine. The origin of that doctrine dates back to the "Revolution in Military Affairs" of 1953-1960. In its original permutation, the doctrine was heavily nuclear in emphasis, stressed the need to prepare the

Soviet armed forces for a global all-out nuclear war with the West by
acquiring military-technical superiority, and emphasized that Moscow,
suitably prepared, can win such a conflict.[11] The impact of nuclear weapons
on warfare, as originally perceived by the Soviet writers, was truly dramatic.
In the prenuclear age:

> Strategic goals were attained through mobilization, unfolding of
> military potential and the operational-tactical utilization of
> weapons on the field of battle. Nuclear "triad" made it possible
> to cause direct massive destruction of the enemy across the
> entire depth of his territory, and erased distinctions between
> front and rear. And the practical absence of effective means of
> defense imbued nuclear weapons with absolute character. All of
> this led to the complete restructuring of perceptions of the
> structure of military might. A sharp decrease in the time needed
> for unfolding military operations practically rendered irrelevant
> the significance of mobilizational capabilities and of the shift of
> economy onto military rails after the beginning of armed
> conflict. The military potential of states began to be determined
> primarily by the availability of nuclear weapons, its quantity and
> technical perfection of the means of delivery.[12]

Despite the early requirement for long-range nuclear delivery systems
capable of destroying U.S. nuclear assets, because of technological and
budgetary considerations, Soviet planners initially opted to concentrate on
fielding theater nuclear forces, slated to attack targets in continental TVD
(*teatr voennykh deistvii* or theater of military operations), and postponed the
large-scale build-up of Soviet central strategic forces until the late 1960s.[13]
Furthermore, as far as Soviet targeting was concerned, even during the nuclear
emphasis days of Soviet doctrine, Moscow had no intention of turning Europe
into a radioactive wasteland. Rather, the Soviet thinking postulated using
discriminatory nuclear strikes against select European targets and preserving
European industry and population as a recovery base to be used by Moscow.[14]
In contrast, Soviet nuclear strikes in the transoceanic TVD would have been
more generous and were designed not only to deplete U.S. nuclear assets and
military forces, but also to destroy U.S. administrative and economic
infrastructure. The new nuclear emphasis in Soviet military planning was
reflected in the establishment, in December 1959, of the Strategic Rocket
Forces (SRF) as a separate military service. The Soviets also began to stress
that nuclear weapons, in addition to being the key indicator of one's military
might, constituted the backbone of deterrence. The essence of the Soviet
deterrence concept *circa* the 1960s was an ability to prevail in any nuclear
conflict with the West. This was to be achieved by limiting damage to the
Soviet homeland, while utterly destroying Moscow's capitalist opponents,
tasks that placed a heavy premium on the Soviet ability to deliver the first
highly effective nuclear blow.

The existence of nuclear weapons also caused changes in the Soviet ground forces, prompting Khrushchev to announce a plan to reduce the size of the Soviet armed forces from 3.6 million to 2.4 million, reductions that were only partially implemented. Force levels aside, the erstwhile principles of Soviet operational art required massing of Soviet forces to break through the enemy lines. Now, massing was to be eschewed, since any large concentration of forces could be expected to attract hostile nuclear fire. To operate successfully in the new "nuclear scared" mode, the Soviets began to emphasize speed and maneuverability enabling their troops to mass rapidly and disperse again. This requirement, combined with the perceived need to protect the troops from radiation, reinforced the traditional Soviet proclivity for armor-heavy ground forces. It was also expected that Soviet nuclear firepower, properly administered, would crush much of the enemy defense, obviating the need to break through NATO lines.

All said and done, however, while the expectations created by new tools of warfare were mighty indeed, the "Revolution in Military Affairs" did not proceed smoothly, with all of the parties involved agreeing on all of the major issues. Atomic and nuclear weapons exerted a powerful impact on warfare, that much was clear. What was being argued about were the nature of that impact and its implications. Such issues as the duration of nuclear war, probability of escalation, proper nuclear strategy, the size and requirements for conventional forces, and continued viability of aircraft in the age of ballistic missiles were heatedly debated. Eventually, despite the view espoused by some technology enthusiasts, namely that nuclear weapons by themselves could accomplish all of Soviet military objectives, a more balanced position was adopted: nuclear weapons were the key to victory, but sizeable "combined arms" forces were required to seize enemy territory and bring about the end of the war.[15]

Nuclear War and Escalation: An Evolving Matrix

By the second half of the 1960s, Soviet military doctrine underwent some further refinements. Having analyzed the impact of NATO's adoption of the "flexible response" strategy and other pertinent trends, Soviet planners began to claim that, while nuclear escalation in an East-West conflict was still likely, it was not inevitable. Specifically, local wars were expected to remain conventional, and even a European conflict was likely to have a conventional phase. As claimed by some Western scholars (most notably Michael MccGwire), the mid-1960s witnessed a key change in the Soviet military planning. Specifically, MccGwire argues that:

> [b]y the end of 1966 the Soviets had reformulated their doctrine
> on the nature of a world war, reversing the 1959 conclusion that
> such a conflict would inevitably be nuclear and would mean
> massive nuclear strikes on the Russian homeland. For the first
> time, the objective of avoiding the nuclear devastation of Russia

might be achievable in a world war. Adopting the objective led to the basic restructuring of Soviet military strategy and the reshaping of their concepts of military operations.[16]

MccGwire attributes these changes to the following factors:

> The shift in Soviet assumptions was made possible by the West's adoption of the policy of flexible response in NATO Europe and by the U.S. emphasis on an assured second-strike capability. Flexible response was by far the more significant, and from the Soviet viewpoint, there were two aspects to this U.S. initiative. First, the policy indicated that if NATO had a choice, the early stages of a war in Europe would be conventional. Second, the debate within NATO that preceded the policy's adoption had certain implications about the U.S. nuclear guarantee of Europe [i.e. the credibility of this guarantee was lowered].[17]

These claims contain a kernel of truth; yet, in their totality, they greatly overstate the magnitude of the change involved.[18] To begin with, Soviet writings, both prior to and post-1966, do not manifest a clear-cut assessment of flexible response and assured destruction notions as indicators of NATO's intention not to "go nuclear."[19] Rather, the essence of these concepts was, in Moscow's view, an intention to wage "war by stages," starting with a conventional phase and later escalating to the use of nuclear weapons.[20] Indeed, both the objective reality in the mid-1960s and the Soviet assessment of it were, at most, that the probability of nuclear escalation in an East-West conflict was somewhat lowered, but not obviated.

Thus, both before 1966 and after that date, Moscow felt that nuclear escalation might be averted, and that realization affected Soviet military planning; the difference was simply one of degree. And even to that extent, the change dates back to the early 1970s, rather than to the mid-1960s. Thus, rather than giving up on nuclear warfighting in the late 1960s, Moscow merely opted to enrich its strategic menu. In fact, the Soviet planners proceeded to acquire a nuclear force structure capable of delivering counterforce strikes against U.S. strategic forces, supporting a separate theater nuclear conflict in Eurasia, and implementing a range of limited nuclear options. Soviet nuclear targeting also evolved and, as the accuracy of Soviet strategic forces grew, became more sophisticated and discriminating.[21]

Developing Conventional Options

During the 1970s, Soviet military thinking also began to feature a full panoply of conventional warfighting options.[22] Specifically, Moscow began to develop a ground, air, and naval force structure capable of defeating hostile forces in Eurasia without resorting to nuclear weapons.[23] Moreover, as the

1970s went on, the Soviets began to deemphasize, at least at the declaratory level, the nuclear aspects of their strategy, stressing that nuclear war was unwinnable and that nuclear superiority was unattainable. These themes were summarized in a path-breaking January 1977 speech by the late General Secretary Leonid Brezhnev, given in the Soviet city of Tula.[24]

By the late 1970s and early 1980s, professional Soviet military officers began to consider a range of further doctrinal innovations. Initially, these were gradual departures, brought about by the Soviet assessment of the changes in military technology and of the evolving capabilities of their potential adversaries. One such innovation was the resurgence of Soviet interest in large mobile formations, the so-called Operational Maneuver Groups (OMGs), which can be rapidly inserted behind the enemy lines in the early phases of military operations.[25]

In many instances, the changes were more a matter of nuance and emphasis, rather than entirely new themes in Soviet military planning. Indeed, given the complexity and evolution of Soviet military doctrine, it is virtually impossible to devise something completely new. Thus, for example, Soviet interest in fine-tuning their conventional warfighting options, which became a major theme of Soviet military planning in the early 1980s, dates back at least to the late 1960s. Likewise, the apparent Soviet desire to deemphasize nuclear warfighting, another major feature of the new Soviet military doctrine, dates back at least to the above-referenced Brezhnev 1977 Tula speech. Nevertheless, as nuanced and gradual as these changes might have been, they began to transform the nature of Soviet military thinking. They covered a range of military matters and affected all Soviet military services.

In the conventional area, the Soviets began to emphasize the ever-growing spatial scope of military operations. According to the then Chief of the Soviet General Staff, Marshal Nikolai Ogarkov, in contrast to past wars in which the largest military operations involved actions by armies and fronts, future conflicts would necessarily entail high speed successive strategic operations spanning entire theaters and continents.[26] To conduct these operations and to cope with the possibility of a rapid transition from peacetime to wartime conditions, the Soviets have established several key command structures at the theater level. Up until 1984, the only intermediate level command existed in the Far East; the rest of military operations were expected to be controlled out of Moscow. In 1987, however, three additional theater commands were set up; the Western TVD, Southwestern TVD, and the Southern TVD, and Marshal Ogarkov, following his ouster as the Chief of the General Staff, assumed command of the most important of the three, the Western TVD.

Yet, according to Ogarkov and other Soviet military leaders, despite the growth in the spatial nature of the fighting, to prevail on the new battlefields one must emphasize quality, rather than quantity, of military forces. The traditional Soviet approach has been to allow flexibility only at the strategic level of warfare, with high command shifting the resources, packaged in fronts (two or more armies under a single command) and armies, from one direction to another, in an effort to uncover enemy weakness and establish a good *schwerpunk*. At the tactical and operational level (divisions, regiments, and battalions) initiative was discouraged and commanders were expected to follow a fairly rigid set of orders. A new and more fluid approach implied greater attention to operations by smaller units and deemphasis of Soviet divisional level warfare, as well as enhancement of the range of options available to unit commanders.[27] The overall trend was in the direction of the more flexible and leaner ground and air forces, led and maneuvered more adroitly by better-educated officers and capable of conducting a high-speed minuet of fire and movement.[28]

The Soviet involvement in Afghanistan provided their military leaders with valuable experience in such key aspects of combat as decentralized command and control, use of indirect fire support, and night operations. The Soviets also invested in such technological counters to NATO anti-armor capabilities and airpower as fitting their main battle tanks with reactive armor and placing additional anti-aircraft guns and missiles on armored personnel carriers and other vehicles.

An apparent Soviet intention also has been to use conventional means, including massive air strikes (dubbed the "air operation"), artillery, and Spetnaz operations, to destroy NATO's nuclear assets. Since most of NATO's nuclear stockpile in peacetime is concentrated at relatively few storage sites, its vulnerability in this state is particularly high. The Soviets would, of course, prefer to attack the stockpile before NATO has an opportunity to disperse it; a plan that requires the Soviets to deliver a series of precise air and ground strikes throughout the entire depth of NATO's territory early in the conflict.

Accordingly, the Soviets began deploying new highly versatile aircraft, capable of delivering ordnance with high accuracy against ground targets. Soviet artillery modernization also proceeded at a rapid tempo, with numerous new self-propelled guns, and rocket and missile systems entering inventory. The new weapons systems were complimented by the development of new projectiles and new and more accurate fire control systems. To better coordinate new artillery assets, these were organized in heavy artillery brigades.[29] If successful, this approach of using conventional means to attack NATO's nuclear inventory was expected both to discourage NATO from escalation insofar as the alliance, with most of its in-theater nuclear assets depleted, was less likely to opt for "going nuclear" and, should escalation still occur, to diminish damage to Soviet forces from hostile nuclear strikes.

Soviet Military Refinements in the 1980s

As the 1980s progressed, even more fundamental doctrinal innovations ensued. The Soviet military began considering the advisability of a major restructuring of its military forces arraigned against NATO. The former Soviet approach had been to cram as much military capability forward as possible, enabling the WTO, in case of war, to break rapidly through NATO defenses and seize territory with such speed and decisiveness as to, hopefully, prevent NATO from resorting to nuclear weapons. This was to be achieved by the carefully choreographed arrival to the frontline of multi-echeloned Soviet forces, capable of maintaining constant pressure on the enemy. Under this approach, the Soviet high command used divisions as drills bits, which were to be replaced as soon as they suffered certain predetermined attrition levels or simply ran out of steam.

The Soviets, however, began to realize that potential proliferation of long-range strike systems and the growing destructive capacity of conventional munitions in the NATO arsenal made both forward deployed Soviet forces and relatively densely packed arriving reinforcing echelons vulnerable to destruction. This threatened the viability of Moscow's earlier operational solution to NATO's doctrinal innovation: OMGs, which were designed to insert large numbers of Soviet troops behind the enemy lines early in the conflict. Now, even these fast moving formations were potentially vulnerable to attack and destruction by NATO "smart" weapons. Moreover, the manifestly offensive emphasis of Soviet forces has been of such concern to NATO that it provided a major impetus for Western military efforts. The Soviet military also began to suspect that, under some scenarios, their political masters might withhold permission to launch an all-out assault against NATO early in the conflict, as they were likely to try settling the confrontation by political means. In short, the erstwhile Soviet *blitzkrieg* force posture in Europe became questionable from both political and military standpoints.

To cope with this problem, the Soviet military began to consider the possibility of conducting a different kind of war. If Moscow thinned out its forward deployed forces, a step reflected in Gorbachev's December 7, 1988, unilateral troop cuts proposal and its subsequent arms control progeny, it could concentrate during the first phase of a conflict on destroying NATO air power, long-range strike weapons, and nuclear systems. During this phase, Soviet forces would remain dispersed and eschew large-scale offensive operations. Once NATO firepower assets were depleted, the Soviet ground forces could go on the offensive. At that time, they would also be able to mass more readily and, thus, would bring a greater combat weight to bear on NATO's defenses. This prospective shift in Soviet thinking has been described by Phillip Petersen as follows: "The intention is not a World War II German blitzkrieg race to the channel ports, but to encircle NATO forward forces, hold on and reduce them with second echelon troops."[30]

In conjunction with rethinking their overall theater posture, the Soviets have been also considering the possibility of evolving a new force mix, featuring a more balanced composition of armor,[31] mobile infantry, and strike systems. The trend has been toward the standardization of Soviet divisions. Thus, for example, according to Christopher Donnelly, head of Soviet Studies Research Center at the Royal Sandhurst Military Academy, the number of tanks in a Soviet motorized infantry division has increased by 50 percent, while the troop contingent in a tank division has increased by 100 percent. The number of artillery tubes assigned to tank and motorized rifle divisions has also increased, albeit not equally. The end result is a nearly identical divisional structure in some 30 frontline Soviet divisions in Eastern Europe.[32] Donnelly argues, however, that even these new Soviet divisions are still too equipment heavy and lack sufficient manpower to operate successfully in combat. This point is not lost on Moscow-based analysts, who argue that new Soviet divisions should have fewer vehicles of all types. Another key area of exploration has been the emphasis on developing forces capable of greater endurance and versatility and trained to execute both offensive and defensive operations.

In many instances, the Soviets have progressed beyond theoretical discussions, introducing actual changes into their troop training, exercises, and even force structure. In the later category, for example, there has been evidence that Moscow has been experimenting with the introduction of such new types of formations as air assault brigades and unified army corps, composed of brigades, rather than regiments. Such army corps have approximately 450 tanks.[33]

Deterrence and Soviet Doctrinal Angst

In the nuclear area, the change and doctrinal ferment have been impressive, albeit somewhat less drastic. By the early 1980s, the Soviet military already appeared to have embraced firmly the notion that nuclear weapons would play a lesser role in the future, both in peacetime and wartime, and that efforts to attain a visible all-out nuclear superiority were fruitless and even counterproductive. In part, this change reflected the Soviet realization, dating back to the late 1970s, that emerging technological trends, U.S. nuclear force diversification, and the growth in third country nuclear forces seriously complicated Soviet strategic preemption in particular and nuclear warfighting options in general. More specifically, the Soviet military seems to believe that, while nuclear warfighting options are useful things to have in one's doctrinal arsenal, the prospects of limiting damage from a nuclear exchange to acceptable levels are quite slim. This implies that nuclear war is unlikely to be won in any meaningful sense. In that regard, as noted in a recent article by three Soviet civilian analysts, "successful offensive and victory is impossible if the attacker cannot prevent nuclear retaliation or, at the minimum, reduce it to acceptable levels."[34]

In recent years, the Soviets began to evidence considerable concern about the stability of the strategic balance and the quality of deterrence. In this area, Soviet views exhibit some fundamental inconsistencies. On the one hand, Moscow asserts that the tremendous destructive power of nuclear weapons makes deterrence highly stable and negates the impact of quantitative and qualitative asymmetries between the U.S. and Soviet strategic forces. Soviet analysts also opine that, as a result of the growth in the survivability of nuclear forces, strategic stability improved during the 1960s and 1970s. Allegedly, a certain, albeit only modest, reversal occurred in the early 1980s, when the U.S. seemed intent on bolstering its counterforce potential. Curiously, the Soviets claim that, objectively speaking, nothing has changed: the U.S. buildup has not resulted in the acquisition of disarming strike options or even in superior counterforce potential for Washington. Yet, in their view, *psychologically*, deterrence was weakened.[35] The presumed remedy, also largely psychological in nature, is arms control and enhanced U.S.-Soviet dialogue.

It is an interesting logical twist that, while manifesting great concern with stability of deterrence, Soviet writers at the same time have been attacking deterrence's fundamental legitimacy, claiming that any reliance on nuclear weapons as a basis for averting war is foolhardy, destabilizing, and cannot serve as a long-term basis for one's security.[36] Indeed, while the generic concept of nuclear deterrence has always been subject to intermittent attacks in the Soviet press, the intensity and even virulence of its recent bashing have been unprecedented. The following statement by Vladimir A. Nazarenko, Deputy Editor in the Department on Disarmament Problems of the Novosti Press Agency, well summarized Soviet views:

> The concept of "nuclear deterrence" is fallacious, dangerous, and immoral. It expresses the essence of militaristic intentions and embodies a myopic egotistic approach to the problem of national and international security. Nuclear deterrence means an unrestrained race for weapons and a chase for military supremacy, a permanent challenge to strategic stability, and perpetuation of international tensions, confrontation, and mistrust. Nuclear deterrence cannot do without the image of a "potential enemy," the ideology and psychology of antagonism and enmity, the subordination of policy to militarism and further militarization of thinking. Nuclear deterrence is urging others to acquire the most destructive weapons to attain a nuclear status, and to get a potential for threatening others. Nuclear deterrence leads to unpredictability and uncertainty. It is much like nuclear brinkmanship and only creates a semblance of security and very shaky peace. Relying on nuclear deterrence means relying on accident, accepting the risk of nuclear disaster which may happen not necessarily due to evil intentions, but as a result of a technical fault. Moreover, technical mishaps will become more and more likely with the further accumulation and sophistication of combat hardware.[37]

The Soviets also seem to discount the political value of nuclear forces. Specifically, they maintain that, as a result of various developments which took place over the last decade, the nuclear threshold is rising and NATO's ability and willingness to use nuclear weapons is increasingly doubtful. In fact, as Moscow well realizes, there are two interrelated trends underway; actual and symbolic denuclearization of western defense (with the latter running well-ahead of the former). All of this has led some Soviet analysts to conclude that "flexible responses" are not to be taken seriously and that something close to a "finite deterrence" has become the West's *de facto* strategy. To capitalize on these trends, the Soviets have been striving to convince the West of their intention to avoid nuclear escalation; an objective served by such Soviet public relations gambits as Brezhnev's June 1982 no-first-use pledge. Meanwhile, they hold that the Soviet's own military objectives can be best obtained on a conventional battlefield.

Yet, this reassessment of the political utility and strategic implications of nuclear weapons has not affected the operational level of Soviet nuclear weapons policy. Specifically, there is no evidence that the Soviet military is any less serious about nuclear warfighting options than it has been in the past. Soviet nuclear procurement continues unabated, and Soviet strategic forces have been steadily improving in quality, diversity, endurance, and flexibility. SRF appears to have lost its premier status among Soviet military services; yet, far from being a sign of Soviet neglect of nuclear warfighting, this change is attributable primarily to the Soviet decision to bolster their air breathing and naval nuclear forces. The end result is a more capable Soviet nuclear triad. Moscow also has accelerated investment in strategic defense, stockpiling thousands of BMD interceptors and radars and bolstering the infrastructure for a country-wide strategic defense system, and appears to strive to produce a more balanced offense/defense mix.

The conclusion that an apparent Soviet disillusionment with nuclear weapons has not been translated into an actual denuclearization of the Soviet military posture may strike one as paradoxical. After all, in the West, the views that nuclear weapons largely lack political utility and that nuclear war is likely to be suicidal have resulted in specific policy consequences. It is now virtually impossible to obtain funding or political support for any major ICBM modernization program in the United States or to deploy new American nuclear weapons on European soil. This, of course, is not the way things evolved in the East. The Soviet military remains convinced that, while nuclear escalation in an East-West war may be unlikely, it cannot be ruled out. It also notes the growth in Chinese and other third-country nuclear forces and the potential spread of nuclear weapons to the unstable Third World countries. And, last but not least, in the view of the Soviet military, nuclear weapons offer the best hedge against the possibility of conventional war gone awry. Overall, both the Soviet military and civilian leaders seem to feel that a robust nuclear posture offers a good insurance policy and is well worth the price for its upkeep.[38]

Gorbachev's New Defense Thinking

Not surprisingly, various changes in Soviet military thinking have not been adopted without resistance and debate pitting different segments of the Soviet military establishment against each other. For example, there is evidence that several key SRF commanders have fought against the diminution in the SRF's status and its subordination to the unified Soviet strategic nuclear forces. There also has been a vigorous debate, involving such senior Soviet naval officers as the late Admiral Sergei Gorshkov, then the Commander-in-Chief of the Soviet Navy, his close associate Admiral Stalbo, Admiral Chernavin, formerly Gorshkov's second in command and subsequently his replacement, and numerous others, over such subjects as the degree of naval autonomy in the Soviet military establishment and the navy's role in peacetime and war.[39]

The ground and air forces also have not been immune from disagreements, pitting, for example, Ogarkov and his supporters, who advocated primary reliance on new high-technology systems, and more "traditional" officers, represented by the late Defense Minister Ustinov, who argued in favor of retaining old and proven systems, while proceeding with the development of more advanced weapons. Despite these debates, there are broad areas of consensus over the new military doctrine in the Soviet military establishment, and a relative harmony has been the order of the day.

It is important to stress that most of the doctrinal innovations described above both precede Gorbachev's tenure and do not have much to do with Gorbachev's domestic and economic reforms. This is not to suggest, however, that Gorbachev has made no changes in the Soviet military arena. Such changes certainly exist. What is still unclear, however, is how substantial or durable they are and how they will mesh with the doctrinal innovations undertaken by the professional Soviet military.

To begin with, Gorbachev has made efforts to introduce glasnost in the discussion of military affairs, of which his recitation of defense budget figures at the inaugural session of the Congress of People's Deputies is a key example.[40] This trend has resulted in some reduction in military secrecy and more frequent and open discussions of national security matters and problems in the media. For example, a recent string of Soviet submarine mishaps has been reported in the Soviet press, complete with critical accounts of existing Soviet safety procedures. There has even been a barrage of articles about deficiencies in Soviet officer training and exercises. In contrast to past accounts, these articles suggest that the entire system is flawed. New light has been also shed on past Soviet military operations, including the official acknowledgement of Soviet combat involvement in Korea, Vietnam, and the Middle East.

Gorbachev also appears intent on reshuffling the top military leadership and on changing organizational arrangements for developing Soviet military policy. The personnel changes alone are sweeping indeed. Since assuming power, Gorbachev has replaced eight out of sixteen military district commanders, three out of five commanders of military services, eleven out of sixteen deputy ministers of defense, including former Soviet Defense Minister Sergei Sokolov and former Chief of the Soviet General Staff Marshal Ogarkov, and retired the Chief of the Soviet General Staff Akhromeev in December 1988. The Commander-in-Chief of the WTO, Marshal Viktor Kulikov, was replaced by Petr Lushev, formerly the Commander of Soviet forces in Germany. Most of the newly promoted officers are reputed to be strong supporters of Gorbachev and his policies. There are also rumors that Defense Minister Yazov may be replaced by a civilian official.

Meanwhile, Gorbachev took some symbolic steps to deemphasize the military's institutional importance by denying both of his defense ministers (Sokolov and Yazov) a full membership in the Politburo. Gorbachev also chose not to promote in rank any of the individuals he elevated to the positions of the Defense Minister or Chief of the General Staff. This represents a notable break with the past practice. Messrs. Ustinov, Sokolov, Ogarkov, and Akhromeev were all Marshals of the Soviet Union. In fact, Akhromeev was promoted to the rank of Marshal in March of 1983, nearly a year before he replaced Ogarkov as the head of the General Staff. Yet, neither Defense Minister Yazov nor Chief of the General Staff Mikhail Moiseev were given the rank of Marshal of the Soviet Union. In fact, the last time anybody was promoted to that level of military hierarchy preceded Gorbachev's tenure,[41] and, following the retirement of Viktor Kulikov, there are no more Marshals left on active duty. Other signs of the relative decline in the military's standing within the Soviet hierarchy are the virtual absence of high ranking military officers at important public functions and the decrease in the military representation in the Central Committee and other key party and state bodies.

Not content only with promoting these military leaders willing to support him,[42] Gorbachev has opted to increase the influence of the Central Committee and the research institutes of the Soviet Academy of Sciences in analyzing military matters. For example, the Central Committee has acquired new arms control staffers,[43] and additional military experts have been placed on Gorbachev's personal staff. Meanwhile, Soviet research institutes have been publishing provocative articles on military issues that challenge many traditional elements of Soviet military doctrine. There also have been some discussions by senior Soviet party leaders, including Foreign Minister Shevarnadze, that military policy might become one of the issues to be reviewed periodically by the newly elected Soviet parliament. Indeed, a special committee to oversee the Ministry of Defense and the KGB has been established in the Supreme Soviet; it, however, is dominated by members of the military, the KGB, and defense industrialists. Overall, while the Soviet General Staff remains a key player in the formulation of Soviet military policies, it no longer enjoys a near total monopoly on military expertise. Gorbachev has also pressed the Soviet military to apply the concept of perestroika to military affairs, so as to eliminate waste and mismanagement and improve efficiency.

In addition to these organizational changes, Gorbachev has also introduced a number of new substantive concepts, collectively referred to as the "new thinking." According to Soviet writers, the inception of this new thinking dates back to the April 1985 Plenum of the Central Committee, and it was refined and elaborated during the 27th Party Congress in February 1986. The Soviets further claim that the new thinking has been translated into a new Soviet military doctrine, which has been worked out by the Main Defense Council during 1987-1988.

This new military doctrine, as enunciated by such Soviet notables as Gorbachev, former Chief of the General Staff Akhromeev, and Defense Minister Yazov, features such themes as reasonable sufficiency, defensive defense (also termed non-provocative defense), primacy of political means in guaranteeing one's security, emphasis on avoidance of war as the key objective of Soviet military policy,[44] and the proposition that war, whether conventional or nuclear, is no longer a viable instrument of policy. The revised Soviet military doctrine is connected with a number of new declaratory themes in Soviet foreign policy, such as the stress on the mutuality of security, the declaration that the Soviets no longer view international relations as a form of class struggle or believe that capitalism is about to perish in the foreseeable future, the assertion that the competition between East and West must take more civilized and benign forms, and the claim that Moscow has altered its erstwhile assessment of the West as being implacably hostile to the Soviet Union and relentlessly aggressive.

Just as in the case of many doctrinal innovations developed by the Soviet military, certain tenets of Gorbachev's new thinking are not entirely new. For example, the war avoidance theme can be traced as far back as Stalin's succession and the Malenkov-Khrushchev struggle in the mid-1950s, when both Malenkov and Khrushchev revised the erstwhile Soviet doctrine and claimed that a military conflict with the West was not fatalistically inevitable. This change was attributable to the "sobering" impact of Soviet nuclear forces on the imperialists. From that time on, Soviet writings have invariably mentioned that the Soviet military might was the key guarantee of preserving peace. The following 1965 statement by Brezhnev offers a perfect illustration of this sentiment: "History has taught us that the stronger our armed forces are, the more watchful we are, the stronger the peace of our frontiers."[45] Thus, Gorbachev's innovation in this area is, at most, a matter of emphasis or a rephrasing of a rather traditional doctrinal theme.

The Soviet admission that capitalism is likely to survive indefinitely and that an outright confrontational policy is likely to harm Soviet interests is also rather unremarkable. It is not only a matter of common sense but is something that has been conceded privately by numerous Soviet officials at least over the last several years. To be sure, the fact that now these sentiments are aired publicly is important; it is not, however, as earth-shattering as some Sovietologists would have us believe.

The Evolution of New Soviet Military Doctrine: Tensions and Debates

While perfect harmony has never attended the promulgation of major doctrinal innovations in the Soviet Union, the degree of tensions in general and the conflict between the Soviet political leaders and the military in particular should not be overestimated.

How Much Is Enough?

Defense spending discussions are the regular fixture of civil-military debates in numerous countries, and Moscow is no exception to this general rule. Soviet civilian analysts, while applauding Gorbachev's announced intent to cut the defense budget by 15 percent and Prime Minister Ryzhkov's claim that 33 percent savings might be possible, have been advocating even deeper cuts. Alexei Arbatov, for example, argues that "by cutting the number of changes in weapons designs and implementing competitive bidding, vigorous cost accounting and penalties for design ministries that go over budget" the Soviet defense budget can be cut by up to 50 percent.[46] Not surprisingly, the Soviet military does not evidence quite as much enthusiasm as civilians about budget cutting. Yet, even they acknowledge that the Soviet military establishment lags far behind in the pace of adaptation to changed economic circumstances and Gorbachev's reforms. In fact, Soviet military leaders themselves have occasionally decried the difficulties involved in implementing Gorbachev's doctrinal innovations, acknowledged past doctrinal errors, and promised to do better in the future. As the former Chief of the Soviet General Staff, Marshal of the Soviet Union Akhromeev, noted in a December 6, 1988, article:

> The new thinking is not penetrating Army and Navy life easily: the outdated, stereotyped cliches are still exerting their influence. In the past, we were often guided by ideas which, in the long run, were by no means the best....Ideas which sometimes involved us in the arms race. The General Staff is aware of the need to adopt a new approach in assessing existing balance of forces. Errors in evaluating the likely nature of aggression and in forecasting the possible results of such an aggression are always dangerous and, especially given the defensive nature of our strategy, may entail serious consequences. The General Staff has the task of ensuring that

this work is of the necessary standard, which makes it possible to make strategic forecasts confidently.[47]

All said and done, the intensity of the present budgetary disagreements should not be exaggerated. The Soviet military is prepared to live with resource constraints, as evidenced by its apparent willingness to cut back on troop training, use of live ammunition, naval out-of-area deployments, and other readiness accounts. It knows well that the Soviet economy is a mess and that, without major economic reforms, the Soviet Union would not be able to support a first-class military establishment in the 21st century. Thus, the claim, often made by Western analysts, that the Soviet military is looking back fondly at the period of Brezhnev's rule as the "golden age" of plentiful resources and institutional autonomy is difficult to accept, since the military knows that, at the end of the day, Brezhnev's policies resulted in economic collapse at home and revitalized Western opposition abroad.

It is also significant that, in the past, the Soviet military was willing to postpone the maximization of immediately available combat power in order to lay a better foundation for the subsequent build-up. This conduct, for example, was evident during the 1920s. As described by Odom:

> The standing Red Army was reduced to about half a million soldiers in active units backed by a large militia force: a policy designed to save manpower in peace time. The Red Army became a school for literacy. Officer education became a top priority....In active combat power, the Red Army was allowed to become quite weak. A foreign observer might have concluded that the Soviet regime was quietly disarming itself, a view that would have been misleading about Soviet military policy....In reality, the Bolshevik leaders were taking a short-term risk in order to have a large, modern military force in the future.[48]

The Soviet military leaders now also acknowledge that major defense cuts can be implemented without jeopardizing Soviet security, provided the quality of remaining forces is improved and suitable doctrinal, operational, and technological adjustments are made. In that regard, as posited by Akhromeev:

> The defense orientation in the structure of the Armed Forces is combined with the new means of maintaining military potential at a level that guarantees our country's reliable security under the conditions of the possible reductions of both nuclear and conventional weapons. Under these circumstances, the combat effectiveness and quality of the arms and military equipment deployed in the Army and Navy assume decisive importance, since they permit us to cope with our military task with a smaller range of military weapons and equipment.[49]

Meanwhile, high-ranking Soviet military officers stress that the General Staff has worked out plans on how to maintain Soviet defense posture in the aftermath of budgetary cutbacks. This is not to say that the military would agree to weakening unduly Soviet military posture or would sign on to any level of defense expenditures: The Soviet officers probably feel that there is a certain minimum level of defense spending that is necessary to guarantee Soviet security. In the past, when they felt that their needs were not being met, the Soviet military officers did not hesitate to bring in a forceful manner this fact to the attention of the Party leaders. This, for example, was the case during the extraordinary October 27, 1982, meeting between Brezhnev and top Soviet marshals, where the military reportedly complained about economic stagnation and a resulting slowing down of the annual growth in defense expenditures. More recently, when a number of civilian analysts advocated deep cuts (50 percent) in Soviet defense spending, Soviet military leaders forcefully reminded the new thinkers that unilateral cutbacks in military spending and force levels cannot go beyond a certain point, without endangering Soviet security.

For example, responding to an article by well-known Soviet civilian analyst Vitalii Zhurkin, who argued in favor of deep unilateral force cuts, Soviet Air Defense Chief General Ivan Tretiak registered strong objections, noting that Khrushchev's 1960s reductions in conventional forces gravely weakened Soviet combat capabilities. There also are numerous indications in the Soviet press that Gorbachev's planned troop cuts (announced in December 1988) and subsequent arms control schemes to reduce further the size of Soviet ground and air forces have provoked great anxiety among the Soviet officer corps, many of whom stand to lose their jobs in the process.[50] Efforts, however, are being made to reassure the Soviet officers that the negative aspects of the 1960s force cuts would not be repeated and that even those who would have to retire would not forfeit their access to special housing and other material perks.

Another subject, closely tied with troop cuts, is the issue of conscription. Presently, some Soviet civilian analysts argue in favor of shortening the present two-year term (three years in the Navy) of compulsory military service and even abolishing the draft altogether in favor of an all-volunteer army backed by militia/reserve forces. Not surprisingly, the military fiercely opposes this idea. It was, however, willing to restore deferment of military service for fulltime students[51] and streamline the present system of compulsory military instruction offered in institutions of higher learning. Overall, while the issues of defense spending and force sizing provoke considerable concern among Soviet officers, there is no evidence of strong opposition to Gorbachev's policies. Moreover, Gorbachev does not appear intent on instituting debilitating cuts in either Soviet defense expenditures or forces, and, as long as the Soviet military feels that Gorbachev's economic reforms are likely to succeed in the long run, it can be expected to support his defense funding decisions.

Professional Autonomy and Threat Assessment

The military also undoubtedly appreciates the advantages of Gorbachev's new astute foreign policy, which promises to weaken defense consensus in the West and result in diminished Western defense efforts. Nor is it a forlorn hope. As observed by Richard Nixon, "For many in Europe and the United States, the fear of the Soviet Union has waned, and what love may exist between economic competitors in the West is a very weak glue to hold an alliance together." In Akhromeev words, "Certain influential circles in the West are more realistic now in evaluating the situation in the Soviet Union and within its Armed Forces, as well as the disastrous consequences which the arms race may produce for world peace."[52] In fact, the military itself has been perfectly prepared to partake in Gorbachev's diplomatic *tour de force*, as evidenced by new accessibility of Soviet military leaders to Western reporters and Akhromeev's July 1988 U.S. visit. Last but not least, the military, as an institution, as distinct from certain elements of the party and state bureaucracy, is not threatened by Gorbachev's stated intention to restructure the Soviet society and state. Overall, it appears that the Soviet military has given their conditional blessing to Gorbachev and his reforms.

This consensus, however, is predicated upon its assumption that Gorbachev does not intend to micromanage Soviet military thought. In essence, the Soviet military is prepared to live with temporary resource constraints and to accommodate itself to Gorbachev's arms control proposals, so long as it is able to retain its professional autonomy. To be sure, numerous civilian "new thinkers" appear to want to enhance civilian control over the military-technical aspects of Soviet military thinking, arguing that, in today's world, such issues exert profound influence on political relations among states and international stability. It does not appear, however, that Gorbachev is prepared to go that far. In fact, it is far more likely that he has been using the prospect of greater involvement by the civilian research institutes in military affairs and some of the more radical ideas developed by them as a leverage to induce military support for his own "middle of the road" position. Moreover, as a practical matter, while Soviet civilians may be able to offer some competing advice on nuclear matters, it is difficult to imagine them developing independent expertise in such areas as naval or conventional forces. Not surprisingly, so far, the professional quality of analysis of conventional force issues performed by Soviet *institutchiki* has been mediocre.

Moreover, in contrast to Khrushchev, Gorbachev does not appear interested in unduly hampering the promulgation of Soviet military thought. In fact, it appears that Gorbachev has not even developed a coherent and comprehensive set of views on military matters; rather, his doctrinal innovations are coming out piecemeal and are largely driven by the imperatives of his economic and political reforms. Thus, for example, the notions of reasonable sufficiency and defensive defense, as articulated by civilian writers, seem to be conceived primarily as devices to justify constraints on defense resource allocations and project a favorable "public relations" impression, rather than as serious military conceptual constructs. Gorbachev also has been frank in linking his defense cuts announced in a December 1988 U.N. speech to the need to reduce budget deficits and channel more resources into the civilian sector. This, however, does not necessarily bother the Soviet military. Thus, while a clear-cut Gorbachev failure, manifested either by an economic collapse or by widespread unrest in the Soviet Union and requiring the use of force to put it down, is likely to strain Gorbachev's relations with his marshals, for the time being, the military's support for him is likely to remain strong.

Despite this relative harmony, there are multiple ongoing disagreements and debates over various Soviet military issues. These debates are difficult to interpret; gone are the relatively simple days of "red hawks" and "red doves." Instead, there is a variety of pronouncements emanating from numerous civilian, military, and party sources, making it difficult to assess how authoritative they really are. The problem is complicated by the fact that the advent of glasnost has contributed to the diversity of Soviet opinions on security issues, resulting in the public elaboration of such unusual stances as the rejection of not only first nuclear use, but even of the second nuclear retaliatory strike and the arguments that the awesome destructive power of nuclear weapons renders the very notion of war inapplicable to situations in which nuclear weapons would be used. Hence, some Soviet writers are now referring to the concept of nuclear catastrophe, rather than nuclear war. Meanwhile, other Soviet analysts have been advocating such unorthodox notions as the elimination of all tanks by the WTO and NATO as a way to establish stable military balance in Europe[53] and the replacement of the present Soviet military structure with a small professional army, backed up by a militia system.[54] Not surprisingly, the Soviet military vehemently attacks such doctrinal heresies, leading some Western analysts to believe that serious debates over these matters are going on. In reality, however, the advocacy by some Soviet civilians of radical notions and vigorous rebuttals of them by the military do not amount to a debate. These are mostly rhetorical flashes in the pan.

There are, however, several specific areas in which some tension between Soviet civilians and military leaders is presently evident and may grow further in the future. The three major areas of possible substantive civil-military disagreements include the concepts of reasonable sufficiency, defensive defense, and relationship between political/arms control measures and military requirements. In fact, the resolution of disputes with regard to these three key issues would largely determine the thrust of Soviet military doctrine and strategy in the 1990s and beyond.

How Reasonable Is Reasonable Sufficiency?

According to the new Soviet military doctrine, reasonable sufficiency constitutes the conceptual basis for Soviet military development. Moreover, it was officially adopted as such by all WTO countries during the May 1987 WTO meeting. Still, the concept of reasonable sufficiency, while universally praised and mentioned in virtually every Soviet statement, is rather vague and has been given different definitions.

The civilian writers have been claiming that reasonable sufficiency means that the Soviet Union should not let the United States set rules of the military competition and that Moscow does not require military forces capable of neutralizing all of its potential adversaries. In contrast, the military has been equating reasonable sufficiency (or the defensive sufficiency as it prefers to refer to this concept) with the maintenance of overall military parity between the Soviet Union and the West, noting that Western threat levels determine the extent of Soviet force deployments, and has been stressing the danger of falling behind in military capabilities. Soviet military writers also evidence lesser exuberance than the *institutchiki* in describing international developments, noting that NATO and the United States continue their "militaristic" policies and arguing that the combat readiness of Soviet Armed Forces should not be allowed to suffer while troop cuts take place.[55] Open attacks on Gorbachev's policies these statements are not. However, they clearly manifest a somewhat different perspective on the issue of reasonable sufficiency than most civilian pronouncements.

Defense That Defends?

With regard to defensive defense, another key component of the new Soviet military doctrine, the civilian writers have been struggling to develop theoretical notions of a military force, capable of defending Soviet territory but incapable of going over on the offensive and seizing enemy territory. Seeking to establish historical legitimacy for their policy preferences, two senior Soviet civilian researchers, A. Kokoshin and V. Larionov, argued in a 1987 article that the key event of the Second World War, the battle of Kursk, proves the ability of a well-prepared defense to parry any offensive thrust.[56] This interpretation of events at Kursk, however, suffers from an overdose of historical revisionism, insofar as it conveniently overlooks the fact that the Germans were defeated in that battle only after a powerful Soviet counteroffensive and not as a result of defensive operations alone. Some scholars also point out that, historically, there has been a strain of Russian military thought that emphasizes defense as the preferred method of military operations. As described by Bruce Slawter, while military academics associated with the Russian General Staff "lobbied for increased modernization using European technological and organizational norms as models, advocates of the nationalist school supported the continued reliance on traditional Russian moral strengths and Kutuzov-style defensive concepts. In a sense, the nationalists won out in determining Russia's order of battle upon entry into World War I."[57] The fact that in the past defense has fascinated Russian military theorists does not, however, support an inference that a purely defensive posture is about to be adopted by Moscow. Nor for that matter is that fact unique; interest in defense can be found in military writings of almost any country, including those which clearly espouse offensive strategy.

Defensive defense fantasies are also supported by Western scholars, who argue that Moscow has fundamentally altered its military objectives in a potential East-West conflict. The most well-known of such analysts is Michael MccGwire, who pioneered the notion that, in the mid-1980s, the Soviets concluded that an East-West conflict in Eurasia would be a *limited one* and that escalation to a global war can be averted. The former Soviet doctrinal requirements, established according to MccGwire in 1964, called for avoiding nuclear escalation but were based on the assumption that an East-West conflict would be global and protracted in nature. To prevail in such a conflict, Moscow had to seize Western Europe, both to exploit its industrial riches and to prevent the U.S. from maintaining a bridgehead on the continent, from which a subsequent invasion of Russia could be mounted. Given its present limited war expectations, Moscow allegedly does not need an ability to mount an invasion of Western Europe.[58]

This theory has a certain intellectual elegance; yet upon closer scrutiny, it turns out to be a strategic chimera. To begin with, there is no compelling evidence even in Soviet writings, much less in the Soviet's force posture, that they consider global East-West conflict to be a contingency not worth hedging against. There is evidence, of course, of the Soviet belief that some types of East-West confrontation *may, but only may,* remain conventional. The Soviets are not certain and cannot possibly be certain that escalation can be averted. Moreover, even if one assumes *arguendo* that the Soviet estimation of the relative probabilities of non-escalation and escalation have recently changed, as MccGwire argues, to conclude from this that Moscow is now prepared to give up for nothing its formidable warfighting options in Europe requires a fertile imagination.

And, given the Soviet's concern about the reliability of their WTO allies and the stability of their empire proper, it is difficult to believe that the Soviet General Staff or the Politburo would view the notion of a limited and possibly indeterminate clash with NATO with much confidence. In fact, one of the most realistic Soviet scenarios for an invasion of Western Europe has always been one of some East European conflagration getting out of hand.

Nor, for that matter, does the version of defensive force posture put forth by Soviet propagandists make sense from a simple military-technical standpoint or even one totally unburdened by Soviet ideology and experience. Any military organization capable of engaging successfully, without the benefit of relying on prohibitive terrain or extensive barrier defenses, a large, well-equipped enemy force in a defensive battle is also inherently capable of mounting a strong offensive. The variables, if any, are how rapidly such an offensive can be launched and its spatial scope. In fact, on the tactical and even operational levels of contemporary maneuver combat, offensive and defensive operations, while not quite twins, look very much alike. In short, the notion that the Soviets may adopt an entirely non-offensive defense suffers from one fatal flaw: it is based on a profound ignorance of realities of war.

Furthermore, the notion of pure defense, its conceptual merits aside, is very much an anathema to the entire post-World War II thrust of Soviet military planning. To be sure, the Soviet military is prepared to eliminate some of its present capabilities for a *blitzkrieg*-style war against NATO. It may even feel that a more balanced posture, featuring a better mix of offensive and defensive options and capable of defeating NATO in a matter of weeks[59] rather than days, is more sound from a military technical standpoint and more likely to lull the West into a false sense of security. Certainly, the Soviet military leaders are prepared to acknowledge that an exclusive preoccupation with planning of solely offensive operations is foolhardy and contributed to major Soviet defeats in the beginning phase of World War II.

Yet, in contrast to civilian writers, the Soviet military stresses that, for a variety of technical, strategic, and historical reasons, offense is an indispensable component of military operations and that defense alone is insufficient to reliably protect Soviet security. They also point out that it is impossible even to conceive a purely defensive force posture. It is unclear how these two contrasting versions of defensive defense can be reconciled.

Arms Control and Soviet Defense Policy: An Uneasy Synthesis

Last but not least, there is the issue of the relationship between arms control and unilateral Soviet military efforts. As far as Gorbachev is concerned, arms control, in addition to scaling down the security threats facing Moscow and bolstering Soviet foreign policy, also serves as a useful tool for constraining defense resource demands. This view is not necessarily shared by the Soviet military. Yet, despite some differences in conceptual approaches, so far, the Soviet military has been strongly supportive of Gorbachev's arms control policies. It understands just as well as Gorbachev the value of "soothing" Western public opinion and decision-makers and frankly acknowledges that such past Soviet decisions as the SS-20 deployment were a mistake, insofar as they failed to take into account Western reactions.

In all encounters with their American counterparts, such senior Soviet military leaders as Defense Minister Yazov and former Chief of the General Staff Akhromeev have been emphasizing the fact that they are prepared to take steps to alleviate the oft-stated U.S. concerns about particular facets of Soviet military posture. In return, however, they expect a similar treatment, that is, "if we humor you, you should be prepared to humor us." (You want our tanks, we want your aircraft.) The Soviet military also indicates that the process of restructuring Soviet military forces, ostensibly to comply with the requirements of the new military doctrine, would be a long process and would require major U.S. concessions. In contrast, Soviet civilian writers seem to emphasize faster and more unilateral Soviet actions. So far, however, the tension between these two positions is largely theoretical.

The INF Treaty, the pending START deal, the Soviet position on strategic defense, and Soviet proposals for conventional arms control are not only good public relations gambits, they also are fully congruent with Soviet military policies. Thus, for example, the INF Treaty has accomplished a longstanding Soviet objective of denying NATO viable options of attacking Soviet territory with nuclear weapons without resorting to the use of central strategic systems and has contributed to the overall denuclearization of European defense. The importance of this development is readily apparent to Soviet planners; they know only too well that nuclear weapons are the ultimate glue that has held the NATO alliance together and ensured the viability of the two key postulates of the post-World War II American military planning: forward basing of U.S. troops and coalition strategy. Ironically, it is precisely this tremendous destructive power of nuclear weapons that, for the first time in history, largely negated the importance of geographical distance, making the population of the continental United States as potentially vulnerable as the population of Europe. This resulted in the equality in risk-sharing, which is the flip-side of coupling; without it American alliances would amount to unilateral and risky guarantees. Nuclear weapons also have played a key role in providing much-needed deterrence of NATO enemies and reassurance of NATO members, as well as performed a key potential warfighting function: holding Soviet maneuver battalions at bay. Even if nuclear weapons were not actually used in a conflict, simply forcing the Soviets to fight in a "nuclear scare" mode would greatly ease the task of NATO conventional defense.

Even more fundamentally, nuclear weapons have served as the ultimate power projection tool enabling a maritime power, like the United States, to hold the lands of Eurasia against the pressure of a heartland power: the USSR. The change in this situation has always been a Soviet strategic objective and remains a *leitmotif* of Gorbachev's policy. In that, the Soviets are greatly encouraged by the fact that the Europeans seemingly no longer wish to live on a continent dense with nuclear weapons; they have lost their zest for coupling, and they want the removal of most of the U.S. troops and nuclear weapons. The seeming assumption that underlies this semi-strategic calculus is that Gorbachev can be readily tamed with economic aid and technology transfers and that U.S. central strategic forces, even in the aftermath of arms control inspired deep cuts, can provide enough of a deterrent of Soviet aggression. The net result is that the West seems to be moving away from a traditional concept of deterrence that leaves something to chance toward a deterrence that leaves a lot to chance.

Not surprisingly, taking advantage of these perceived trends has been the highest Soviet priority. It is not by accident that Gorbachev used Secretary of State Baker's May 1989 visit to Moscow as an opportunity not only to announce his conventional force reductions proposals, but also to outline the Soviet plan to retire unilaterally some 500 warheads from its inventory of short-range nuclear forces in Europe. Given the fact that Moscow has nearly 10,000 such warheads in Europe, including 3,000 missiles on 1,400 launchers, the reductions involved are minuscule indeed. Yet, what matters at this juncture is the symbolism involved.

The Soviets already succeeded in derailing, perhaps irreversibly, the Lance modernization, and chances that Germany would agree to accept any new nuclear weapons on its soil are rather slim. And the prospects of a totally denuclearized Germany are no longer just the gleam in the eye of the Politburo; they are very real indeed. Meanwhile, the inclusion of aircraft in conventional arms control talks is bound to produce major strains in the alliance over the question of the British and French dual-capable aircraft, all part and parcel of the long-standing Soviet objective to bring, even if only gradually, the British and French nuclear arsenals into the East-West arms control talks. The Soviets can be also expected to push their old standbys of nuclear free zones in Europe, as a first step toward the full denuclearization.[60] Most recently, the denuclearization theme was asserted in Gorbachev's July 6, 1989, Strasbourg speech to the European Parliament. The speech contained such carrots as "further deep cuts in Soviet conventional forces, the Soviet embrace of the concept of the common European home," the end of the Brezhnev doctrine, and even the implicit promise of Soviet disengagement from Eastern Europe; all, of course, contingent upon NATO's elimination of remaining short-range nuclear weapons. All in all, Gorbachev's astute diplomacy is directed at fulfilling a long-standing Soviet strategic objective and, to that extent, is overwhelmingly supported by the Soviet military.

Meanwhile, the Soviet negotiating position on SDI is also fully compatible with the Soviet objective of delaying and obstructing the U.S. strategic defense program, if not killing it outright. As described in a Soviet publication, Moscow's position in the Space and Defense Talks is as follows:

> Strengthening the ABM Treaty regime on the basis of assuring of a mutual obligation not to withdraw from the ABM Treaty for ten years, while strictly complying with all of its provisions; agreement regarding the boundary between activities, permitted and proscribed by the Treaty, by agreeing on the list of items which cannot be launched into space for any reason, including for research purposes; agreement regarding permissible research activities on earth.[61]

Meanwhile, in START, the kinds of reductions presently being envisioned (6,000 nuclear warheads and 1,600 strategic delivery vehicles) would not greatly interfere with the present Soviet nuclear weapons employment policy and might, in some respects, further shift the nuclear balance in Soviet favor. In particular, a START treaty may well increase the ratio of Soviet warheads to U.S. targets, a key determinant of strategic stability, and may lead to a virtual eradication of a U.S. capability to attack a vast array of hardened Soviet targets. And, just as has been the case in the past, the sins of START are certain to haunt the U.S. with a vengeance in looming START II. Specifically, further deep cuts in strategic forces without strategic defenses to pick up the slack (a reasonable supposition given the present state of SDI and related political attitudes) are certain to increase the importance of asymmetries in target arrays, long an area of Soviet advantage, and further worsen deterrence quality.

To be sure, reductions in strategic forces down to the numbers presently being discussed at a semi-official level by Soviet pundits (600-1,000 nuclear charges)[62] are bound to cause a drastic change in Soviet nuclear weapons policy. However, even assuming *arguendo* that such arms control musings find favor with the Soviet military, the implications of such a regime for Western security are not necessarily favorable. On the plus side, Moscow, with its strategic arsenals curtailed, would have to give up on targeting most economic, administrative and military targets in Eurasia and the United States. Arguably, under this approach, instead of trying to limit damage to the Soviet homeland through preemption, Moscow would have to rely on "virtual" damage limitation, based on arms control and strategic defenses. On the negative side, cuts in central strategic arsenals down to the level of several hundred warheads are bound to enshrine the process of denuclearization and, in the absence of large-scale strategic defense deployments and conventional forces augmentations, would make the world safe for Soviet conventional aggression.

A lot of Western commentators have argued that the Soviet military is bound to be unhappy about Gorbachev's concessions on verification measures. Yet, unless one assumes that the Soviet military is blindly obsessed with secrecy, it is unclear why it should object to trading improved verification measures for substantive arms control provisions it finds beneficial. In fact, the desirability of such a linkage has been acknowledged by a number of senior Soviet military leaders, including the Deputy Minister of Defense for Armaments, General Shabanov.

But what about Gorbachev's concepts for conventional arms control; concepts that, if implemented, would remove millions of men and dozens of thousands of tanks, armored vehicles, artillery tubes, and aircraft from the Soviet inventory? Surely, the Soviet General Staff must be extremely unhappy about such sizeable cutbacks in the Soviet military muscle. This supposition, however, while plausible, ignores the profound changes in the Soviet military's thinking about European war, threat assessment, and, last but not least, about the impact of resource constraints on defense posture.

On paper, Gorbachev's conventional force concepts and proposals look impressive enough. To begin with, in December 1988, Gorbachev announced his intent to pull out 50,000 troops from Eastern Europe, remove six tank divisions and 3,000 additional tanks from the area, and cut the size of the Soviet Armed Forces by some 500,000 men. Significantly, this unilateral initiative appeared to respond, in part, to NATO's oft-stated concerns about the Soviet standing-start attack capability. Specifically, Moscow indicated that among the troops being withdrawn were a number, albeit unspecified, of specialized assault and engineering units crucial to the success of any Soviet *blitzkrieg*. Furthermore, according to Major-General Valentin V. Larionov (retired and now at the Institute of U.S.A. and Canada), four out of six tank divisions being withdrawn would come from the OMGs based in Eastern Europe.

The Soviet unilateral troop withdrawals are not limited to Europe. In May of 1989, Moscow indicated its intent to pull out two divisions from Mongolia. Eventually, up to 75 percent of 50,000 Soviet troops stationed in Mongolia are to leave.[63]

Following on the heels of his December 1988 unilateral initiatives, Gorbachev unraveled even more sweeping conventional arms control proposals. These were originally unveiled during Secretary Baker's May 1989 trip to Moscow and amplified in the weeks and months that followed. Moscow proposed major cuts in military forces stationed in and around Western Europe. Specifically, it suggested the following overall force ceilings for NATO and WTO: 1,350,000 troops, 1,500 attack aircraft, 1,700 helicopter gunships, 20,000 tanks, 24,000 artillery tubes, and 28,000 armored vehicles. The Soviets further indicated their intent to satisfy NATO's long-standing request that constraints be imposed on troops and weapon systems to be maintained by any single member of the two alliances; agreeing, in effect, to impose separate limits on Soviet forces. Specifically, under this proposal, the Soviet forces cannot exceed 920,000 troops, 1,200 attack aircraft, 1,350 helicopter gunships, 14,000 tanks, 17,000 artillery pieces, and 18,000 armored vehicles.

Additional limitations are also being envisioned for the troops and equipment stationed by any one alliance member in the territory of another; in effect, establishing limits for Soviet forces in Eastern Europe. These include 350,000 troops, 250 attack planes, 600 helicopter gunships, 4,500 tanks, 4,000 pieces of artillery, and 7,500 armored vehicles.

At the first glance, the implications of Soviet proposals seem monumental; Moscow is considering retiring additional (above and beyond its December 1988 plan) hundreds of thousands of soldiers and dozens of thousands of tanks, artillery pieces, aircraft, and helicopters from its inventory. The end result seems to be a genuine numerical parity between NATO and Warsaw Pact, albeit at greatly reduced force levels. And even more radical schemes are being propounded. Moscow has repeatedly called for the eventual dissolution of the opposing alliances in Europe, for the establishment of additional geographic limitations on troop deployments in Europe, and, last but not least, for the creation of the special "zones of reduced level of armaments."

To be fair, one must acknowledge that, in many key respects, the Soviet proposals are rather close to NATO's own arms control schemes, at least as far as the air and ground force equipment is concerned. NATO, for its part, agreed to modify its erstwhile stance by accepting two key Soviet demands: that reductions include troops (i.e., manpower) and aircraft. Herein, however, lies the first major problem. Soviet proposals on how to limit aircraft have been extremely one-sided. Specifically, they have sought to exclude from limitation thousands of Soviet air-defense aircraft, skewing the tally in their favor. The ostensible reason for this approach, as enunciated by the Soviet Deputy Minister of Foreign Affairs Victor Karpov, is that interceptor aircraft are allegedly strictly defensive weapons and "there is a common understanding that it is offensive systems insuring a surprise attack capability that should by reduced."[64] This casuistry does not bode well for the future.

The issue of aircraft aside, the problems with the Soviet proposal and the kind of arms control regime it envisions, remain fundamental. To begin with, verification requirements associated with conventional reductions being proposed are daunting and may be even insurmountable. This implies that we have to place much trust in the alleged Soviet moderation and their embrace of the rule of law. Yet, both of these offer a shaky foundation for Western security. The problem is complicated by the fact that any evidence of Soviet cheating is bound to be highly technical and uncertain. Thus, Fred Ikle's famous "sixty-four thousand dollar" question of arms control: "after detection, what?" is likely to be answered in the case of conventional arms in Europe: "nothing."

Even more fundamentally, the problem is that, even if no cheating occurs, the spectre of Soviet conventional superiority in Europe has dominated the minds of NATO decision-makers for so long that we tend to forget a fundamental maxim of military art: even perfectly matched forces do not ensure stability and do not avert the possibility of a decisive defeat of one side by another. The Soviet proposals certainly do not remove a possibility of a decisive defeat of NATO by the WTO, albeit after a period of weeks rather than days. This, however, should offer scant comfort to NATO.

The Soviets also indicate a strong interest in using the conventional arms control process to curtail U.S. naval operations and forces and reduce forward deployed U.S. airpower. An equally strong Soviet desire is to constrain large-scale NATO exercises.

In exchange, the Soviets appear willing to eliminate some of their armor, "thin out" their forward deployed units in Europe, and reduce their capabilities for prompt initiation of large-scale offensive operations. Yet, these changes, even if all faithfully implemented, would still leave Moscow with an ability to launch an offensive against NATO within two and three weeks from the day of the outbreak of conflict, while reducing precisely those NATO assets (air and naval power) that can be used to slow down Soviet mobilization and secure the arrival of U.S. reinforcements. Thus, the net impact of the present Soviet conventional arms control proposals is highly advantageous to the Soviet Union. Consequently, despite oft-repeated Western speculations about the Soviet military's opposition to Gorbachev's arms control schemes, harmony appears to reign between Soviet security requirements, as defined by the military, and Soviet political and foreign policy imperatives, as enunciated by Gorbachev.

Whether or not this harmony will last depends, to a large extent, on Western actions. Should the U.S. and NATO clearly outline proposals which seriously cut into Soviet nuclear and conventional muscle and hold firm at the negotiating table, the Soviet leaders might have to face a choice between military and political requirements. Indeed, it is conceivable to envision cuts in Soviet nuclear arsenals which go beyond the present START guidelines or some conventional arms control regimes which would give pause to the Soviet military. If and when the Soviet civilian leaders decide to embrace them, there is likely to be a major debate over whether alleged political benefits of such agreements outweigh the military risks. There are no indications at present, though, that anything of this nature is in the offing.

Conclusion

The end result of the new ongoing revolution in Soviet military affairs is far from clear. Many specific issues remain unresolved, and there are a number of conflicting and contradictory trends in Soviet doctrinal developments. Not surprisingly, we have witnessed a number of debates involving various elements of the Soviet military establishment and pitting, in some instances, Soviet military leaders against each other. Extrapolating from all the evidence available at this time, however, it is likely that the relative harmony between the Soviet military and party leaders would be maintained and that the new Soviet military doctrine and policy would produce more capable and sophisticated Soviet military forces.

Notes

[1]The opinions contained within this chapter are those of the authors and do not necessarily represent the views of the U.S. government.

[2]General Wolfgang Hefenburg, "Arms Control and the Needs of NATO Armed Forces," *RUSI*, Autumn 1988, p. 11.

[3]William E. Odom, "Soviet Force Posture: Dilemmas and Directions," *Problems of Communism*, July-August 1985, p. 1.

[4]See, for example, Dimitri Volkogonov, et al., *Marksistsko-Leninskogo uchenie o voine i armii*, (Moscow: Voenizdat, 1984).

[5]Odom, *op. cit.*, p. 5.

[6]Significantly, the Soviet writers claim that technology has always been a major driver of military innovation and that technological changes often caused dramatic shifts in military balance. See, for example, G. Kochetkov, V. Sergeev, "Iskustveni intellect i problemi strategicheskoi stabil'nosti," *MEMO*, September 1987, p. 71. This view also has been expressed by Engels. See *Izbranie voennie proizvedeniia*, (Moscow, 1956), pp. 17-18.

[7]Kochetkov, *op. cit.*, p. 72.

[8]Soviet writings posit that the level of armaments adopted by states is "a direct consequence of corresponding policies and political relations among them." Accordingly, in their view, Western policies toward the Soviets form the basis for NATO defense efforts and have to be considered carefully. See E. Pozdiakov, "Vzaimosviaz ekonomiki i politiki v mezhdugosudarsvennykh otnoshenie," *MEMO*, October 1987, p. 32.

[9]For a useful discussion of the Soviet assessment of SDI, see David B. Rivkin, Jr., "What Does Moscow Think?" *Foreign Policy*, Summer 1985; Stephen M. Meyer, "Soviet Views on SDI," *Survival*, November-December 1985.

[10]V. Petrovski, "Doverie i vizhivanie chelovechestva," *MEMO*, November 1987, pp. 15-16.

[11]See, for example, V.D. Sokolovski, (ed.), *Voennaia strategiia*, Second Edition, (Moscow: Voenizdat, 1962).

[12]Kochetkov, *op. cit.*, p. 71.

[13]See, for example, Robert P. Berman and John C. Baker, *Soviet Strategic Forces: Requirements and Responses*, (Washington, D.C.: Brookings Institution, 1982).

[14]See, for example, M. Shirokov, "Voennaia geographii na sovremenon etape," *Voennaia Mysl'*, November 1966.

[15]See, for example, Raymond Garthoff, *The Soviet Image of Future War*, (Washington, D.C.: Public Affairs Press, 1959); Peter H. Vigor, *The Soviet View of War, Peace, and Neutrality*, (London: Routledge Press, 1975).

[16]Michael MccGwire, *Military Objectives in Soviet Foreign Policy*, (Washington, D.C.: Brookings Institution, 1987), p. 29.

[17]*Ibid*, pp. 29-30.

[18]For a comprehensive critique of MccGwire's thesis, see Christoph Bluth, "The Evolution of Soviet Military Doctrine," *Survival*, March-April 1988, pp. 149-161.

[19]See, for example, V.D. Sokolovski, (ed.), *Sovetskaia voennaia strategiia*, Third Edition, (Moscow: Voenizdat, 1968).

[20]See, for example, Vitalii I. Zemskov, "Characteristic Features of Modern Wars and Possible Methods of Waging Them," *Voennaia Mysl'*, July 1968.

[21]See, for example, David B. Rivkin, Jr., "Evolving Soviet Approaches to Arms Control: Continuity and Change," *Survival*, October-November, 1987.

[22]It should be noted that this process generated some controversy and became entangled with a power struggle leading to Khrushchev's ouster and the subsequent struggle for control among the members of the Politburo troika: Brezhnev, Kosygin, and Podgorny. Specifically, Khrushchev appeared fixated on his heavily nuclear "new look" policy, originally announced in 1960, and was hostile to the idea of investing in conventional options, a view highlighted by his 1964 decision to disband Ground Forces as a separate service. This decision was reversed only in 1967. Khrushchev also reportedly favored some cutbacks in defense expenditures, and debates over this issue continued for several more years after his ouster.

[23]See, for example, Amoretta Hoeber and Joseph Douglass, *Conventional War and Escalation: The Soviet View*, (New York: Grane, Russak and Co., 1981).

[24]*FBIS-SOV*, January 18, 1977, pp. R3-13.

[25]See, for example, Christopher W. Donnelly, "The Soviet Operational Maneuver Group: A New Challenge for NATO," *Military Review*, March 1983.

[26]See, for example, N.V. Ogarkov, *Vsegda v gotovnosti k zashchite otechestva*, (Moscow: Voenizdat, 1982).

[27]It is important to note that the Soviets have a distinct approach to the issues of flexibility and initiative in combat. Soviet marshals also look upon tactical flexibility in a manner unfamiliar to most Western soldiers. Flexibility, for the Soviet commanders, is that which you have to do when you are "off plan." Getting back "on plan" is a function of selecting from a known set of options, all of which are products of repetitive testing. Soviets use their academies and field exercises to play tactical problems and to update the solution-suites.

[28]See, for example, Phillip A. Petersen and John G. Hines, "The Conventional Offensive in Soviet Theater Strategy," *Orbis*, Fall 1983.

[29]For a discussion of these trends, see Scott Gourely, "The Soviet Army: Artillery and Fire Control," *Defense Electronics*, January 1989.

[30]*Washington Times*, December 9, 1988.

[31]Some Soviet writers have criticized the Soviet preoccupation with building up tank forces as being cost inefficient, politically provocative, and unnecessary for genuine defense. These alleged problems were caused by such factors as the "cavalry mentality" of Soviet army commanders, the emphasis on fighting a European war with the use of nuclear weapons, and the simple inertia of piling new tanks on top of old ones. In contrast, the U.S. is lauded for avoiding

costly large-scale tank buildup and for emphasizing ATGMs. See V.V. Schlykov, "Tankovaia asimmetriia i real'naia bezopasnost'," *Mezhdunarodnaia Zhizn'*, November 1988.

[32]Christopher Donnelly, *Red Banner*, (England: Janes Publishing Service, 1988).

[33]*Washington Times*, December 9, 1988. According to Donnelly, the Hungarian Army was converted to the corps/brigade structure in 1987 and is serving as a test-bed for the Soviet reorganization.

[34]A.G. Arbatov, A.A. Vasileev, A.A. Kokoshin, "Iadernoe oruzhne i strategacheskaia stabil'nost'," *SShA*, No. 9, 1987, p. 7.

[35]*Ibid*, pp. 8-9.

[36]See, for example, Petrovski, *op. cit.*

[37]Vladimir Nazarenko, "Soviet and U.S. Military Doctrines and Progress in Arms Control," in Elizabeth J. Kirk, (ed.), *Technology, Security and Arms Control for the 1990s*, (AAAS, 1988), p. 147.

[38]Interestingly enough, even at the declaratory level, while disparaging the concept of nuclear warfighting, Moscow also rejects the entire notion of deterrence. Soviet writers posit that assured destruction is inconsistent with truly stable international relations and is rejected by the new political thinking. See *MEMO*, October 1987, p. 10.

[39]See, for example, David B. Rivkin, Jr., "No Bastions for the Bear," *U.S. Naval Institute Proceedings*, April 1984. For a fascinating Soviet discussion of the future of naval warfare see Nikolai Gorshkov, (ed.), *Voenno-morskoi flot: rol', perstpektivy razvitiia, ispol'zovanie*, (Moscow: Voenizdat, 1988). The book stresses that submarines are the most capable type of naval vessels and describes futuristic submarines, capable of diving to great depths, travelling faster than surface ships, displaying great endurance and superior concealment capabilities, and carrying armament that can engage air, land, and naval targets.

[40]Gorbachev's figure of 77.3 billion rubles amounts to roughly nine percent of the Soviet GNP. See the *Washington Post*, May 31, 1989, pp. A1, A17. This figure, however, is still much less than the Western estimates of Soviet defense spending: 15 to 20 percent of Moscow's GNP. Assuming Gorbachev's sincerity, the difference may be attributable to the arbitrary nature of the Soviet pricing system, that does not reflect the true costs of Soviet military activities.

[41]In March of 1983, three Soviet generals were promoted to the rank of Marshal: Petrov, Kurkotkin, and Akhromeev.

[42]Most of the Gorbachev-appointed senior officers are relatively junior in rank and all hail from the Far Eastern military district. These include such officers as Yazov, Moiseev, Tretiak, and Govorov. All of them reportedly impressed Gorbachev when he toured the Far East and have been outspoken supporters of perestroika and glasnost.

[43]Until the recent Central Committee reorganization in September 1988, the International Department had a special arms

control section.

[44]According to Bovin, "Today, military doctrine, corresponding to requirements of the times, is first and foremost a political-theoretical foundation for averting nuclear war." A. Bovin, "Ot iskustva voin k iskustvu peregovorov," *Izvestiia*, June 4, 1987, p. 5.

[45]L.I. Brezhnev, "Speech to Soviet Officers," Radio Moscow Domestic Service in Russian, July 3, 1965, quoted in Bluth, *op. cit.*, p. 154.

[46]*Wall Street Journal*, April 25, 1989.

[47]*Rabotnichesko Delo*, (Sofia), December 6, 1988, p. 1, translated in *FBIS-SOV*, December 9, 1988, p. 1.

[48]Odom, *op. cit.*, p. 7.

[49]*Rabotnichesko Delo*, *op. cit*, p. 1.

[50]Soviet officials predict that some 83,000 officers would be retired as a result of Gorbachev's troops reductions. Cited in *New York Times*, December 23, 1988, p. 1.

[51]Such deferments were abolished in 1982 and recently restored.

[52]*Rabotnichesko Delo*, *op. cit.*, p. 1.

[53]See, for example, Shlykov, *op. cit.*

[54]See, for example, A. Savinkin, "What Kind of Armed Forces Do We Need?" *Moscow News* (English Edition), No. 45, November 1988.

[55]*Krasnaia Zvezda*, January 8, 1989, p. 3.

[56]A. Kokoshin and V. Larionov, "Kurskaia bitva v svete sovremenni obornitel'noi doktriny," *MEMO*, August 1987.

[57]Bruce D. Slawter, "Geopolitics: A Framework for Analyzing Soviet Regional Behavior," *Global Affairs*, Winter 1989, p. 67.

[58]Michael MccGwire, *op. cit.*

[59]In fact, in a meeting with a group of American experts, Marshal Akhromeev, when asked by one of the authors to describe "defensive defense," replied that it was the Soviet intent to eschew large-scale offensive operations for 5-9 weeks. During this time, political leaders on both sides can explore the possibility of settling the conflict. Should the settlement prove impossible, Soviet forces would then be prepared to launch an offensive against NATO. Akhromeev also remarked that his scenario has been tested in several Soviet staff exercises. The view that Moscow is shifting to a "delayed offensive" strategy has been embraced by a number of Western experts, including Paul Nitze.

[60]For example, Czechoslovakia and GDR, under the Soviet auspices, have proposed a creation of a 300-mile-wide nuclear free zone along the WTO-NATO borders. Meanwhile, Bulgaria and Romania have proposed turning the Balkans into a zone free of nuclear and chemical weapons.

[61]*MEMO*, October 1987, p. 109.

[62]See, for example, R. Sagdeev, A. Kokoshin, et al., *Strategic Stability Under the Conditions of Radical Nuclear Arms Reductions*, (Moscow: Committee of Soviet Scientists for Peace and Against the Nuclear Threat, April 1987).

[63]*Washington Times*, May 12, 1989, p. 1.

[64]*New York Times*, June 12, 1989, p. 19.

9

Soviet Military Reference Works as a Guide in Soviet Military Doctrine

William C. Green

For over a decade, Western analysts of Soviet military affairs extensively used a number of Soviet military reference works in their research. Since the appearance of the first volume of the *Soviet Military Encyclopedia* in 1976, these analysts are the unintended beneficiaries of a Soviet urge to systematize the entire corpus of military knowledge. But important questions concerning this reference literature remain to be answered.

All reference works of any sort must be prepared under strong editorial guidance in order to have any sort of coherence. But the relationship of the editorial supervision of these Soviet military reference works to any centrally approved set of views remains to be explored. How rigidly are the definitions and synopses set forth in these works scrutinized for doctrinal and ideological conformity? What indicators are there that consensus is or is not forged on a particular issue? Above all, what is the relationship between these carefully worded articles and actual Soviet military practice? Such questions can only be answered by closer examination of how the works are prepared.

This chapter begins with a review of the role of Marxism-Leninism in Soviet military theory. It then proceeds to an assessment of some important Soviet sources that explain the reasons for the appearance of this literature. After a consideration of the question of disinformation, this chapter concludes by evaluating possible changes in the role of Soviet military reference works as the Gorbachev reforms affect the Soviet Armed Forces.

The Role of Ideology

Much ink is spilt in the West over the question of whether the Soviet political and military leadership really "believes" in communism. For the most part this is an unproductive and polarized debate, caught between individuals who assert that almost all Soviet behavior can be traced directly to Marxist-Leninist ideology and those who cite numerous examples of cynicism, opportunism, or pragmatism among members of the Soviet elite. Mikhail Gorbachev's reforms, under the slogans of perestroika (restructuring) and new thinking (*novoe myshlenie*) accelerate the Western debate. An assortment of bewildering and contradictory explanations of Soviet motives for undertaking these reforms appear, which under one guise or another represent attempts to bolster various positions in this Western debate over the role of ideology in the Soviet system.

The extreme positions in this debate lose sight of two important issues. The first is whether there are ways in which Soviet behavior differs because of the demands of Marxist-Leninist ideology. The second is the possibility of using these patterns to predict future Soviet behavior.

One important way that Marxism-Leninism affects Soviet behavior is its insistence that concepts and terminology be defined according to the arcane "laws" of dialectical materialism. This term encompasses the philosophical and methodological assumptions and procedures that by definition make Marxism-Leninism "scientific" and "objective." It also serves as a useful mechanism for standardizing and coordinating public and academic thought in a wide variety of fields. As a result, even the most useful and pragmatic of state actions must eventually be justified in terms of the official ideology.

Much energy is put into these exercises by both Party officials and specialists in various professions, since poor or restrictive definitions can seriously hamper future action, while loose definitions lead to a deterioration of the value of this procedure as a controlling mechanism. Under Gorbachev, this process continues. Far from being the non-ideological "pragmatists" envisioned by some Western commentators, he and many of his subordinates seem at times to be almost obsessed with the ideological implications and justifications of their policies.

For a number of reasons, the Soviet military is particularly active in this process of defining and redefining terminology and concepts. Moreover, in recent years it vigorously encouraged and enforced the proper usage of military terms and concepts in publications and official usage. This activity is reflected in the large number of military reference works published in the Soviet Union, particularly dictionaries and encyclopedias. By examining them, one can uncover important ways in which ideology constrains and modifies Soviet military vocabulary and thought patterns. This, in turn, can be used to develop some observations on possible future Soviet military behavior, particularly given the atmosphere of political ferment current in the Soviet Union.

The Importance of Authorized Terms and Concepts

The Soviet Union, like Imperial Russia before it, always possessed a lively and energetic military press. This military publishing tradition included both dictionaries and encyclopedic works. But prior to the 1950s such reference materials tended to reflect the sometimes idiosyncratic views of their editors rather than any consensus in party-military opinion. Primarily, this was because a consistently thought-out and centrally approved set of views on military affairs had not yet been formulated in the Soviet Union. The sharp military debates between People's Commissar of War Leon Trotski and the more radical advocates of a "proletarian military science" during the 1920s led to, in turn, the Great Purges, the turmoil of the Second World War, and finally the public stagnation of military thought in Stalin's final decade.[1]

It was not until the so-called "Revolution in Military Affairs," brought about by the introduction of nuclear weapons and accurate delivery systems, that the Soviet Union began to develop a systematized approach to the analysis of military problems. The experiences of the Second World War and subsequent developments in military science were studied carefully, especially at the General Staff Academy, for general principles that would have universal significance in the nuclear age. As a result of this review, the revision of Soviet military theory became necessary. A new doctrine, adopted in 1959, rested on the principles of surprise (*vnezapnost'*) and preemption (*preuprezhdenie*). The Soviet military completely reorganized to conform to this doctrine, with a new service, the Strategic Rocket Forces, having pride of primacy. By 1962 a strategy for execution of this doctrine was worked out; since then, only relatively minor changes in emphasis or elaborations of principles not fully developed have occurred in this body of theory.

Part of this change in military theory involved the adoption of an entirely new military vocabulary, specially intended to fit with the new thinking. The way in which the General Staff Academy operated to evolve this vocabulary is now being revealed in the memoirs of recently retired Soviet military officers. For example, retired General-Lieutenant Vladimir D. Lavrinenkov served as a mid-level Air Force officer on the faculty of the Academy of the General Staff in the early 1950s. In his memoirs he describes the way in which military operations of the Second World War were closely scrutinized by the faculty and students in order to develop and refine concepts and terminology. He concludes:

> The aviation offensive was conducted by Soviet forces in all operations and was one of the most important conditions for their success. By character of mission and time of action this offensive could be divided into two periods: aviation preparation [preliminary and direct] and aviation support [accompaniment] of troops in the course of an offensive. As a result, from my seat at the General Staff Academy, I began to examine this and that incident at the Front with different eyes, and began to evaluate my personal role in them differently. From 1954 the term "aviation offensive" disappeared from usage, its place taken by the concepts "aviation preparation," "support," and "accompaniment."[2]

Of course, the older terms often continued to be used even after replaced. For example, in his *Soviet Military Encyclopedia* article "Operation in Depth," Marshal Nikolai Ogarkov noted that after the Second World War the introduction of nuclear weapons, more powerful conventional weapons, and effective means of delivery made it possible to strike deep behind the enemy's frontlines without the effort needed to mount an operation in depth. This "transformed the essence of the means of organizing and conducting an operation or combat. [Therefore] the term "operation in depth" has not been used in official documents since the 1960s."[3] In short, military policy makers abolished or modified terms that were confusing or carried implications that misled or were irrelevant.

Maintaining Uniformity

General-Lieutenant Mikhail Kir'ian, the Deputy Director of the Institute of Military History for the USSR Ministry of Defense and a member of the Main Editorial Commission for the *Soviet Military Encyclopedia* and *Military Encyclopedic Dictionary*, published two accounts of how the Soviet military prepares authoritative military reference works.[4] In addition, several articles in the *Soviet Military Encyclopedia* offer helpful insights on its repair.[5] Kir'ian placed great emphasis on how an attempt to produce a Soviet military encyclopedia in the early 1930s failed because of inadequate preparation and because "in the 1930s great changes occurred in all areas of military affairs."[6] Hence, it was not possible to form definitions based on a unified set of views. Only two volumes of this encyclopedia appeared out of the twelve originally planned.

An important element in maintaining this uniformity was the extensive publication of military dictionaries. *The Concise Dictionary of Operational-Tactical and General Military Words* was published during the course of the extensive reorganization of military forces and doctrine carried out in the late 1950s.[7] The *Dictionary of Basic Military Terms* was published after this reorganization had been completed.[8] It was closely followed by a more detailed work, the *Explanatory Dictionary of Military Terms*.[9]

The third edition of the *Great Soviet Encyclopedia*, which appeared between 1970 and 1978, also developed an appreciation of the need for uniformity and active military participation. As a result of this participation, states Kir'ian:

> Many new concepts emerged. They found expression in corresponding articles on military themes. The scientific-technical revolution and the effects of its radical changes in all areas of military theory and practice was a major reason for making more precise formulations of many military concepts.[10]

Nearly every Western publication on the Soviet military that appeared in the past ten years cites the *Soviet Military Encyclopedia* in defining Soviet terminology or uses it as a source of data. Other Soviet military reference works are also extensively used by Western analysts in their assessments of a wide variety of issues concerning the Soviet military. Recent publications from the Soviet Union, as well as a thorough review of the Soviet military reference works themselves, make it possible to address a wide variety of questions about these works, including their purpose, authoritativeness, and reliability.

The *Soviet Military Encyclopedia* is easily the single most important Soviet military work of the late 1970s. According to Kir'ian, the concept of a Soviet military encyclopedia grew out of the frustrations in the preparation of the third edition of the *Great Soviet Encyclopedia*, since it "did not include articles on many special questions of strategy, operational art, and tactics, or much information on the armed forces and military art of the capitalist nations."[11] He states that it lacked specific information because "many officers, especially in small garrisons, were unable to obtain full access" to the "enormous issues of material, addressing new problems of military affairs."[12] Finally, the non-standardized use of language presented a problem. As previously discussed, since the mid-1950s the Soviet military had been striving for standardized terms and concepts. But apparently these earlier efforts were not adequate; Kir'ian complains that, as late as the mid-1970s, many terms and concepts were still misused.[13]

As a result, in 1972 the decision was made to prepare a *Soviet Military Encyclopedia*. Both Kir'ian and the work itself lay great stress on the collective and authoritative nature of its editorial staff and authors. The Main Editorial Commission, chaired by then Soviet Minister of Defense Marshal Andrei Grechko, also included twenty high-ranking officers; after his death in 1976, Marshal Ogarkov, the Chief of the General Staff, took his place. Eight thematic subcommissions formed, addressing "War and Politics," "Ground Forces," "Air Forces," "The Navy," "Military-Technical Sciences," "Military Personages," "the Rear of the Armed Forces," and "Military History." The subcommissions were chaired by the CINC (commander-in-chief) of the corresponding service, by the corresponding Deputy Minister of Defense, or in some cases by other prominent military officers. The same principle was followed in the preparation of articles: whenever possible, the officer most directly involved became the author. In short, nearly every high-ranking officer in the Soviet Armed Forces participated in the preparation of the *Soviet Military Encyclopedia*. According to Harriet Fast Scott, the Soviet military's preoccupation with preparation and production of articles for the encyclopedia and the great delays occasioned by the need to obtain approval from numerous authorities for each article possibly contributed to the relative scarcity of other important military-theoretical works during the late 1970s.[14]

This preparation began in 1973 with the development of a word guide (*slovnik*), a task that took over a year.[15] Initially twenty thousand words and names were selected as subjects for possible articles. Eventually the list tightened to include slightly more than eleven thousand articles. Volumes One and Two appeared in 1976, Volumes Three and Four in 1977, Volumes Five and Six in 1978, Volume Seven in 1979, and Volume Eight in 1980.

In the effort to make the encyclopedia as inclusive and professional as possible, the Main Editorial Commission apparently authorized some departures from general practice. For example, there is an article devoted to each of the major United States and British campaigns of the Second World War, including the Lend-Lease effort, which by and large present an accurate picture of the action, forces, and motives involved. Biographies, including photographs, are provided of many contemporary Soviet military leaders.

On the other hand, politics often intrude; for example, there is no article on Trotski, the founder of the Red Army. There are scores of biographies of officers who perished in Stalin's purge of the military in 1937-38; not once is any reason given for the great mortality among Soviet officers in those years. And as Harriet Fast Scott pointed out in her review of the first volume, there are many omissions of information which were available for many years outside the Soviet Union in the *Soviet Military Encyclopedia*: "Data which in the West would be ordinary facts fall into the realm of state or military secrets in the USSR, and this situation places great limitations on what the Soviet contributors can write."[16]

Developments Since 1980

The *Soviet Military Encyclopedia* betrays no sign that the Soviet Union made any significant changes in its military theory during the late 1970s or that any dissent among the authors and editors existed over the broad outlines of Soviet military doctrine and strategy. As Albert Weeks wrote in his review of the entire series:

> It should come as no surprise to the really serious student of Soviet military policy that not a single major position on strategy proposed by professional military thinker/writers, since the 1960s has been "revised" by the current SVE [*Soviet Military Encyclopedia*].[17]

However, volumes of the *Soviet Military Encyclopedia* published after 1976 (Nos. 31-38) were subjected to the insertion of undeveloped assertions. William Lee's assessment argued that this change resulted from the replacement of the chief editors:

Although the *Military Encyclopedia* remains a vast storehouse of useful information, some disinformation was introduced after Ogarkov replaced the late Marshal Grechko as editor....Volume Three of the *Military Encyclopedia* was published in the same year (1977), but with a new editor in place of Marshal Grechko (who had died in 1976). That volume and all subsequent ones were edited by N.V. Ogarkov, whose performance in the SALT negotiations and as head of the *Maskirovka* (deception) program government-wide was rewarded in January 1977 by appointment as chief of the General Staff and promotion to Marshal of the Soviet Union.[18]

But it is unlikely that Grechko put forth any impediment to modifications of the *Soviet Military Encyclopedia* for political reasons. More probably, the beginning of Ogarkov's tenure as Chairman of the Main Editorial Commission simply coincided with a change in Soviet statements on the nature of Soviet strategy often known in the West as the Tula line.

The Tula line is featured prominently in some of the major articles in the encyclopedia. Its most concise formulation appears in Marshal Ogarkov's article "Military Strategy," where he states:

Soviet military strategy, as well as Soviet military doctrine as a whole, has an especially defensive tendency; it does not provide for any preemptive [*uprezhdaiushchie*] strikes or premeditated attacks. Its main task is to elaborate methods to repel an aggressor's attack and to defeat him utterly by means of decisive operations....Soviet military strategy takes into account the capabilities of the USSR and other socialist countries to prevent military-technical superiority on the part of a probable enemy, but at the same time it does not have as its own objective the attainment of military-technical superiority over other countries.[19]

The nature of the Tula line is hotly debated by Western analysts of Soviet military affairs. One group affirms that a shift occurred in Soviet military thinking away from nuclear weapons towards a broader array of conventional options. The other sees it merely as a Soviet reaction to heightened Western sensitivities towards nuclear weapons issues during the SALT II debate and 1980 presidential election, unconnected with changes that may or may not be occurring in the Soviet military. Whichever view is correct, the *Soviet Military Encyclopedia* showed no sign in the contents of its articles of any great debate taking place over military theory. A high level of continuity remained with the military writings of the 1960s and 1970s.

Unfortunately, Soviet military reference works issued since 1980 are not helpful in resolving this issue. In 1983 a massive single volume *Military Encyclopedic Dictionary* appeared, also under the editorial supervision of Marshal Ogarkov. It is a condensed, one-volume summary of the *Soviet Military Encyclopedia* and is slightly updated, especially in the area of biographical information. Most of the articles are shortened versions of the *Soviet Military Encyclopedia* articles, ofter employing identical wordings. The latest development is an announcement made in April 1988 by the Military Publishing House that it plans to issue a second edition of the *Soviet Military Encyclopedia* at some undisclosed future date. This announcement was confirmed by Soviet Defense Minister Dmitri Yazov in a recent interview where he stated, "We are revising our military encyclopedia. One aim of the new edition is to depict the defensive character of Soviet doctrine."[20]

Soviet Military Reference Works and Perestroika

Mikhail Gorbachev is in his fourth year as General Secretary of the Communist Party of the Soviet Union. During this time dramatic changes continue to occur in Soviet upper and mid-level leadership personnel and in official rhetoric. To a lesser extent, changes also occur in Soviet political and economic policy along the lines suggested by his slogans. The Soviet Union is not immune to these changes; indeed, a "restructuring" of the military appears to be an important part of his overall program.

The role that Soviet military reference works will have in perestroika is not yet clear. In principle, they could serve as a powerful tool to communicate new policies and enforce adherence to them. In practice, there are a number of impediments to this. The first is that the full ramifications of changes in policy most likely are not sufficiently explored for them to be amenable to the authoritative encapsulation required for reference works. The second is that the lengthy lead-times needed to prepare and edit such reference works makes them unsuitable tools of communication during transition periods, such as the present. Finally, current Soviet military reference publications are firmly oriented towards explaining and promoting conformity to the doctrine and strategy adopted in the late 1950s and early 1960s. As a result, the future publication of Soviet military reference works is dependent on developments in Soviet military theory. If Gorbachev's policy initiatives can be implemented within the existing framework of this body of work, follow-up editions to current Soviet military reference works can be issued with relatively minor changes. If, however, the imperatives of Gorbachev's reforms require major changes in the form and content of Soviet military doctrine and strategy, there may be long delays while completely new publications are prepared. In the extreme case, that Gorbachev's reforms lead to current military strategy being discarded but that no consensus can be formed for a new doctrine and strategy to take its place, a complete halt in the preparation and publication of Soviet military reference works can be expected.

Thus far, it is unclear which of these paths will be taken. One major Soviet military reference work, the *Military Encyclopedic Dictionary*, had a second, slightly revised edition appear in 1986. This implies that the Soviet military is trying to adapt to Gorbachev's reforms without undertaking major changes in military theory. However, aside from a few dictionaries, no important military reference works have appeared since.[21] The announcement of a successor edition for the impressive but aging *Soviet Military Encyclopedia* means that we will now have an important indicator of which path events in the Soviet Union are taking. An edition appearing speedily with few doctrinal changes will indicate that Soviet military theory will not be undergoing major revision. Serious delays, on the other hand, will indicate that Soviet thinking is undergoing important substantive change.

Notes

[1]See, for example, William C. Green, "The Future Through the Past," *Naval Intelligence Quarterly*, January 1987, pp. 32-36.

[2]Vladimir D. Lavrinenkov, *Bez voiny*, (Kiev: Izdatel'stvo Politicheskoi Literatury Ukrainy, 1982), p. 185.

[3]Nikolai Ogarkov, "Glubokaia operatsiia," *Soviet Military Encyclopedia*, (Moscow: Voennoe izdatel'stvo, 1976), p. 576.

[4]M.M. Kir'ian (ed.), *Istoriia otechestvenoi voennoentsiklopediicheskoi literatury*, (Moscow: Voennoe izdatel'stvo, 1980); *Problemy voennoi teorii v sovetskikh nauchno-spavochnykh izdaniiakh*, (Moscow: Izdatel'stvo Nauka, 1985).

[5]I.A. Korotkov, "Entsiklopedii voennie," *Sovetskaia Voennaia Entsiklopediia*, (Moscow: Voennoe izdatel'stvo, 1980), pp. 602-603.

[6]Kir'ian, *op. cit.*, p. 14.

[7]*Kratkii slovar' operativno-takticheskikh i obshchevoyskovykh terminov*, (Moscow: Voennoe Izdatel'stvo, 1958).

[8]*Slovar' osnovnykh voennykh terminov*, (Moscow: Voennoe Izdatel'stvo, 1958).

[9]P.I. Skuybeda (ed.), *Tolkovyi slovar' voennykh terminov*, (Moscow: Voennoe Izdatel'stvo, 1966).

[10]Kir'ian, *op. cit.*, pp. 33-34.

[11]*Ibid.*, p. 34.

[12]*Ibid.*, pp. 34-35.

[13]*Ibid.*

[14]Interview, October 11, 1985.

[15]Kir'ian, *op. cit.*, p. 35.

[16]Harriet Fast Scott, "Insights into the Soviet Military," *Problems of Communism*, January-February 1977, p. 71.

[17]Albert Weeks, "The New Soviet Military Encyclopedia," *Survey*, Spring 1982, p. 203.

[18]William T. Lee and Richard F. Starr, *Soviet Military Policies After World War II*, (Stanford, CA: The Hoover Institution Press, 1986), p. 31.

[19]Nikolai Ogarkov, "Strategiia, voennaia," *Sovetskaia Voennaia Entsiklopediia*, (Moscow: Voenizdat, 1978), p. 563.

[20]*U.S. News and World Report*, March 13, 1989, p. 34.

[21]Recently, *Slovar' voennykh terminov*, (Moscow: Voenizdat, 1988) appeared. However, it reportedly has few major changes in definitions.

10

Conclusions:
The Unresolved Agenda

Thomas Nichols

The contents of this book should be understood as an unresolved Soviet *and American* agenda: Changes in the Soviet defense picture are forcing American analysts to reconsider long-held beliefs about Soviet politics and foreign policy, and the contributions in this volume therefore represent both foresight and frustration. On one hand, the direction of military development is in some areas clear enough. Many aspects of military technology are universal, and therefore certain trends (such as the further development of space technologies) seem irresistible. There is little mystery over these and other generally logical developments, although some disagreement emerges around questions of detail, implementation, or timing.

On the other hand, clarity gives way to confusion when we look at the *politics* of military development in the USSR. Daniel Goure's analysis of nuclear strategy, for example, is tempered by a recognition of the fracturing of military opinion on this issue; William Green suggests the need to turn to military reference works in order to trace the development of thought on a range of military/technical issues; Theodore Karasik and I argue that the debate over new military concepts at this point is more political than operational. Even authors less impressed by Soviet divisions on these issues, such as Paula Dobriansky, David Rivkin, and Stephen Blank, admit that there are alternative futures to be considered even where the Soviet path seems clear. (Dobriansky and Rivkin accept the existence of a debate but do not see it as representative of a deep civil-military cleavage.) Among our contributors, only William Scott argues directly that "change" in Soviet defense policy is no change at all and that previous concepts derived from an expansionist view of the USSR are still valid.

Like the Soviets, we are left without a framework for the future. Our traditional conceptions of the Soviet Union no longer seem to fit. Our expectations and predictions are rendered irrelevant after a wave of retirements or reassignments. Likewise, the Soviets themselves are searching for a common framework, a way of looking at the world and its challenges that makes sense to politicians, academics, analysts, and military officers alike. Neither we nor they appear to have a solution in sight.

We can offer little to the Soviets in their search for a paradigm; the Western analytical community, however, should consider the methods and beliefs by which our own impending reassessment of the USSR will be guided. Specifically, there is a need to differentiate the problem. Until now, many analyses of Soviet defense policy and politics have aggregated factors like technological change, foreign threat, and internal politics. In part, this was due to the limitations of the research base. It was also because of a belief, however, that our view of the nature of Soviet foreign policy was "settled" and that there was no need to discuss first principles. This was incorrect; the issue was not so much settled as ignored.

Untying the Knot

In every state, defense policy is an amalgam of pressures. Moreover, the counter proposition, that all aspects of state policy are an amalgam of pressures (and that there is therefore nothing overwhelmingly unique about defense), is inadequate. The defense of the nation, often regarded by soldiers and statesmen alike as tantamount to the question of survival, touches on almost every aspect of state policy, and it is an often repeated criticism that national security has become the overriding concern of the modern nation-state. Agriculture, industry, culture, and ethnic issues all have their place in the daily life and workings of a government. Only national security, however, lays claim credibly to all those areas and more as being within its legitimate purview.

There are several dimensions to Soviet military and security policy that provide useful foundations for analysis. The first is specifically Marxist-Leninist, the second is specifically Soviet, the third is specifically Russian, and the fourth is universal.

Ideology and Defense

It is popular now to ring the death knell of ideology in the Soviet Union, to argue that Marxism-Leninism is no longer useful (if it ever was) in understanding Soviet behavior. As a general proposition, this is more or less correct; there is little use in defining what is "Bolshevik" and what isn't, and the writings of Lenin and Stalin on defense are probably no better a guide to the Soviet Union of the 1990's than they were to the Soviet Union of the 1930's. Much of the well-intentioned and well-reasoned attempts to use an "operational code" approach in the 1950's and 1960's revealed the limitations of the all-encompassing ideological approach when they resulted in sets of "codes" that seemed no more "Bolshevik" than any other set of common-sense realpolitik ruminations.

What is important about ideology is not that it defines the mindset of the entire Soviet political system but that it provides valuable insights into the thinking of a crucial portion of the national security elite. Specifically, it is necessary to understand the ideological orthodoxy of key members of the military establishment in order to understand the dialogue between military professionals and civilian leaders. It could be argued, for example, that the military depicts the Western threat as unyielding in order to protect institutional budgets and privileges. This is to a degree accurate. But the military chooses to frame that view using powerful ideological language; they argue that the threat is continual not because of the characteristics of this or that administration but because a scientific, Marxist-Leninist analysis proves that the tensions between classes (and therefore wars) are endemic. In Soviet debate, this is seizing the rhetorical high ground, and it puts opponents of this kind of thinking in the position either of responding in ideological terms or of being labeled un-Marxist.

The fact that Gorbachev partisans have spoken so often of the need to "de-ideologize" conflict is testimony to the importance of this factor, and any analysis of the development of Soviet defense policy has to take into account that ideology, especially in this area, is far from dead. A kind of "duck test" must be applied; if a Soviet walks and quacks like a Marxist-Leninist; i.e., if he defends his views on ideological grounds, takes an ideological line, and claims that ideology is crucial, then for the sake of analysis he is a Marxist-Leninist, and we must take his concerns seriously. If he puts forth a class-oriented analysis of current affairs, we are as mistaken to ignore or dismiss it as we would be to assume that it defines the position of the entire Soviet leadership. Until now, these two extremes, disregard and obsession, have dominated our view of the place of ideology in national security. Among our authors, William Scott makes the clearest case for the importance of ideology, although I find that I disagree with his evaluation of the extent to which ideology provides for uniformity among the views of Soviet elites.

The middle way is to recognize the importance of ideology *to a specific speaker* or his group. This axiom is better appreciated in analyses of Soviet domestic politics but appears less often in studies of foreign policy. When we understand the relative emphases placed on ideology in the Soviet debate, we will understand the tone and direction of the debate more completely.

Politics and Defense

The internal struggles produced by the Gorbachev reforms should remind us of the importance of the *political* dimension of Soviet national security. Again, I am cognizant of William Scott's dissent on this issue, but I suggest that recent events cast strong doubt on so monolithic a view of the Soviet leadership. We know that Khrushchev's attempts to seize the military agenda resulted in civil-military conflict, and there is no reason to suspect that the present period is any different. If anything, the removal of certain barriers to the expression of criticism has made disagreement even more open and intense. In this volume, Theodore Karasik and I place the greatest explicit emphasis on the role of politics.

The question that arises, of course, is what we mean by the "role" of politics. Is the intention to describe Soviet national security policy as the result of political competition, the *kto kogo* of Kremlin life? Or is it even more formally an attempt to describe the Soviets in the language of "bureaucratic politics" models of policymaking? Neither is satisfying; both oversimplify the problem and remove it from its context. (After all, every participant in the national security process has personal, political, and institutional interests. The more interesting question is when and how they act based on those interests).

Almost every major industrial nation formulates national security policy through the give and take, the "pulling and hauling" of politics. In the Soviet Union, however, this is an especially important part of the process because there are few clear limits on participation among political and military elites. In the United States, by comparison, the boundaries of military participation in the policy process are defined by tradition and law. When military officers overstep those bounds (as Billy Mitchell, Douglas MacArthur, and Oliver North can attest), there is publicity and prosecution. The Soviets are in a quite different situation: Their senior officers also hold high Party and state offices. If these officers cannot voice their opinions as generals and admirals, they are certainly free to do so as members of the Central Committee, the Supreme Soviet, the Council of Ministers, or even the Politburo.

This cannot be underestimated; how much importance would Americans attach to the political processes of national security policy formulation if the Chairman of JCS, the service chiefs, and dozens of other active-duty officers were also U.S. congressmen and senators? This is the uniquely Soviet aspect of the problem, and it casts doubt upon assertions that Soviet soldiers are obedient officers like any others in the industrial world. They live in the board room as well as the barracks, and the lack of clear boundaries on military participation in politics in the USSR means that the Soviets have a First World military organization and, at least potentially, a Third World civil-military relationship. This is not meant to suggest that a military coup is likely in Moscow but only to recognize that military officers in the Soviet Union have political privileges and options available to them that are not available to their Western counterparts.

Culture and Defense

It is a tradition in Western writings on Soviet foreign policy to speak of "Great Russian" or "messianic" objectives, of a "Byzantine" or even "Asiatic" approach to security. We gravitate to these terms because they have an intuitive appeal; we suspect that there is something in Russian culture and history that explains current Soviet behavior. Unfortunately, these cultural explanations are impossible to operationalize, and in the end they tend to be rhetorically useful assertions rather than analytical guidelines or categories.

Does this mean that culture is useless in the analysis of Soviet national security policy? No, although culture is a concept that has been abused for decades. Again, comparative studies of other nations have generally been more careful in their use of terms like "political culture." If culture is thought of as a dynamic set of images and traditions that have evolved from the early confluence of ethnic characteristics and historical experiences, then it is undeniable that there is something culturally "Russian" about the security policy of the Soviet Union. Specifically, Russian culture, like Soviet ideology, provides images and terms through which Soviet elites communicate. Moreover, cultural experience imbues the national security process with a distinct character: Great Russian racism, for example, no doubt affects the Soviet relationship with Asian countries (just as German culture affected the relationship of the Third Reich with Anglo-Saxon countries or American legal culture affects U.S. behavior in the world today).

Like ideology, culture can say much about the structure and terminology of debate, even if it does not provide an all-encompassing explanation. The Western analyst must be sensitive to the use of culturally powerful images in Soviet rhetoric; resort to concepts like the *Rodina* ("Motherland," a word that carries a visceral charge for many ethnic Russians) indicates an attempt on the part of the speaker to convey the emotional intensity and moral rectitude of his position. We cannot dismiss the use of such language as propaganda; it means something to them, and it should mean something to us.

Technology and Defense

Finally, it is important to consider an influence on security policy shared by the United States and the Soviet Union: technology. Although technology is central to the Soviet-American security relationship, Americans tend to believe that technology is the *defining* characteristic of that relationship. This technological determinism is an American cultural problem, with roots in a traditionally Western belief in the universality of science. It views defense policy, including military doctrine, as the inevitable result of the nature of a given technology. It assumes that technology is subject only to very narrow parameters of interpretation and that "doctrines" are inherent in the weapons; universal rationality allows a similarly universal interpretation of international realities and technological developments, regardless of circumstance.

This tendency is understandable but dangerous. Technologies do not simply appear and then work their way into a system of national or international security. They appear either as a result of pure research or specific request. In both cases, the resultant development must be interpreted by individual policymakers and filtered through individual prisms; the challenge for the Western analyst is to deduce the structure and influence of those conceptual prisms in order to understand the Soviet purpose in pursuing this or that system.

Stephen Blank and Daniel Goure both wrestle with this problem in this book; Goure in particular points out that there can be different interpretations of technological advance even in strategic matters. Nuclear strategy is often thought to be the area least subject to cultural or political prejudices, but Goure's research (as well as that of specialists on China) has shown that the American view of deterrence and strategy is by no means universal, any more than the Soviet view is monolithic.

Still, technology is of obvious importance in understanding Soviet policy. The answer may be to shift our focus away from the details of development and procurement (a process with a life of its own in any country) and toward a concern with competing Soviet interpretations of technology. How can weapons systems be evaluated as "offensive" or "defensive?" How can we know if the Soviets really see SDI as a "defense", or medium-range strike aircraft as part of the "offense?" The technology itself will not provide solutions, as any participant in technical discussions with the Soviets quickly learns. In the end, perceptions are paramount, and Westerners must overcome their own cultural obsession with the objective characteristics of technology if we are to understand Soviet views on the flood of technological developments that will affect the East-West relationship into the next century.

Suggestions for Developing a Framework

Criticism is easy; construction is difficult. Still, I will attempt briefly to present a framework or agenda for research derived from the admittedly abbreviated discussion above. In general, what follows is a suggested set of concerns to bear in mind when conducting the kind of content analysis that is the basic method of Sovietology.

1. Marx and Lenin Are Not Dead: Ideology Matters

Analysts of Soviet security policy cannot share the luxury afforded their colleagues in domestic politics of tossing a shovel of dirt on the grave of ideology and moving on to more interesting subjects. When listening to the Soviet debate, we must continue to ask: Who is appealing to ideology? That is, who is seeking to elevate his own preferences to the level of Marxist-Leninist scripture? In what way? To what end? (And with what success?) If we "tune out" ideology in our analyses, we might as well cease to read Soviet military literature and concentrate instead on the hard data of budgets and weapons systems.

2. Stalin Is Dead: Politics Matter

The subfield of Soviet national security policy is the last bastion of the totalitarian paradigm in Soviet studies. Where defense is concerned, Western analysts are often willing to posit a monolithism and sinister unity of purpose to a degree that would never be accepted or even considered with regard to other issues. This recognition of the importance of politics adds depth to our view of the participants and serves as a reminder of the parallel agendas, political as well as altruistic, that may be present in the speeches or writings of Soviet leaders. Advocacy carries a price in the Soviet Union; if we forget that Soviet policymakers represent personal and institutional interests, then we are left with a two-dimensional picture of "Marxists" vs. "Westernizers" or "hawks" and "doves" or even "conservatives" and "liberals." These terms become unintelligible without a sensitivity to the fact that domestic politics and foreign policy are intimately related. In this volume, this caveat is reflected in attempts to provide meaning to such terms as "reformers," "moderates," "pro-" or "anti-" leadership, and the like.

This "palace politics" vs. "rational actor" division is not endemic only to Soviet studies. It is in fact a result of the artificial division of labor in political science, in which comparativists study domestic politics and international relations theorists study foreign policy. The results too often are domestic studies that take place in an international vacuum and foreign policy studies that treat the "State" only in rational-actor terms (and thus reach conclusions that are based in logic but not particularly informative about the particular country involved).

Therefore, analysis of Soviet statements must consider the position and interests of the speaker. What is his agenda? How do the images and rhetorical defenses employed relate to other, perhaps more prosaic goals?

3. The Coloration of Culture

Students of Soviet security policy must overcome their alternate fascination with and disdain for culture. Rather than seek the direct line between ancient history and modern policy, we must become more attuned to the use of cultural imagery by the Soviets themselves. The details of the Battle of Borodino are less interesting than the fact that a modern-day Soviet writer may feel the need to use that incident to elicit a certain feeling from his readers. This kind of reference is the impact of history and culture on modern events, and understanding the rhetoric of culture is crucial to understanding the tone, the feel, of Soviet debate.

In particular, a sensitivity to cultural themes in turn illuminates the intensity with which a given subject is being debated. Cultural images do not define the debate, but they do serve to differentiate the debate; an issue that is being debated in explosive cultural terms is of a different species than issues discussed in more routine language. Recognizing the use of culture in Soviet dialogue will help Western analysts to avoid ascribing importance to issues based on inductive criteria and instead provide a truer reading of the hierarchy of issues within the Soviet context.

4. Putting Technology in Perspective

The landing gear of the MiG-29 or the treads of the T-80 tank will not speak for themselves. Amassing technical specifications of Soviet systems is a necessary function of the Western intelligence effort, but specs will not explain Soviet intentions. Reams of paper have been devoted to the arcane art of tracing political motives from technological characteristics with (at least in my view) virtually no success. The remedy is to reinstate a division of labor between engineers and political analysts. It is understandable that the long-standing criticism of political science as more "political" than "science" has led to the desire to buttress analysis with the comfortable data of technology, but this has neither enhanced our knowledge of the USSR nor improved the credibility of political science among the "hard" scientists.

To be fair, there is an encouraging trend, as this and other volumes show, toward more careful consideration of Soviet views on technological issues and the political consequences of those views. However, this is a fairly recent development, coming after a long period in which it was assumed that the political implications of technology (especially nuclear technology) were universal. The coming deluge of technological developments could lead to a revival of the techno-centric analysis of Soviet security affairs, and this would be unfortunate.

Because the next two decades will be characterized by what the Soviets would call the "stormy" development of technology, there is a danger that the study of Soviet security and defense will become highly technical. Instead, Sovietology should do what it does best: analysis of the perceptions of the political, military, and technocratic leaders who are tasked with interpreting and implementing changes in technology. Only then will the impending changes in Soviet military technology make sense in a greater political context.

Like all initial research outlines, this one is subject to amendment. The coming decade in the USSR, with unsettled tensions between soldiers and civilians, untested changes in strategy, unstoppable technological developments, and an unresolved domestic political agenda, will provide (in many cases for the first time) ample opportunity to examine these and scores of other hypotheses, new and old. There have been warnings for some years now that the United States will face unusual political challenges in the wake of Soviet changes in the 1990s; we must also, however, be prepared for the intellectual challenges that may eventually guide Western policies in the next decade.

APPENDIX 1

The Soviet Military Leadership

Grey Burkhart

The study of Soviet leadership personalities is of primary importance in Soviet studies. While glasnost (openness) increased the volume and variety of information available to researchers, there remain gaps that can be filled only through more "traditional" analysis. We may no longer be reduced to counting the heads lined atop Lenin's tomb for the May Day parade, but cataloging and following the Soviet leadership still requires the collection and collation of myriad bits of data from every source available.

A key area of analysis that benefits from personnel studies is the reconstruction of Soviet leadership organizations, including their relationships to one another and their respective spans of control.

Despite being virtually inundated by the volume of data released under glasnost, we find that the Soviets remain very circumspect regarding key organizations. Unlike the United States, where anyone interested can readily buy a copy of the Pentagon telephone book and a wealth of other source material regarding the organization and leadership of the United States Armed Forces, the Soviets do not release specific information regarding the attributes of such critical organizations as the Defense Council or General Staff.

The recent discussions by the Congress of People's Deputies and Supreme Soviet suggested there will be substantive discussions within those bodies in the near future regarding defense issues, including the composition and activities of the Defense Council, Ministry of Defense, and the General Staff. The subject of opening up defense issues to public scrutiny is also debated. If these investigations and revelations do in fact occur, which is far from guaranteed, and the records are made public, we will likely achieve the deepest and most authoritative look into the Soviet defense establishment. Also tantalizing are recent references to the establishment of a formal national security staff. If such a staff exists, former top officials such as Marshal Sergei Akhromeev and former Ambassador Anatolii Dobrynin are likely key members. It remains to be seen, however, just how such an organization might be integrated into the existing leadership structure and how much authority it might wield. Although there is little information available as yet, initial indications suggest this national security staff will comprise both military and civilian representatives, especially those from the foreign policy field, and may supplant the General Staff as the primary advisory body for the Defense Council.

The following is a partial list of key Soviet personnel comprising the strategic leadership of the Soviet Armed Forces as of October 1, 1989. Some information, such as the personnel of the Military Districts, is readily available. The higher one goes in the Soviet hierarchy, however, the less data is available. Departmental meetings, visits by foreign dignitaries, Party gatherings, and even obituaries all provide pieces of the puzzle. Each places a named person with an activity, a class of people, or a certain type of specialist, from which informed judgments can be made regarding overall organizational structures. Logic and historical analysis (both Soviet and Western) help fill in the picture of the complex interrelationships and respective spans of control. For the reader's use, date of announced appointment or appearance (if available) appears after the subject's position.

SUPREME HIGH COMMANDER

M.S. Gorbachev   General Secretary (3/11/85)

STAVKA OF THE SUPREME HIGH COMMAND

K.A. Kochetov   First Deputy Minister of Defense (MoD) (2/15/89)
P.G. Lushev   Commander-in-Chief (CINC), WTO (2/2/89)
M.A. Moiseev   Chief of the General Staff (12/15/88)
D.T. Yazov   Minister of Defense (5/30/87)

A.V. Kovtunov   CINC, Forces in the Far East (2/89)
V.I. Osipov   CINC, Southwestern TVD (2/89)
N.I. Popov   CINC, Southern TVD (2/89)
S.I. Postnikov   CINC, Western TVD (11/88)

DEFENSE COUNCIL

O.D. Baklanov   Junior Secretary, Defense Industry (2/18/88)
M.S. Gorbachev   General Secretary, Chairman (3/11/85)
V.A. Kryuchkov   Chairman, KGB (10/1/88)
Iu.D. Maslyukov   Chairman, GOSPLAN (2/7/88)
N.I. Ryzhkov   Chairman, Council of Ministers (9/27/85)
E.A. Shevardnadze   Minister of Foreign Affairs (7/1/85)
D.T. Yazov   Minister of Defense (5/30/87)
L.N. Zaikov   Senior Secretary for Defense Industries (3/6/86)

MINISTRY OF DEFENSE OF THE SOVIET UNION

D.T. Yazov   Minister of Defense (5/30/87)

First Deputy Ministers

K.A. Kochetov   First Deputy Minister (portfolio unknown) (2/15/89)
P.G. Lushev   CINC, WTO (2/2/89)
M.A. Moiseev   Chief of the General Staff (12/15/88)

Deputy Ministers (Service CINC)

V.N. Chernavin   CINC of the Navy (12/11/85)
A.N. Efimov   CINC of the Air Forces (12/22/84)
Iu.P. Maksimov   CINC of the Strategic Rocket Forces (7/85)
I.M. Tretiak   CINC of the Air Defense Forces (7/2/87)
V.I. Varennikov   CINC of the Ground Forces (2/16/89)

Deputy Ministers (DM)

V.M. Arkhipov   Chief of the "Rear" Services (5/15/88)
N.V. Chekov   DM for Construction and Billeting (11/23/88)
Iu.A. Iashin   Deputy Minister (portfolio unknown)
V.L. Govorov   Chief of Civil Defense (7/86)
A.D. Lizichev   MPA Chief (7/24/85)
V.M. Shabanov   DM for Armament and Equipment (6/78)
M.I. Sorokin   Inspector General (7/22/87)
D.S. Sukhorukov DM for Cadres (7/22/87)

Ministry Staff (Chiefs of Troops, Main Directorates, and Directorates)

V.A. Achalov   Airborne Troops (4/26/89)
V.N. Bab'eev   Central Finance Directorate, Rear Services (10/88)
I.V. Balabay   Main Automotive Directorate
E.V. Boichuk   "12th" Main Directorate
A.A. Galkin   Main Armor Directorate (9/3/87)
G.N. Gorski   Affairs Directorate
V.R. Iashchenko   Main Directorate of Geodesy and Cartography
I.D. Isaenko   Central Food Directorate, Rear Services (8/27/88)
V.A. Kuznetsov   Engineer Troops (12/25/87)
Iu.M. Lazarev   (Unidentified) Main Directorate (11/29/83)
N.I. Lutsev   Central Archives Directorate (8/8/87)
M.K. Makartsev   Railroad Troops (3/15/85)
A.P. Mikhailovski Main Directorate of Navigation and Oceanography
A. Muranov   Directorate of Military Tribunals (12/8/88)
M.E. Penkin   Main Missile and Artillery Directorate
F.P. Petrov   Central Clothing and Equipment Directorate

S. Petrov	Chemical Troops (2/19/89)
B.S. Popov	Main Military Procuracy (1/31/86)
V.S. Riabov	Military Publishing House (Voenizdat) (2/23/88)
N.G. Sadovnikov	Main Trade Directorate (7/3/86)
N.F. Vasil'ev	Central Military Motor Vehicle Directorate (11/88)
K.M. Vertelov	State Examination and Inspection (3/5/88)
D.A. Volkogonov	Institute of Military History (5/4/88)
Iu.K. Vorontsov	Central Military Transport Directorate (4/23/88)
V.A. Vostrov	Main Military Educational Institutions (9/2/88)
V. Zakimatov	Main Military Construction Directorate (11/26/88)
Unknown	Central Institute of Military and Technical Information
Unknown	Main Directorate of Special Construction

GENERAL STAFF

M.A. Moiseev	Chief of the General Staff (12/15/88)
V.N. Lobov	Chief of Staff, WTO (1/26/89)
B.A. Omelichev	First Deputy Chief (1/26/89)[1]
V.G. Denisov	Deputy Chief (portfolio unknown)
S.A. Dikov	Chief, Main Operations Directorate
E.A. Evstigneev	Deputy Chief (portfolio unknown)
M.A. Gareev	Deputy Chief, Doctrine
K.I. Kobets	Deputy Chief for Communications
G.F. Krivosheev	Chief, Organization-Mobilization Directorate[2]
V.M. Mikhailov	GRU Chief (12/6/88)
Iu.A. Sysoev	Deputy Chief for Naval Matters
A.N. Agafonov	Chief, Political Department
G.A. Borisov	Chief, External Relations Directorate
V.S. Ermin	Chief, (Unidentified) Directorate (5/19/88)
A.I. Losev	Chief, Military Topographic Directorate
N.F. Chervov	Chief, Treaty and Legal Directorate (1/82)
L.S. Chuvakhin	Chief, Administration of Affairs Directorate
M.A. Kozlov	Chief, Censorship Directorate
E.E. Kondakov	Chief, Foreign Military Assistance
A. Koskin	Chief, Administrative-Economics Directorate (12/88)
E.A. Kuznetsov	Chief, Military Science Directorate (10/9/88)
O.S. Kupriianov	Chief, Cadres Directorate
A. Iniakov	FDC, Military Science Directorate (10/9/87)
Iu.V. Lebedev	Deputy Chief, Treaty and Legal Directorate
Iu.A. Markelov	General Staff Representative to MFA
G.I. Salmanov	Chief, General Staff "Voroshilov" Academy
G.P. Skorikov	Counsellor to Military Science Directorate
V.M. Tatarnikov	Representative to CSCE (8/16/88)

CHIEF INSPECTORATE

M.I. Sorokin	Inspector General (7/22/87)

I.I. Alekseev	former Deputy Minister for Armaments
I.A. Gerasimov	former CINC Southwestern TVD (1/89)
V.M. Grishanov	former Chief, Navy Political Directorate (7/80)
I.I. Gusakovski	former Deputy Defense Minister for Cadres (6/71)
S.P. Ivanov	former Chief, General Staff Academy
E.F. Ivanovski	former CINC Ground Forces (2/89)
I.N. Kozhedub	former DC of the Air Force Main Staff (7/87)
V.G. Kulikov	former CINC WTO (2/89)
S.F. Kurkotkin	former Deputy DM for Rear Services (5/88)
P.N. Liashchenko	former First Deputy CINC Ground Forces (2/88)
V.F. Margelov	former Chief, Airborne Troops
G.I. Obaturov	former Chief, Ground Forces Academy (2/86)
N.V. Ogarkov	former CINC Western TVD (10/88)
I.G. Pavlovski	former CINC Ground Forces
V.I. Petrov	former First Deputy Defense Minister (4/10/87)
A.P. Silant'ev	
A.F. Shcheglov	former Warsaw Pact Representative to Poland (9/89)
I.N. Shkadov	former Deputy Defense Minister for Cadres (2/87)
N.I. Smirnov	former First Deputy CINC of the Navy (5/88)
S.L. Sokolov	former Minister of Defense (7/87)
M.M. Zaitsev	former CINC Southern TVD (1/87)
A.S. Zheltov	former Chief, Military Political Academy (3/72)

MAIN POLITICAL ADMINISTRATION

A.D. Lizichev	Chief (7/26/85)
A.I. Sorokin	First Deputy Chief (11/81)
V.S. Nechaev	Deputy Chief (3/19/85)
G.A. Stefanovski	Deputy Chief; Chief, Agitprop Directorate (5/5/85)
V.P. Khrobostov	Chief, Agitprop Department (6/19/88)
V.D. Lukinykh	Chief, OPW Directorate (7/10/86)
A.I. Maslov	Chief, Cadres Directorate (2/4/89)
N.V. Shapalin	Deputy Chief, Agitprop Directorate (11/27/87)
A.I. Shirinkin	Senior Secretary, Party Commission (10/22/88)

L.L. Batekhin	Chief, Air Forces Political Administration
N.F. Kizyun	Chief, Military Political Academy
V.I. Panin	Chief, Navy Political Administration (6/27/87)
M.D. Popkov	Chief, Ground Forces Political Administration
V.S. Rodin	Chief, SRF Political Administration (11/19/87)
V.A. Silakov	Chief, Air Defense Administration (11/1/87)

SERVICE COMMANDERS

STRATEGIC ROCKET FORCES

Iu.P. Maksimov	CINC of the Strategic Rocket Forces (7/85)
V.M. Vishenkov	First Deputy CINC; Chief of Staff (11/76)
Unknown	First Deputy CINC

GROUND FORCES

V.I. Varennikov	CINC of the Ground Forces (2/16/89)
D.A. Grinkevich	First Deputy CINC; Chief of Staff (8/81)
A.V. Betekhtin	First Deputy CINC (9/13/88)

AIR DEFENSE FORCES

I.M. Tretiak	CINC of the Air Defense Forces (7/2/87)
I.M. Mal'tsev	First Deputy CINC; Chief of Staff (4/85)
V.V. Litninov	First Deputy CINC (9/13/88)

AIR FORCES

A.N. Efimov	CINC of the Air Forces (12/22/84)
V.E. Pan'kin	First Deputy CINC; Chief of Staff (6/85)
E.I. Shaposhnikov	First Deputy CINC

NAVY

V.N. Chernavin	CINC of the Navy (12/11/85)
K.V. Makarov	First Deputy CINC; Chief of Staff (1/86)
I.M. Kapitanets	First Deputy CINC
Iu.A. Sysoev	Deputy CINC
V.G. Novikov	Deputy CINC
N.I. Khovrin	Deputy CINC for Warsaw Pact Naval Forces (11/83)
K.V. Makarov	Chief of Staff (7/26/86)
D.M. Komarov	First Deputy Chief (6/9/89)
V.P. Potapov	First Deputy Chief for Naval Aviation
A.A. Kuz'min	Deputy Chief for Combat Training (1/17/89)
V.S. Liakin	Deputy Chief (portfolio unknown)
F.I. Novoselov	Deputy Chief for Shipbuilding and Armament
E.V. Semenkov	DC for Naval Educational Institutes (1/89)
V.V. Sidorov	Deputy Chief for Rear Services (1/14/88)
V.V. Zaitsev	Deputy Chief for Maintenance

O. Anikanov	Chief, Main Engineering Directorate (5/10/87)
V. Belov	Chief, Finance Service
Ye. Ermakov	Chief, Cadres Directorate (9/3/87)
M.M. Krylov	Chief, Communications Directorate
V.N. Kharitonov	Chief, Political Department (11/86)
V. Zatula	Chief, Unidentified Department (4/1/89)

FLEET CINCS

BALTIC FLEET

V.P. Ivanov	Commander (7/29/86)
V. Egorov	First Deputy Commander
V.A. Kolmagorov	Chief of Staff (7/28/85)
A.I. Kornienko	Head of Political Administration (2/19/87)

BLACK SEA FLEET

M.N. Khronopulo	Commander (7/30/85)
Unknown	First Deputy Commander
V.E. Selivanov	Chief of Staff (7/87)
V.P. Nekrasov	Head of Political Administration (8/22/86)

CASPIAN SEA FLOTILLA

V.E. Liashchenko	Commander
B.Ia. Zuev	First Deputy Commander
Unknown	Chief of Staff
V.G. Kalinin	Head of Political Administration

NORTHERN FLEET

F.N. Gromov	Commander (5/15/88)
I.V. Kasatonov	First Deputy Commander
Iu.N. Patrushev	Chief of Staff
S.P. Vargin	Head of Political Administration (11/5/85)

PACIFIC FLEET

G.A. Khvatov	Commander (11/8/87)
E.D. Baltin	First Deputy Commander (8/2/88)
G. Vasil'yov	Chief of Staff
B.N. Pekedov	Head of Political Administration

V.N. Sergeev   Commander, Indian Ocean Squadron (11/23/88)

JOINT ARMED FORCES OF THE WARSAW TREATY ORGANIZATION

P.G. Lushev   CINC, WTO (2/2/89)

V.N. Lobov	Chief of Staff, WTO (1/26/89)
V.N. Verevkin	First Deputy Chief of Staff
F.F. Krivda	Representative to Hungary
V.A. Makarov	Representative to Romania
V.K. Meretskov	Representative to GDR
V.I. Sivenok	Representative to Poland
N.A. Zotov	Representative to Czechoslovakia
A.M. Zvartsev	Representative to Bulgaria

REGIONAL COMMANDS

M.P. Burlakov	Southern GSF (Papa, HU) (1988)
V.F. Ermakov	Leningrad MD (Leningrad) (1987)
I.V. Fuzhenko	Turkestan MD (Tashkent) (1989)
B.V. Gromov	Kiev MD (Kiev) (1989)
N.V. Kalinin	Moscow MD (Moscow) (1989)
I.I. Korbutov	Northern GSF (Legnica, PL) (1987)
A.V. Kovtunov	Forces in the Far East (Ulan Ude) (1987)
A.I. Kostenko	Belorussian MD (Minsk) (1989)
F.M. Kuz'min	Baltic MD (Riga) (1989)
A.M. Makashov	Urals-Volga MD (Sverdlovsk) (1989)
I.S. Morozov	Odessa MD (Odessa) (1987)
V.I. Novozhilov	Far Eastern MD (Khabarovsk) (1989)
V.I. Osipov	Southwestern TVD (Kiev) (1989)
V.A. Patrikeev	Transcaucasus MD (Tbilisi) (1989)
N.I. Popov	Southern TVD (Baku) (1989)
S.I. Postnikov	Western TVD (Legnica, PL) (1988)
B.E. P'iankov	Siberian MD (Novosibirsk) (1987)
V.M. Semenov	Transbaikal MD (Chita) (1989)
L.S. Shustko	North Caucasus MD (Rostov-na-Donu) (1987)
V.V. Skokov	Carpathian MD (L'vov) (1986)
B.V. Snetkov	Western GSF (Wunsdorf, GDR) (1987)
V.G. Tsarkov	Moscow Air Defense District (1987)
E.A. Vorob'yov	Central GSF (Milovice, CZ) (1988)

THEATER HIGH COMMANDS

WESTERN TVD

S.I. Postnikov	CINC (10/88)
I.F. Zarundin	First Deputy CINC

M.N. Tereshchenko Chief of Staff
B.P. Utkin   Head of Political Administration

SOUTHWESTERN TVD

V.I. Osipov   CINC (2/89)
Unknown   First Deputy Commander in Chief
Unknown   Chief of Staff
Unknown   Head of Political Administration

SOUTHERN TVD

N.I. Popov   CINC (2/89)
I.V. Sviridov   First Deputy CINC
Unknown   Chief of Staff
A.I. Ovchinnikov   Head of Political Administration

FORCES IN THE FAR EAST

A.V. Kovtunov   CINC (2/89)
Unknown   First Deputy Commander in Chief
E.A. Touzakov   Chief of Staff
A.N. Kolinichenko   Head of Political Administration

GROUPS OF FORCES

WESTERN GROUP OF FORCES (formerly Group of Soviet Forces, Germany)[3]

B.V. Snetkov   CINC (12/8/87)
M.N. Kalinin   First Deputy Commander in Chief (9/88)
V.I. Fursin   Chief of Staff
N.A. Moiseev   Head of Political Administration (1/86)

NORTHERN GROUP OF FORCES

I.I. Korbutov   Commander (2/20/87)
B. Usachev   First Deputy Commander (3/30/88)
V.P. Nikityuk   Chief of Staff
I.M. Titov   Head of Political Administration (1/30/85)

CENTRAL GROUP OF FORCES

E.A. Vorob'yov   Commander (12/87)
V.S. Malashkevich   First Deputy Commander (3/88)
Yu. Shchepin   Chief of Staff (5/89)
V.A. Grebenyuk   Head of Political Administration (12/88)

SOUTHERN GROUP OF FORCES

M.P. Burlakov   Commander (7/88)
I.N. Vodolazov   First Deputy Commander (10/17/87)
I. Chumak   Chief of Staff (10/87)
R.V. Gorelov   Head of Political Administration (11/87)

MILITARY DISTRICTS

BALTIC MILITARY DISTRICT

F.M. Kuz'min   Commander (1/89)
F.I. Mel'nichuk   First Deputy Commander (9/30/88)
P.G. Chaus   Chief of Staff
O.V. Zinchenko   Head of Political Administration (12/28/88)

BELORUSSIAN MILITARY DISTRICT

A.I. Kostenko   Commander (1989)
Unknown   First Deputy Commander
V.S. Sokolov   Chief of Staff (2/23/85)
N.M. Boiko   Head of Political Administration

CARPATHIAN MILITARY DISTRICT

V.V. Skokov   Commander (11/8/86)
Unknown   First Deputy Commander
V.T. Shevtsov   Chief of Staff (11/5/85)
E.N. Makhov   Head of Political Administration (12/30/88)

FAR EASTERN MILITARY DISTRICT

V.I. Novozhikov   Commander (2/17/89)
Unknown   First Deputy Commander
V.P. Kovalev   Chief of Staff (8/2/88)
A.I. Voronin   Head of Political Administration (11/1/87)

KIEV MILITARY DISTRICT

B.V. Gromov	Commander (2/15/89)
V. Tsvetkov	First Deputy Commander (12/88)
Unknown	Chief of Staff
V.A. Sharygin	Head of Political Administration (7/87)

LENINGRAD MILITARY DISTRICT

V.F. Ermakov	Commander (1/31/88)
V.I. Mironov	First Deputy Commander (5/23/89)
S.P. Seleznev	Chief of Staff (5/7/89)
I.M. Pavlov	Head of Political Administration (2/15/87)

MOSCOW MILITARY DISTRICT

N.V. Kalinin	Commander (2/16/89)
A.A. Golognev	First Deputy Commander (6/88)
Unknown	Chief of Staff
A.I. Makunin	Head of Political Administration (11/1/87)

NORTH CAUCASUS MILITARY DISTRICT

L.S. Shustko	Commander (10/17/86)
D. Mokshanov	First Deputy Commander (1/6/87)
G.A. Andresian	Chief of Staff
G. Donskoi	Head of Political Administration (1/88)

ODESSA MILITARY DISTRICT

I.S. Morozov	Commander (2/87)
S.A. Suyudeev	First Deputy Commander
V.A. Semenov	Chief of Staff (1/26/86)
V.F. Plekhanov	Head of Political Administration (5/85)

SIBERIAN MILITARY DISTRICT

B.E. P'iankov	Commander (5/25/89)
E.I. Krylov	First Deputy Commander
Iu. Shavrikov	Chief of Staff (1/86)
B.O. Mukul'chuk	Head of Political Administration (5/88)

TRANSBAIKAL MILITARY DISTRICT

V.M. Semenov	Commander (4/89)
V. Tret'iakov	First Deputy Commander (5/17/89)
Unknown	Chief of Staff
I.Ia. Solodilov	Head of Political Administration (3/19/86)

TRANSCAUCASUS MILITARY DISTRICT

V.A. Patrikeev	Commander (8/89)
Iu. Kuznetsov	First Deputy Commander (4/20/89)
V.N. Samsonov	Chief of Staff (9/88)
A.N. Novikov	Head of Political Administration (6/88)

TURKESTAN MILITARY DISTRICT[4]

I.V. Fuzhenko	Commander (2/17/89)
B.P. Shein	First Deputy Commander (6/87)
Unknown	Chief of Staff
Unknown	Head of Political Administration

URALS-VOLGA MILITARY DISTRICT [5]

A.M. Makashov	Commander (4/89)
O. Komarov	First Deputy Commander
B.S. Perfil'yov	Chief of Staff
B.V. Tarasov	Head of Political Administration

Notes

[1]Traditionally, there are three First Deputy Chiefs of the General Staff; the third is also the Chief of the Main Operations. Since the transfer of General Valentin Varennikov to the Ground Forces, this position apparently remains vacant. Of interest, during his tenure as a First Deputy Chief, Varennikov apparently relinquished the post as chief of operations to personally oversee military operations in Afghanistan. The withdrawal of Soviet forces, coupled with the long separations of the First Deputy Chief and Main Operations positions, suggests there is no longer a perceived need for a third First Deputy.

[2]Krivosheev was identified as acting Chief of the General Staff on August 12, 1989, while Moiseev was on vacation.

[3]The USSR Defense Ministry announced this name change on

June 29, 1989.

[4]Includes former Central Asian Military District (abolished June 1, 1989).

[5]Includes former Volga Military District (abolished on September 1, 1989).

APPENDIX 2

Gorbachev and the
Soviet Military: A Chronology

Randall E. Newnham

1985

March 11, 1985: Mikhail Gorbachev becomes General Secretary of the Communist Party of the Soviet Union (CPSU) following the death of Konstantin Chernenko.

April 1985: Marshal Nikolai Ogarkov's book *History Teaches Vigilance* appears. It compares the present period to that preceding the Second World War and argues for an urgent military buildup.

April 23, 1985: Gorbachev outlines his reform strategy at a plenum of the CPSU Central Committee. He clearly stresses civilian matters and holds out an olive branch to the United States. Marshal Sergei Sokolov is promoted to candidate member of the Politburo.

May 8, 1985: The 40th anniversary of the end of the Great Patriotic War.

May 9, 1985: Sokolov delivers a fiery speech at the Victory Day Parade. In this and other speeches in the spring and summer of 1985, he fails to mention Gorbachev or the results of the April plenum.

July 3, 1985: Gorbachev announces that he has assumed the position as head of the Defense Council.

July 10, 1985: Gorbachev addresses military officers at an unpublicized meeting in Minsk, Belorussia. Secretary for Defense Industry Lev Zaikov also attends.

July 24, 1985: Colonel General Dmitri Lizichev becomes Main Political Administration chief. His predecessor, General Aleksei Epishev, retires from that post after 23 years of service.

July 26, 1985: General Iurii Maksimov becomes head of the Strategic

218

Rocket Forces. Marshal of Artillery Vladimir Tolubko is removed.

October 4, 1985: Gorbachev mentions reasonable sufficiency for the first time during a visit to Paris, France.

November 27, 1985: Gorbachev again mentions reasonable sufficiency in a speech delivered to the Supreme Soviet.

November 19-20, 1985: Gorbachev meets with United States President Ronald Reagan.

December 11, 1985: Admiral of the Navy Sergei Gorshkov retires after 29 years of service. Admiral Vladimir Chernavin succeeds him.

1986

February 16, 1986: Lizichev promoted to Army General.

February 27-March 6, 1986: 27th Party Congress of the CPSU. Gorbachev speaks of a "purely defensive" military strategy and of political control over strategic decisions. He gives the first definition of the concept of "reasonable sufficiency." The following military leaders are either retained or were elected to the Central Committee:

FULL MEMBERS

A.T. Altunin	Deputy Minister for Civil Defense
V.M. Arkhipov	Commander, Moscow Military District
S.F. Akhromeev	Chief of Staff
V.N. Chernavin	Deputy CINC, Navy
A.N. Efimov	CINC Air Defense Forces
I.A. Gerasimov	Commander, Southwestern TVD
V.L. Govorov	Chief, Main Inspectorate
S.G. Gorshkov	Member, Main Inspectorate
A.I. Gribkov	FDC General Staff
E.F. Ivanovski	CINC Ground Forces
A.I. Koldunov	CINC PVO
V.G. Kulikov	CINC WTO
S.K. Kurkotkin	Deputy Minister for Rear Services
A.D. Lizichev	Chief of MPA
P.G. Lushev	Commander GSFG
Iu. P. Maksimov	Deputy Minister SRF
N.V. Ogarkov	Commander, Western TVD
V.I. Petrov	First Deputy Minister
V.M. Shabanov	Deputy Minister for Armaments
S.L. Sokolov	Minister of Defense
V.F. Tolubko	Member, Main Inspectorate

| I.M. Tretiak | Commander, Far East Military District |
| M.M. Zaitsev | Commander, Southern TVD |

CANDIDATE MEMBERS

V.A. Belikov	Commander, Carpathian Military District
G.M. Egorov	Chairman, DOSAAF
I.M. Kapitanets	Commander, Northern Fleet
A.U. Konstantinov	Commander, Moscow PVO District
V.V. Osipov	Commander, Kiev Military District
M.D. Popkov	Commander, Turkestan Military District
M.I. Popov	Chief, Political Administration, Ground Forces
V.S. Rodin	Chief, Political Directorate, SRF
V.M. Shuralev	Commander, Belorussian Military District
V.V. Sidorov	Commander, Pacific Fleet
B.V. Snetkov	Commander, Leningrad Military District
A.I. Sorokin	First Deputy Chief, MPA
V.I. Varennikov	First Deputy Chief, General Staff
D.T. Yazov	Commander, Far East Military District

March 1986: General Ivan Tretiak, Commander of the Far East Military District, becomes Chief of the Main Inspectorate. His deputy, General Dmitri Yazov, takes command of the district.

June 1986: In an article in *Kommunist*, Anatolii Dobrynin becomes one of the first Party leaders to call for a greater civilian role in the debate over national security issues.

July 30, 1986: Gorbachev visits the Far East Military District HQ in Khabarovsk. Several officers from this command are later called to Moscow to fill high military posts (Yazov, Moiseev).

July 1986: First Deputy Minister of Defense Marshal Vasilii Petrov retires. General Petr Lushev replaces him.

October 6, 1986: A Soviet Yankee I SSBN sinks in the western Atlantic Ocean 600 miles north of Bermuda.

October 11-12, 1986: Reykjavik Summit. Akhromeev plays a prominent role on Gorbachev's negotiating team.

October 27, 1986: Ogarkov calls for conventional force readiness in an article released by *Novosti*.

Fall 1986: The *Soviet Military Dictionary* is published; Akhromeev is the editor.

1987

February 8, 1987: Colonel General Mikhail Moiseev becomes chief of the Far East Military District.

February 19, 1987: *Krasnaia Zvezda* identifies Yazov as the new Deputy Minister of Cadres.

February 23, 1987: In speeches on Army-Navy Day, Sokolov, Akhromeev, and Marshal Viktor Kulikov call for continuing the military buildup in opposition to Gorbachev's plans.

February 25, 1987: Gorbachev, speaking to the Trade Union Congress, stresses reasonable sufficiency.

March 1987: Writing in *Kommunist*, Lizichev tries to defend Gorbachev's peace initiatives from military criticism. He forcefully argues that the proposed changes will not threaten real defense needs but rejects unilateralism.

March 18, 1987: Sokolov speaks to a meeting of the Ministry of Defense Party Aktiv and calls for perestroika in the military.

March 30, 1987: Colonel General Vladimir Lobov replaces Colonel General Ivan Gashkov as First Deputy Chief of the General Staff.

May 1987: In *Kommunist*, Politburo Member Aleksandr Yakovlev calls for a more open debate on defense issues.

May 9, 1987: Kulikov, in his Victory Day speech, argues against any concessions to the "reactionary, militaristic, aggressive" West.

May 22, 1987: Volkogonov, head of the Agitprop Directorate of the MPA, ridicules unilateral disarmament in a *Krasnaia Zvezda* article. He likens it to "trying to clap with one hand."

May 28, 1987: Mathias Rust lands his Cessna airplane in Red Square.

May 28-29, 1987: Meeting in Berlin, the Warsaw Treaty Organization approves a military doctrine. It supports Gorbachev's arms control proposals.

May 30, 1987: Sokolov and Marshal of Aviation Aleksandr Koldunov (PVO CINC) are fired by the Politburo. General Dmitri Yazov becomes Minister of Defense.

June 3, 1987: A *Literaturnaia Gazeta* article by Deputy Chief of the

General Staff Colonel General Makmut Gareev criticizes pacifistic tendencies in the press and criticism of the military.

June 17, 1987: Moscow Gorkom First Secretary and Candidate Member of the Politburo Boris Yeltsin harshly criticizes officers responsible for the Rust affair. In addition, Moscow Air District Commander Marshal of Aviation Anatolii Konstantinov and his subordinates are fired.

June 26, 1987: At a plenum of the CPSU Central Committee, Yazov becomes a candidate member of the Politburo while Sokolov is released.

July 1, 1987: Tretiak replaces Koldunov.

July 18, 1987: In a major speech, Yazov takes a pro-reform line. He speaks of "negative tendencies" in the armed forces and calls on its leaders to admit past mistakes.

July 20, 1987: Gorbachev tells Najibullah of his determination to withdrawal from Afghanistan within a year.

October 1987: Yazov publishes *Na strazhe sotsializma i mira* that argues the need for a strong offensive capability. Later, Deputy Foreign Minister Petrovski acknowledges that this is inconsistent with Gorbachev's reform efforts.

December 1987: Akhromeev calls for "defensive sufficiency" rather than merely "reasonable sufficiency" in *Problemy Mira i Sotsialisma*. He also decries unilateral disarmament.

December 8, 1987: Gorbachev and Reagan sign the INF Treaty at the superpower summit in Washington, D.C.

1988

January 16, 1988: Yazov and Volkogonov criticize the press on Soviet TV. *Ogonyok* and *Literaturnaia Gazeta* are mentioned by name.

February 8, 1988: Gorbachev announces that Soviet troop withdrawals from Afghanistan will begin by May 15, 1988, if United Nations-sponsored negotiations proceed quickly.

February 9, 1988: Yazov limits his praise for Gorbachev's recent decision to withdraw from Afghanistan.

February 23, 1988: 70th anniversary of the Soviet Army and Navy. Zaikov and Yazov deliver major speeches.

February 28, 1988: Tretiak criticizes the "defensive doctrine" concept and unilateral disarmament in a *Moscow News* interview.

March 13, 1988: The "Andreeva letter" is published in *Sovetskaia Rossiia* and quickly reprinted in local military newspapers.

April 14, 1988: In Geneva, U.S., Soviet, and Pakistani representatives sign an agreement calling for a Soviet withdrawal from Afghanistan by February 15, 1989.

May 1, 1988: Commander of the Transcaucasus Military District Konstantin Kochetov is promoted to Army General due to his handling of riots in Armenia and Azerbaijan.

May 15, 1988: Colonel General Vladimir Arkhipov is appointed as Chief of Rear Services, replacing Marshal Semen Kurkotin, who served in that position for 16 years.

May 29-June 2, 1988: Gorbachev and Reagan meet in Moscow.

June 1988: Gareev advocates "reliable defense" in *Argumenty i Fakty* #39.

June 28-July 1, 1988: 19th All-Union CPSU Conference. Only one military representative spoke: CINC of Soviet forces in Afghanistan Colonel General Boris Gromov.

July 1988: *Molodaia Gvardiia* publishes a conversation between writer Ivan Shevtsov and Marshal of Aviation Ivan Pstygo. Both agree on the need to fight "Western, cosmopolitan, and Zionist influences" on Soviet society.

July 10, 1988: Aleksandr Prokhonov, cited as an ideological model by Andreeva, publishes an article in *Krasnaia Zvezda* which praises the Polish army's 1981 coup and draws implicit parallels to present Soviet conditions.

July 26, 1988: *Pravda* reports a major statement made by Soviet Foreign Minister Eduard Shevardnadze at a Foreign Ministry Conference. He says that a "nationally elected body" should monitor military budgets and deployments.

August 31, 1988: Lobov, in a speech in Hungary, notes that unilateral disarmament measures "can only work to our detriment."

September 30, 1988: A plenum of the CPSU Central Committee demotes Politburo Member Egor Ligachev. This is a blow to conservatives in the military.

October 1988: Ogarkov retires as head of the Western TVD.

October 13, 1988: The Politburo warns the Ministry of Defense about abuses in the treatment of recruits and other infractions of military rules.

October 29, 1988: Gorbachev, speaking to leaders of the Komsomol, hints that the current two-year period of mandatory military service may be reduced.

November 3, 1988: In *Moscow News*, Lieutenant Colonel Savinkin calls for an end to the traditional draft. He feels the army should have a small professional core augmented by territorial militia in time of crisis.

November 7, 1988: Speaking at the Revolution Day parade, Yazov seems to endorse the concepts of "reasonable sufficiency" and "defensive defense."

December 6, 1988: Akhromeev, in an interview in the Bulgarian press, again warns against "one-sided" Soviet action.

December 7, 1988: In a major address at the UN, Gorbachev announces a unilateral cut of 500,000 men in Soviet troop strength. The speech is broadcast live on Soviet television.

December 7, 1988: Akhromeev resigns as Chief of the General Staff.

December 15, 1988: Akhromeev transfers to a strictly advisory position on Gorbachev's personal staff. Moiseev becomes Chief of General Staff despite his lack of seniority.

December 20, 1988: Swedish newspaper *Dagens Nyheter* reveals Soviet plans to create a new "ministry for the armed forces" which would include the military, the KGB, and the MVD. The new head of the ministry would be a civilian.

December 21, 1988: Shevardnadze criticizes the military for its opposition to perestroika in refusing to disclose the defense budget.

December 28, 1988: General Staff Party Conference. A report from the conference criticizes Gareev and three other Deputy Chiefs (Krivosheev, Omelichev, and Evstigneev) for slowing the pace of perestroika.

December 30, 1988: Yazov criticizes the performance of the Army during the Armenian earthquake cleanup effort.

1989

January 14, 1989: In *Sovetskaia Rossiia* Akhromeev rejects a volunteer army.

January 18, 1989: Gorbachev announces defense cuts. 14.2% is to be cut from the military budget overall, with a 19.5% drop in procurement and a 12% fall in troop strength.

January 19, 1989: Shevardnadze announces that the 50,000 troops to be withdrawn from Eastern Europe will take their tactical nuclear weapons with them.

February 1989: The CINCs of the Far Eastern, Southwestern, and Southern Forces are replaced.

February 2, 1989: Marshal Viktor Kulikov retires as CINC of the Warsaw Treaty Organization and First Deputy Minister of Defense. Lushev replaces him.

February 8, 1989: Moiseev's speech to General Staff Party Aktiv seems critical of Gorbachev's defense policies.

February 15, 1989: Completion of the withdrawal from Afghanistan. On the same day, CINC of the Ground Forces General Evgenii Ivanovski retires and is replaced by General Valentin Varennikov, a former First Deputy Chief of Staff who helped supervise the Afghan withdrawal. Moiseev is promoted to the rank of General.

March 21, 1989: The Supreme Soviet issues a decree removing border troops, internal security forces, and railroad troops from military jurisdiction. Thus, these forces are not to be counted as "troops" in arms control negotiations.

March 26, 1989: Elections to the Congress of People's Deputies. 121 military personnel run in this first election with 76 elected and six more gaining seats after runoff (82). Military representation does not drop but many senior officers do not win seats.

April 7, 1989: A Soviet Mike Class SSN burns and sinks north of Norway. This was the only submarine of its class.

April 11, 1989: A *Krasnaia Zvezda* report announces the appointment of Iurii Iashin, a strategic missile expert, as a Deputy Minister of Defense. It is believed that his appointment may signal a reappraisal of Soviet nuclear strategy.

April 25, 1989: At the April Plenum of the CPSU Central Committee, many military "dead souls" are retired while a minority retain their seats. The move reduces military leadership in the Central Committee from 7.5 percent to 5.2 percent. Only one military officer was promoted: V.V. Osipov.

FULL MEMBERS

V.M. Arkhipov	Rear Services
S.F. Akhromeev	Defense Advisor to Gorbachev
B.P. Bugaev	Inspector in the MOD
V.N. Chernavin	Deputy CINC, Navy
A.N. Efimov	CINC Air Defense Forces
V.L. Govorov	Chief, Main Inspectorate
A.I. Koldunov	Inspector
A.D. Lizichev	Chief of MPA
P.G. Lushev	CINC WTO
Iu. P. Maksimov	CINC SRF
V.V. Osipov	CINC Southwestern TVD
V.M. Shabanov	Deputy Minister for Armaments
I.M. Tretiak	CINC PVO
D.F. Yazov	Minister of Defense

CANDIDATE MEMBERS

I.M. Kapitanets	Commander of Northern Fleet
M.D. Popkov	Commander, Chief of Political Directorate
V.S. Rodin	Chief, Political Directorate, SRF
V.M. Shuralev	Advisor to Soviet Armed Forces
V.V. Sidorov	Deputy Chief for Naval Rear Services
B.V. Snetkov	Commander of Group of Soviet Forces Germany
A.I. Sorokin	First Deputy Chief, MPA
V.I. Varennikov	CINC Ground Forces

May 1989: Lev Semeiko of the Institute for USA and Canada defends reasonable sufficiency in *Kommunist*.

May 1989: Elections to the Supreme Soviet. Seven military officers are elected (Akhromeev, Kulikov, Shabanov, Gorbatko, Tutov, Sokolova, and Goliakov) to the Council of Union while three (Ochirov, Podziruk, Golovnev) are elected to the Council of Nationalities.

May 30, 1989: Gorbachev states that the Soviet Union spends 77.3 billion rubles a year on defense.

June 1, 1989: The Central Asian Military District is abolished. Its units are absorbed by the Turkestan Military District.

June 2, 1989: Andrei Sakharov denounces atrocities committed by Soviet forces in Afghanistan in a speech delivered before the Congress of People's Deputies. He is shouted down by other delegates.

June 7, 1989: In a speech to the Congress of People's Deputies, Prime Minister and Politburo Member Nikolai Ryzhkov says that the defense budget will be cut by one-third to one-half by 1995. He states that the current budget of 77.3 billion rubles can be broken down as:

32.6 billion	Armaments/Hardware
15.3 billion	R&D
20.2 billion	Upkeep of Army and Navy
4.6 billion	Military construction
2.3 billion	Pensions
2.3 billion	Other

June 10, 1989: The Supreme Soviet creates a Committee on Defense and State Security.

June 26, 1989: In *Izvestiia*, Vladimir Lapygin, chairman of the Committee on Defense and State Security, argues for an all-volunteer military and asserts that his commission will vigorously oversee the military budget.

June 29, 1989: The Group of Soviet Forces in Germany is renamed Western Group of Forces.

July 1989: The work of the Supreme Soviet continues. While Gorbachev reveals that he faced military opposition to restructuring, members of the Supreme Soviet grill Yazov during his confirmation hearings.

July 6, 1989: A strong note from the CPSU Secretariat, a body believed to be inactive, calls on the Soviet media to rein in criticism of the military. *Izvestiia*, *Komsomolskaia Pravda*, *Sovetskaia Rossiia*, *Literaturnaia Gazeta*, and *Ogonyok* are among the publications singled out for criticism.

July 11, 1989: Ryzhkov proposes the release of students from military duty.

July 18, 1989: Ligachev, at a CPSU conference, states that the military "will receive whatever it wants."

July 21, 1989: Akhromeev testifies before the U.S. Armed Services Committee.

August 12, 1989: Colonel General G.F. Kirvosheev is identified as "Acting"

Chief of the General Staff while Moiseev is on vacation.

September 1, 1989: The Urals Military District is abolished. Its responsibilities are taken over by the Volga Military District, now known as the Urals-Volga Military District.

September 16, 1989: In an *Izvestiia* interview, Yazov claims that Soviet military troops were cut by 149,000 men in the first half of 1989. He praises reasonable sufficiency, but warns that draft deferments and a lack of funding for modern weaponry will hurt the Soviet Armed Forces.

September 20, 1989: Speaking at the Central Committee Plenum on nationality issues, Yazov warns that the "imperialist" threat is still present and calls for "not only a sufficient defense, but an unconditionally reliable one."

September 25, 1989: The Supreme Soviet announces an 8.3 percent reduction in military spending. Spending on weapons development and military construction will be cut more sharply than that on the production of tanks, aircraft, and helicopters.

Contributors

Stephen J. Blank is a National Security Affairs Analyst at the Strategic Studies Institute (U.S. Army War College). He is the author of articles on the Soviet military in foreign and domestic policy.

Grey Burkhart is a Senior Analyst and Political-Military Advisor for the Naval Analysis Group in Washington, D.C.

Patrick Cronin is a Member of the Research Staff of the Center of Naval Analyses and an Adjunct Professor at the Paul H. Nitze School for Advanced International Studies at Johns Hopkins University and is the author of a forthcoming book on superpower summitry.

Paula J. Dobriansky is the Deputy Assistant Secretary of State for Human Rights and Humanitarian Affairs. Previously she served as the Director of European and Soviet Affairs at the National Security Council, White House.

Daniel Goure is Senior Scientist at SRS Technologies in Arlington, Virginia, and the author of numerous studies on the Soviet military.

William C. Green is Associate Professor of International Relations at Boston University and the author of the book *Soviet Nuclear Weapons Policy: A Research and Bibliographic Guide* (1987).

Theodore Karasik is a Staff Member in the Political Science Department of the RAND Corporation and a Research Associate at the Center for Russian and Soviet Studies in Monterey, California. He is the author of articles on Soviet politics and specializes in leadership analysis.

Randall E. Newnham is a Doctoral Candidate in the Political Science Department at UCLA and a Fellow at the RAND/UCLA Center for Soviet Studies.

Thomas Nichols is an Assistant Professor of Political Science at Dartmouth

College and the author of articles on Soviet civil-military relations and military doctrine.

David B. Rivkin, Jr., is the Legal Advisor to the Honorable C. Boyden Gray, Counsel to the President. Previously, he was at the Department of Justice, in private practice, and worked for a number of years as a defense analyst.

William F. Scott is former U.S. Air Attache to Moscow and the author of numerous works on the Soviet military, including the recent *Soviet Military Doctrine* (1988), coauthored with Harriet Fast Scott.

Fred Wehling is a Doctoral Candidate in the Political Science Department at UCLA and a Fellow at the RAND/UCLA Center for Soviet Studies.

Index